D1126595

THE CLASS CHOREGUS

Nancy,

Welcome back to the sixties. I hope that we learned something!

your friend,

Dunn Morrison

THE CLASS CHOREGUS

by

David E. Morine

Sabrina Books
Great Falls, Virginia

Also by David E. Morine:

GOOD DIRT: Confessions of a Conservationist

The Class Choregus

Copyright © 1993 by David E. Morine and Paul H. Flint, Jr.
ISBN 1-55643-122-8

Published by
Sabrina Books
Great Falls, Virginia

Distributed by
North Atlantic Books
2800 Woolsey Street
Berkeley, California 94705

Cover and book design by Paula Morrison
Printed in the United States of America

Strang-ers once, we came to dwell to-geth-er
Sons of a moth-er wise and true
Now we're bound by ties that can-not se-ver,
All our whole life thro'.
                              —Senior Song 1906
                              J. S. Hamilton '06

To the Class of '66
"Never sit down"

PREFACE

Most of the events recorded in this book actually happened; many were my own experiences, the rest those of other students in college during the sixties. I would like to claim that I am all of Ed Morley, but in fact, I am just a large part of him. Paul Flint, Amherst College '63.5, is responsible for much of the wrinkle in Morley's character, and it is because of this wrinkle that Paul and I have spent the last twenty-five years trying to figure out what Morley should have done when Robert Strange McNamara was awarded an honorary degree at Amherst's 145th Commencement. It was this award by Amherst to McNamara in the spring of 1966 that initiated the first institutionalized dissent to the war in Vietnam and brought into question the morality and legality of America's foreign policy.

Although this book is intended primarily for the enjoyment, and possible enlightenment, of those who were in college during the sixties, it might be of interest to those in college today. The war in Vietnam forced the students of my generation to ask difficult questions about themselves, their role in society, and the integrity of their government. Even without the war, these questions still exist, and if students today can learn something from Morley, maybe it won't take them twenty-five years to find the answers.

Most of the names in this book have been changed to protect the not so innocent. This is especially true of the Beta Honeys. Remembering those wonderful women has made me feel young again. I hope *The Class Choregus* will have the same effect on all of you who were in school during these times. As for today's students, if you find Morley somewhat insensitive and tasteless, don't be too critical of him. That's the way things were in the sixties.

D.E.M.
Great Falls, Virginia 1991

PROLOGUE

If you had sons, lived around Boston, and cared about education, you wanted them to go to Harvard. J.P. Morley had three sons. He lived in Arlington, just outside of Boston, and was the Director of Vocational Guidance for the Commonwealth of Massachusetts. All through the fifties and sixties, he harbored the hope that his boys would go to Harvard: that they would play in the Stadium, that they would catch the pass or kick the field goal that beat Yale.

J.P. Morley had booted his own chance to attend Harvard. It had come during the Depression. His parents were hurting financially, so if J.P. was going to attend college, he'd need a full scholarship. Fortunately, that was no problem. J.P. was an exceptional shortstop who could hit. His slick fielding and powerful bat made him a hot prospect. Many schools sent him feelers; Alabama offered him a full ride. J.P.'s game shone in the Southern sun. He not only started at short, but captained a freshman team that included Dixie Howell at second, Don Hudson in left, and Bear Bryant in right.

J.P.'s career with the Tide turned during the middle of his sophomore year. Money had gotten so low back home that J.P. knew he'd have to ebb back north. Harvard said it would take him as a second semester sophomore, but there was a catch. At Harvard, understanding why a ball curved was just as important as hitting it, and J.P. was only carrying a C average in Physics. Harvard required nothing less than a B. If J.P. could lever that C up to a B, he was in.

Not so at Tufts. They didn't care about a C in Physics. Tufts had plenty of physicists. What they wanted was a shortstop who could hit. Tufts accepted him on the spot but demanded an immediate answer. J.P. wasn't sure that he could ever move that C to a B so he played the percentages. He went to Tufts.

It was a decision he always regretted. He got his B in Physics, and while he was scooping grounders out of the mud in Medford, Harvard was touring the Far East with a very mediocre shortstop.

J.P. steered all three of his sons into sports. He was a firm believer that, in their case, athletics was key to getting into Harvard. "Harvard wants to be the best," he'd tell them, "at sports as well as academics."

It was generally acknowledged that Ted, the oldest son, stood the best chance of making Harvard. Ted was smart, athletic, and even looked a little like his namesake, the "Splendid Splinter." But, realizing that football had become far more popular than baseball, J.P. steered Ted away from the diamond and onto the gridiron. By senior year in high school, Ted had matured into a very respectable end. There was no question he could have played for Harvard, but J.P. had made one big error. He hadn't properly pitched the Crimson. When it came time to apply, Ted announced that he had no interest in Harvard. He thought that Harvard was full of jerks. He liked Tufts, and during the four years he spent playing in the Medford mud, he was the Jumbos' leading receiver.

Behind 0–1 in the count, J.P. turned to his second son, Edward. Edward didn't have Ted's natural ability. While Ted was long and lean, Edward was a 'husky.' While Ted had perfect vision, Edward, even in the fourth grade, was myopic. While Ted was a good student, Edward spent much of his elementary education sitting on a bench outside the principal's office. But what could J.P. do? He had to play the card he'd been dealt, and while Edward wasn't an ace, he was J.P.'s next to last hope.

"You're going to Harvard," he told Edward in the fall of 1957. Edward had just started the eighth grade.

"I don't want to go to Harvard," he protested. "Ted says it's full of jerks."

"Your brother doesn't know anything," J.P. replied firmly. "The best people in the world go to Harvard. You can see for yourself. I've gotten you a job as an usher at the Stadium."

Every fall, Harvard hired about three hundred kids from the Greater Boston area as ushers. Thanks to its big stately stadium, Harvard played six of its nine games at home. The prestige and financial rewards of playing at the Stadium were enough to convince lesser schools like Bucknell, UMass, and even Dartmouth to give up the home field advantage. J.P. wasn't going to make the same mistake he had made with Ted. He figured that six Saturdays at the Stadium ought to be enough to imbue Edward with the Harvard spirit.

For the first couple of games, young Morley was not happy with his new job. Before he left home, his father would inspect his attire and give him a brief unflattering synopsis of Harvard's opponent. "Columbia? You wouldn't like Columbia; it's in the middle of New York City." "Cornell? You wouldn't like Cornell; it's in the middle of nowhere." "Brown? You definitely wouldn't like Brown. It's not in the middle of anything. It's at the bottom of the Ivy League."

Properly clothed and prejudiced, young Morley would trudge down to Arlington Center and catch the MTA to Harvard Square. As the bus picked its way down Mass. Ave., he'd stare out the window wishing he was off playing with his friends. But he did enjoy Harvard Square. That was the home of Joe and Nemo's, the Hot Dog King. For 15 cents, or 2 for 25¢, he'd buy a boiled dog in a steamed roll, smothered with mustard, relish and onions. A stop at Joe and Nemo's was the high point of any husky's week.

From Joe and Nemo's, Morley would shuffle his way through the sycamore leaves that covered the brick sidewalks along Boylston Street, cross Lars Anderson Bridge over the Charles, and head for the usher's entrance to the Stadium. The banks of the Charles were lined with tailgaters. The smell of Leavitt & Pierces'

3

custom-blended pipe tobacco hung heavy in the air. Morley cleaned his clear-framed glasses so his myopic eighth-grade eyes could get a better look at the patrician breasts sprouting beneath fields of cashmere sweaters.

By the third game, he had figured out the routine and began to enjoy his afternoons at the Stadium. He was becoming imbued with the Harvard spirit. He'd come home whistling "Veritas" and proudly present his father with a used program. Whereupon J.P. would sit him down and grill him about the game. "How did Hank Keohane do?" he'd ask, pleased that his plan seemed to be working. "You know, Hank went to Arlington High," implying that there was hope for young Morley.

J.P. was particularly encouraged after the Cornell game. It was played on October 5, 1957. Harvard won, 20–6, but that wasn't the big news. The big news was that the Russians had launched Sputnik. On his way to the bus, Morley passed a crowd huddled around the kiosk in Harvard Square. They were waiting nervously for the latest news. No one was talking about Harvard's victory. All they wanted to know about was Sputnik. Everyone was sure that Sputnik was going to drop a bomb on America.

J.P. had the same worried look on his face when Morley ran into the house. He didn't even ask Morley about the Cornell game. He was glued to the radio listening to an update on Sputnik. "I want to go to Harvard and become a physicist," Morley said. "I want to build our own Sputnik."

"That's great," J.P. assured him. "I know for a fact that Harvard has a fine Physics Department."

By the Dartmouth game, Morley had forgotten all about Sputnik. When he arrived at the Stadium, his thoughts were refocused on fields of cashmere sweaters. It was going to be an overflow crowd. Dartmouth was undefeated.

He checked in and was disappointed when the head usher gave him a badge that said Section 32. Section 32 was midfield on the visitor's side. For an usher, it was the worst draw in the entire Stadium. Unlike the Harvard side, where most people had held the same seats since the Mayflower, nobody knew what they were doing on the visitor's side. For the big games like Dartmouth, Princeton, and Yale, nobody wanted to work Section 32.

Morley assumed that Dartmouth fans would be the usual assortment of preppy students and alumni. Except for the color of their scarves, he had come to the conclusion that all Ivy Leaguers looked the same. But the students coming into Section 32 weren't wearing scarves. They weren't wearing much of anything. Even though the temperature was hovering around freezing, a green loincloth was the standard dress. Green paint covered the rest of their bodies. Feathers stuck out of their heads. These students didn't look very studious. They looked like Indians.

The main war party arrived just before the kickoff. They were led by an Indian Princess. He was a dark, hairy little guy with thick coke bottle glasses, sucking on a big cigar. His attire consisted of a pigtailed wig and a scanty pair of buckskin panties. Two footballs stuffed into a huge bra easily qualified him as the most hypermammarific maiden ever to enter Harvard Stadium.

Morley watched in amazement as the Indian Princess headed right for the best seats. He proferred no ticket; he asked for no help.

People began to complain. "Usher! Usher! Check this guy's ticket! He's in the wrong seat."

The Indian Princess did not take these complaints sitting down. He jumped up onto his seat, put his hand to his mouth, extended two fingers, and proclaimed, "White man speak with forked tongue! Once Indians own whole section. John Harvard stole ancestral seats. Now braves reclaim them!" The braves whooped and howled as they chugged from jugs of firewater. It was obvious that the Indian Princess and his war party weren't moving.

A new cry of "Usher! Usher!" was the immediate response. Morley tried to melt into the crowd. The Indian Princess's ancestral seats were in his part of Section 32. A pompous paleface spied his badge. He was wearing a crimson scarf. For big games, Harvard stuck many of its young alumni in section 32. It wasn't until they were older and giving lots of money that they moved them over to the Harvard side.

"Hey, usher, get over here," the pompous paleface demanded. "We need some help."

"Is there some problem, sir?" young Morley asked timidly.

"You bet there's a problem," he huffed indignantly. "I don't believe that these, er, gentlemen are in the proper seats. Here are our tickets." He handed Morley some stubs.

The pompous paleface was wearing a jaunty touring cap and smoking a pipe. Even at thirteen, Morley could tell that this guy was a jerk. Did he really think that some kid armed only with a badge that said "USHER" was going to move these drunken Indians?

Morley did the only thing he knew how to do. He tapped the Indian Princess on the shoulder. "May I see your tickets, please?"

The Indian Princess ignored him. He had settled in next to the jerk's date and was offering her a slug from his jug of firewater. She must have been a blind date. She accepted. Her eyes began to water. "Pretty good stuff, huh?" the Indian Princess said, smiling as he tipped the ash from his cigar.

"Sir. Excuse me, er, ma'am. Sir. May I please see your tickets?"

"Here you go, kid," the Indian Princess said, handing Morley the jug. "Take a swig of this, it'll make your whosiwhatsis grow. And when you go to college, go to Dartmouth." He aimed his cigar at the Harvard guy. "You don't want to end up like this stuffed shirt."

"I beg your pardon?" the pompous paleface protested.

"Hey fella. Siddown and have a pop," the Indian Princess ordered. "If you're a good boy, I'll let you play with THESE for a while." He stood up and thrust his humongous breasts into the Harvard guy's face. The little touring cap disappeared into the huge bra. There was a muffled protest, but at that moment, everyone stood up for the kickoff. Morley used this opportunity to melt back into the crowd. As far as he was concerned, the Indians were welcome to their ancestral seats.

Fueled by firewater, the Indians got more and more rambunctious as the game went on. By halftime, they were set to go on the warpath. They booed lustily as the Harvard band came strutting onto the field. They erupted wildly when they saw the Harvard drum.

The Harvard drum was at least ten feet tall and had a big block "H" on either side. It was mounted on a wagon pulled by two goons that Harvard probably had accepted just for that purpose. Two more huge guys banged the drum with enormous drumsticks. All four were dressed in white bucks, white pants, and crimson letter sweaters. It was all very impressive, what with the drum banging, the glockenspiel chiming, the band playing, and more than ten thousand men of Harvard singing and waving their little white handkerchiefs.

Morley was so absorbed by the show that he didn't realize what was happening until he heard the cry, "Charge!" The Indian Princess was leading an assault onto the field. Hundreds of Indians poured out of the stands. A few cops moved over to try and stop them. They were too late. The Indian Princess was the first over the wall. He still had his big stogie clenched firmly in his mouth. A cop at the foot of Section 32 stepped up to block him. The Indian Princess knocked him flat with a beautiful forearm shiver. He was headed straight for the Harvard drum.

The drum was right in front of the Harvard bench, which meant that the Indian Princess would have to lead his war party through the entire Harvard band. The flutes were no problem, but the going got rougher when they hit the trombones. Band members, instruments, and Indians were flying all over the place. The Indian Princess lost his cigar somewhere among the tubas, but he kept pressing on.

The goons ushering the drum quickly sized up the situation and initiated an early but orderly retreat. They started pulling the drum down the Harvard sideline towards the exit. The remains of the band valiantly kept tootling "Ten Thousand Men of Harvard" while the Harvard partisans frantically waved their white handkerchiefs and screamed, "Save the drum! Save the drum!"

Only the Indian Princess made it through the band. He was wobbling like a bent arrow. He had lost one of his footballs, he had been scalped of his wig, his buckskin panties hung tattered from one ankle. But now there was nothing but open field between the Indian Princess and the drum. The whole Stadium was focused on his solitary charge.

The Indian Princess broke into a sprint. The goons pulling the drum picked up their pace. They weren't going to make it. The Indian Princess was going to catch them. Just as he reached the drum, the Princess extended his arms, lowered his head, and launched himself at the block "H." There was a collective gasp from the crowd. The Indian Princess was going to dive through the Harvard drum.

He didn't make it. One of the drummers beat him off in midair with a perfectly executed stroke. It knocked the Princess cold. A cheer filled the Stadium as he crumpled to the turf and the drum rolled unscathed towards the exit. A couple of loin-clothed braves ran onto the field, scooped the Princess up, and lugged him back to Section 32. A few shots of firewater seemed to revive him, but his day ended on another sour note. Dartmouth was routed by Harvard, 26–0.

J.P. listened to every Harvard game on the radio. When Morley got home, the first thing he said was, "Quite a game! Harvard sure taught those heathens a lesson. Imagine trying to dive through the Harvard drum. Who would ever want to go to Dartmouth?"

"Me!" exclaimed Morley. "Ted's right! Those Harvard guys are jerks!"

J.P. slumped into his chair. His plan had backfired. He knew he'd never be able to salvage Morley. The count was now 0–2. "Go find your little brother," he told Morley, obviously dejected. "I need to talk to him."

8

I

The sun was shining, it was 78°, a warm breeze blew over the Connecticut Valley. Ed Morley lay in his bed at Amherst. He scanned the room. The walls were covered with pictures from Janson's *History of Art*. He was lying in the middle of one big collage.

In less than 51 hours, he had to take his comprehensive exams. This was his second and last shot. If he flunked again, which was quite likely, he wouldn't graduate. If he didn't graduate, he wouldn't get his job with AT&T. If he didn't get his job with AT&T, he'd have to join the Army. If he joined the Army, he'd have to go to Vietnam. If he went to Vietnam, he'd probably get his ass shot off. But going to Vietnam and getting his ass shot off wasn't the worst of it. If he didn't graduate, what would he say to his father?

That was the thought that really bothered him.

The Damned Cast Into Hell by Luca Signorelli stared down at him. Signorelli was not one of the great names of the early Renaissance, but at least Morley had no trouble recognizing his work. Signorelli always made the skins on his people too tight. They all looked like the muscle charts down at the gym.

Janson stated that Signorelli used the human body as an expressive instrument. That explanation didn't mean much to Morley. What Morley remembered most about Signorelli was an aside that Professor Merrill had thrown into one of his lectures. According to the Professor, Signorelli dissected his own son when the boy died shortly after reaching puberty. The Professor claimed that Signorelli used this untimely death to learn more about the structural anatomy of young men. Now, every time Morley looked at a Signorelli, he didn't see a painting. What he saw was young Signorelli, skinned like a rabbit.

Unfortunately, after three years as a Fine Arts Major, this one aside on Signorelli comprised the bulk of Morley's knowledge of the history of art. The rest of the pictures taped to his walls were nothing more than an annoying blur. Why had he ever become a Fine Arts Major?

Then he remembered. At one time he was going to be an architect. That was before he realized that architects had to know things like stress and torque, the stuff they taught in Physics. There was another problem; he couldn't draw. The ink was always smearing, and his letters never conformed to rule. By the mid-point of his junior year, Morley knew he'd never be an architect; only by then, it was too late to change his major. Now he had to pass his comps.

But he wasn't dead yet. He had drawn one last plan. It too was smeared and didn't conform to rule, but if it worked, he was home free. If it didn't, Luca Signorelli wouldn't be the only father to skin his son.

Morley looked out his window at the clock on top of Johnson Chapel. Its big black face with gold hands and Roman numerals were visible throughout the Valley, but from Morley's room, he could hardly see them. That's because his room was almost directly under the clock. Due to the bells in Johnson Chapel, no one ever signed up for 402 North. That's why Morley was able to have a double all to himself. And this wasn't even where he lived. His official residence was at Beta. He just used this room in North for studying and getting laid.

He craned his neck seeking a better angle. The hands looked like they were trying to say 11:30. That was close enough. It didn't matter what the hands said. It was the bells that told the time at Amherst.

He heard his typewriter pecking away in the next room. The GE slogan, "Progress Is Our Most Important Product," flashed through his mind. He had interviewed with GE but they had not been impressed with his progress. Fortunately, Ma Bell had made him a decent offer, one that carried a military deferment. Once he graduated and got hitched to Ma Bell, there would be no war in Vietnam for Morley.

"Damn it, Morley, you're the world's worst speller." It was Margie in the other room. Morley became aware that the comforting click, click, click had stopped. That was not good. Margie was typing his final paper for Psych 39. The paper had to be in by 5:00 P.M. He'd already gotten two extensions. If he didn't meet this deadline, he wouldn't have to worry about his comps. He'd flunk Psych 39, and he needed those credits to graduate.

Margie had been typing for over two hours. She was still a long way from done. He knew that he had to keep her going. He slowly pulled himself out of bed, and walked into the other room. Margie was erasing yet another misspelled word. The desk was covered with bits of eraser. He wondered how much more had fallen into his typewriter. He was amazed that it still worked.

"Come on, Margie, you're almost done. Just knock out these last couple of pages and we'll go to the game."

"Right, I'm almost done. I'll be here the rest of the day. You know, I can't believe you ever got through Amherst."

"Hey, I'm not through yet, and I've gotta play this game. Get the paper done and I'll make it up to you. Just let me graduate, and we'll go to the Cape." Morley hoped that the thought of going to the Cape would take Margie's mind off of his spelling. Margie loved the Cape. He had taken her there once before and banged her eyes out. Surely she could never forget that trip. She wouldn't let him down. She'd get the paper done and it would be perfect.

Margie was one of Morley's better finds, even though she wasn't a classic beauty. Early in his freshman year, Morley had learned not to fool around with the classic beauties. They were nothing but trouble. Thanks to those freshmen photo books, every classic beauty's picture was hung in every phone booth at every men's college in the Northeast. They expected their dates to buy them expensive dinners, take them to plays, and chauffeur them around in fancy cars. And who could blame them? They got more recognition than the FBI's ten most wanted. If you were a classic beauty from Smith or Holyoke, there was always some jerk from Williams or Yale just dying to squire you around. Looking good was all these guys cared about.

Morley didn't buy that act. He couldn't afford dinners, plays, or a fancy car. He enjoyed getting laid and the best way to get laid was to stick with the second-liners. These were the girls who were a little too short, too tall, too thin, too fat, had a lousy set of pins, or, more likely, little boobs. They knew they weren't classic beauties; they just wanted a good time. A few beers and a roll in the rack was fine with them. These were the Beta Honeys.

Margie's problem was that she was slightly stoop-shouldered. It wasn't anything physiological; she was just shy. From the way she walked around you would never have guessed that she was stacked. On their first date Morley discovered that Margie had one of the best bodies in the Four College area. Her legs were those of the *Prima Ballerina* (Edgar Degas, c. 1876); her breasts, Rubenesque (*Marie de' Medici, Queen of France landing at Marseilles*, 1622–1623). When he got her on the workbench, he couldn't believe his eyes. Those two beautiful mounds literally burst from her blouse. He knew that if Margie ever threw back her shoulders, he could kiss her goodbye. Every guy in the Northeast would want to turn on those headlights. But as long as she walked around like Quasimodo, Margie was all his. Well, almost all his.

Margie had a boyfriend; some stiff from Yale that she had met as a freshman. She had been going with him for two and a half years. Morley had never met this warhorse, but he had seen dozens like him—lots of money, and all boola boola. He'd probably gone to Hotchkiss. Hotchkiss specialized in turning out rich jerks.

This Yalie was the only guy besides Morley that Margie had dated while she was at Smith. She would go down to New Haven one weekend and he would come up to Smith the next. Morley knew the routine. When he came to Smith, Margie might give him a tweak. When she went to Yale, he might give her a little poke, provided he got drunk enough and Yale beat Harvard. Morley didn't even have to meet him to know he was a touchhole.

Margie had made the necessary corrections and was stooped over the typewriter. She was wearing a loose fitting halter. As she punched the keys, Morley could see those magnificent breasts bouncing up and down. He looked back at the collage of pictures. The hell with his comps. He snuck up behind her. She was preoccupied with correcting yet another mistake. He slipped his hand into her halter and gently kissed her neck. He could feel her nipples getting hard.

"Watch it, Morley, or I'm not going to finish this paper."

There was a definite challenge in her voice. It was Morley's call. He could get laid, but if she came, she might not be able to finish the paper. Decisions, decisions. Morley reluctantly removed his hand.

"Discovering Yourself" was the official course title for Psych 39. It was commonly known as "Jerkoff 101." The course generally was considered a gut for seniors. All you had to do was write a halfway credible paper for your final and the Psych Department would give you your college average. In Morley's case, that would amount to a 71, but "Discovering Yourself" was good for three credits and Morley needed those credits to graduate.

The course actually was kind of interesting. The students took a battery of psychological tests, and then using these tests as a reference, wrote a paper describing themselves and how they had changed over the last four years. Morley looked at the page that Margie was typing. She was just finishing the part where he introduced his Asshole Theory. That was still Freshmen year. She did have a long way to go.

As Margie continued typing, Morley started to reread the Asshole Theory. "I developed my asshole theory soon after I arrived at Amherst. I didn't know a soul at Amherst, so quite naturally I was a little nervous."

Morley should have said overwhelmed. He'd never felt that he was smart enough to be at Amherst. He'd been all set to go to Dartmouth, but when he was accepted at Amherst, his father had told him to forget about Dartmouth. There was no way he was going to matriculate with those heathens.

He focused on the paper.

> My main claim to fame was being named "All-Scholastic" in football as a senior at Arlington High. Everybody in Massachusetts knew what it meant to be selected "All-Scholastic." If you were "All-Scholastic," you were on top of the world. It opened up a lot of doors.

Morley couldn't believe all the attention he'd received from college recruiters. B.C., Duke, and Penn State had made him offers. There was often a green station wagon sitting in front of the house; those guys from Dartmouth were fanatics when it came to football. He really should have gone to Dartmouth. If he had, he wouldn't have to worry about taking his comps. Playing ball would have been enough to get him through Dartmouth.

Morley read on as Margie typed.

> In high school, it was all very simple: to be cool, you had to play football. Guys who played ball could do no wrong. They were treated like kings. That's why I loved wearing my Arlington High Varsity Football Jacket. It was my security blanket. It told everyone that I was a cool guy.

Wasn't that the truth. In high school, his varsity football jacket had been his ticket to respect. When he put it on, there was no way that anyone could mistake him for an asshole. It had his letter on the front, the words Arlington High Football on the back, his nickname, "Morley," on one sleeve, with a little football and his number on the other. If it rained, not to worry. The Arlington High Varsity Football Jacket was reversible. It really was a thing of beauty.

14

After Arlington High, my father sent me to Deerfield Academy for a year. There I noticed that my jacket had lost some of its mystique. People still realized that I played ball, but playing ball at Deerfield wasn't such a big deal. Other things like swimming, squash, skiing, and even debating were considered just as important as football. Plus, Deerfield had its own Varsity Jacket and you could get one for doing almost anything. A guy on the debating team might be an asshole, only at Deerfield, he didn't know it. He actually thought that he was as cool as a guy who played ball. And why not; he had a Varsity Jacket to prove it.

Morley wondered what Margie thought about the Asshole Theory. Now was not the time to ask. He kept reading.

When I got to Amherst, I was in for a rude awakening.

Perfect. The Psych Department loved rude awakenings.

My second night here, I decided to walk up and see a guy from Manhasset named Ken Howard. Howard had been a big basketball star for Manhasset. He was so good that he got invited to play in the Greater New York All Star Tournament, which was played in Madison Square Garden. When the New York press saw that he was the only white guy on the floor, they dubbed him "The White Shadow."

Morley figured that it wouldn't hurt to give Howard a plug, not that Howard needed it. Ken was an excellent student.

Fortunately, there was a chill in the air that evening, so I had an excuse to put on my Arlington High Varsity Football Jacket. It felt good, especially around all these smart guys at Amherst.

When I got to what I thought was Howard's room, the door was open, so I knocked and walked in. A little guy with frizzy hair was sitting on a box reading a book. The box was full of more books. Howard wasn't there.

15

I stood there shifting from foot to foot, but the little guy didn't bother to look up. He just kept reading. I put my hands into the pockets of my jacket and pulled it closer. I recognized him. His name was Slosher. He had made a big scene at the first History 1 lecture.

Morley didn't have to explain the scene in his paper. Everybody at the College knew it.

That first lecture was supposed to focus on the summer reading assignment. In reality, the faculty used this lecture as a way to establish their superiority over the freshman class. The assigned reading list was about two miles long, and just in case there were any freshmen gung ho enough to do all of the assigned reading, the faculty had tacked on a suggested reading list that was four miles long.

Professor Kinsey relished giving the opening lecture to the freshmen class. He had been doing it for the past seventeen years. It confirmed his status as the prima donna of the department and allowed him to instill a fear and respect for the entire faculty into each new class. Prof. Kinsey's favorite trick was to let some unsuspecting freshman challenge him with a question. Kinsey then would urge the eager student on as if he had discovered a legitimate chink in the department's armor. Then, when all of the class was sure that their new hero had him on the run, Kinsey would turn and shred the poor guy into academic confetti. After that, very few freshmen were willing to challenge the Amherst faculty.

The Professor had just finished chopping up Lawrence Myers Mudd, III, some very smart kid with a real deep voice from the Hill School, when Slosher raised his hand. Professor Kinsey couldn't believe it. No student in his right mind would dare ask another question after seeing what he had just done to Mudd. All he could figure was that this little guy with the frizzy hair must be looking for the men's room.

Slosher's question hit him like a two-by-four: "Why had the Amherst faculty chosen to present only one theory of Western

Civilization, while most of the academic community recognized two valid theories on the subject?"

Unbeknownst to the other 286 freshmen in the room, there were two somewhat different theories on the development of Western civilization. The traditional theory maintained that there was a great Dark Age between the fall of Rome and the early Renaissance one thousand years later. The alternative theory, which was much less popular but still had a few respected disciples within academia, was that there was no Dark Age; that the Roman civilization had just shifted to Constantinople, where it continued its decadence. Judging from the assigned and suggested reading, the Amherst faculty had chosen to ignore the alternative theory.

The honest answer was that the Amherst faculty felt most freshman wouldn't care about one theory of Western Civilization, let alone two, but Professor Kinsey couldn't admit that in front of 287 of the brightest kids in the world.

His only recourse was to state, in a condescending tone, that "the Amherst faculty considered the 'second theory' to be of little consequence, and had decided not to confuse the issue by presenting it." He thanked Slosher for bringing it to everyone's attention and prayed that Slosher would sit down. But Slosher had no intention of sitting down. You could see that he was getting upset.

"Isn't that somewhat presumptuous?" he said. The sincerity of his indignation was apparent to everyone in the room. Professor Kinsey conceded that maybe the faculty had been a bit negligent in not suggesting reading from the other school of thought.

This explanation did not appease Slosher. Now he was pissed. "It's a bit more than negligent," Slosher said. "I think that it's intellectually dishonest." He then suggested that the faculty immediately add readings on the second theory to the syllabus and even recommended several texts. Kinsey was devastated. From that moment on, it was open season on the Amherst faculty. After that first lecture, Slosher had left them as naked as Signorelli's son.

Margie stopped typing. As she leaned over to make another erasure, Morley was tempted to slip his hand down the back of her drawers. But instead he kept reading about his first meeting with Slosher.

> Slosher finally raised his head. A look of disgust came over his face as he studied my jacket. When I asked him where I could find Howard, he said, "Howard who?"
>
> "You know, the big guy from Manhasset."
>
> Slosher's look changed from disgust to contempt. "He's probably down at the gym." Then the final blow. "Why? Are you some friend of his from high school?"
>
> What Slosher had really meant was, "That's the stupidest-looking jacket I've ever seen. You must be a real asshole."
>
> I had come full circle. At Arlington High, playing ball meant everything. At Amherst, it meant less than nothing. I went back to my room and stuffed my Arlington High Varsity Football Jacket into the bottom of my trunk. I was about to have a major identity crisis.

Not bad. Not bad at all. The paper would go on to explain that understanding other people was the key to discovering yourself. That was the basis of his Asshole Theory, and the Psych Department would love the part about Slosher. Most of the faculty had been delighted when Slosher abandoned Amherst after sophomore year for the University of Chicago. His departure had removed the greatest threat to their superiority.

Morley slipped one hand under Margie's halter and the other down the back of her drawers. She began to moan as he stroked her tits and ass. Her head leaned against his crotch. That excited Morley. There was going to be a slight interruption in "Discovering Yourself." He undid Margie's halter and steered her onto the workbench.

The workbench was a daybed that his mother had found for him. She'd fitted it with a bright new red corduroy cover. It had looked pretty good when it first arrived at Amherst, but now, after three years of hard labor, it was covered with pecker tracks.

Morley was not a Catholic but he practiced coitus interruptus religiously. He constantly worried about knocking someone up, especially since his taste in women dropped off dramatically after a few beers. Most guys used a safe, but Morley felt awkward rolling one on in front of a date. It was particularly embarrassing if he didn't know her. Thus, coitus interruptus had become his standard operating procedure and the red corduroy cover showed it.

Once Morley was inside Margie, he stopped. Margie liked it that way. She had read a book called *The Harrod Experiment* which explained how kids could screw for hours at a time. The Harrod technique was tough on Morley. It required a lot of stamina and patience. He fought to hold his load as Margie nibbled on his ear and ground her pelvis hard into his crotch. Morley usually thought of baseball scores, the traditional cure for premature ejaculation, but today, he had other things on his mind. He had to finish this paper, pass his comps, and get that job with AT&T. If he could do those three things, he'd be a winner. But passing his comps was going to be a major problem.

He started reviewing his plan. His comprehensive exam in Fine Arts would consist of twenty slides. Those twenty slides were all that stood between him and graduation. They would come from the Art Department's collection of thousands. To pass, he was going to need help. If his plan worked, he'd have it.

Margie must have felt him drifting away. He seemed to be shrinking. "Say, when's your game?" she asked.

"I don't have to leave until twelve."

He saw a slight smile come over her face. "I thought you weren't supposed to get laid before a game."

"It's O.K. We won't come."

At that moment, the bell on the clock of Johnson Chapel started to clang. It was noon. With each chime Margie twitched. So much for the Harrod Experiment and not coming. Margie was going wild; he could feel her fingernails ripping into his back; her legs pulling him in, deeper and deeper. He pulled out just in time to spill one more trail on the corduroy cover.

19

Normally, Morley was good for another shot, but he had no time today. He had to stop by the Beta House and pick up the brothers. Eight of Amherst's starting side were Betas. Besides, he couldn't afford to put Margie out of commission. She'd already come once; if she came again, she might be out for the entire afternoon.

Morley got up, dressed and looked at Margie. She was conked out. He left, disgusted with himself. Why had he stopped to get laid? Margie had been moving right along. All he'd had to do was leave her alone. Now there was a chance that she might not finish "Discovering Yourself." Slosher was right. He was an asshole.

As Morley ran out of the dorm, he noticed a group of protesters on the steps of Johnson Chapel. That was not unusual. There were always some nuts hanging around the Chapel protesting something. A banner wrapped around one of the Chapel's massive Doric columns said, "Stop the War." Yeah, right, thought Morley, and tomorrow we'll go to the moon.

A girl that looked like Mary Travers, long straight blonde hair, no makeup, cut-off jeans, and very serious, was playing a guitar. Morley recognized the song; it was "Blowing in the Wind." Standing next to her was Elliot Ginsberg.

For four years, Elliot had been protesting. First it was civil rights, then rights for migrant workers, now the war in Vietnam. Elliot was the self-proclaimed conscience of the College, but Morley couldn't see where Elliot ever accomplished anything. Did he really expect to change what was happening in Mississippi, California or Southeast Asia by sitting on the steps of Johnson Chapel singing songs with a bunch of fruitcakes? If the answer, my friend, was blowing in the wind, Elliot wasn't producing so much as a breeze.

As Morley headed down the path towards Beta, he thought about Elliot. Why didn't he join a fraternity, get drunk, get laid, and get into graduate school like everyone else? That's what you did at Amherst. Why was he wasting his time protesting? Elliot had to be an asshole.

II

As soon as he saw the House, Morley knew something was wrong. There were no brothers on the porch. On a nice spring day like this, the Betas should have been outside working on their tans. The empty porch could mean only one thing; the brothers were too screwed up to get up.

When he opened the door, he could see that the brothers had done some serious ratfucking. Queen Anne chairs and Chippendale sofas were heaped into a pile in the middle of the hall. The TV was balanced precariously on top of the heap. A group of brothers were lying on the floor. No one seemed too concerned. They were watching "Rocky and His Pals."

"Rocky and His Pals" was far and away the brothers' favorite show. Everyone liked the fact that Rocky, the flying squirrel, had gone to Harvard, but Bullwinkle, the moose, had gone to Dartmouth. That's because he wasn't smart enough to get into Harvard. The writers of "Rocky and His Pals" had to be Betas.

Before Morley could say anything, the sinister voice of Boris Badenoff focused his attention to the TV. As usual, Boris and his sidekick, Natasha, were up to no good. It soon became clear that what the Russkies were after was a precious metal known as Upzadazium. Upzadazium was the only solid lighter than air. Whoever controlled Upzadazium would control the world.

Morley pulled a chair from the pile. By the time he sat down, Boris and Natasha had made off with the Upzadazium. The vertical hold was way out of whack, so Boris and Natasha kept rolling over and over as they floated away with their prize. None of the brothers bothered to fix it. Morley could see that Boris

21

and Natasha were wearing big smiles. Natasha was saying, "Boris dahling, we did it. Mr. Big will be very pleased." Good thing for them. Mr. Big had been plenty pissed with their past foul-ups. If they messed up again, it would be one-way tickets to Gulag City.

Just when all seemed lost, Rocky came flying into the screen. With all the flickering and rolling, it was tough to tell exactly what happened next, but he must have knocked the Upzadazium out of Boris's hands. The Russkies came crashing back to earth. They landed right on Bullwinkle and Capt. Wrongway Peachfuzz, one of Rocky and Bullwinkle's befuddled friends. The world was saved, if only Bullwinkle didn't do anything stupid. But that was impossible. Bullwinkle had gone to Dartmouth.

Bullwinkle and Captain Peachfuzz started apologizing to Boris and Natasha. They saw nothing strange about two Russians falling out of the sky and landing on their heads. Somehow, they thought it was their fault. Bullwinkle very kindly offered to throw Boris and Natasha back up to the floating piece of Upzadazium. The last shot was of Boris and Natasha fighting with Rocky over the Upzadazium, while the shadow of Mr. Big flickered ominously over the screen. The announcer said, "Stay tuned for our next episode, 'Two for the Rock,' or 'Up Your Dazium.'

Rocky and his pals were replaced a couple of cannon shooting Quaker Puffed Wheat and Quaker Puffed Rice. Morley hated Puffed Wheat and Puffed Rice. They were like Upzadazium. When you poured on the milk, they floated out of the bowl.

The bodies on the floor began to stir. Shortpecker, the House's custodian and father-figure, was stretched out on the couch. He didn't move. Shortpecker had been the House custodian for a generation of Betas. During that time, he had seldom left the couch, but no one ever complained. The brothers knew that Short had earned his position. During the war, he had saved a half dozen guys by falling on a German grenade. Most of Short's right hand had been blown off, he took considerable shrapnel in both legs, and according to Beta lore, lost half his pecker. This last injury was very much open to question, because after the war

Shortpecker had come back to Amherst, married his high school sweetheart, and fathered six little shortpeckers.

"Hey, Short, what happened?" Morley said, surveying the pile of furniture.

Shortpecker didn't hear him. He was mesmerized by the puffed wheat and puffed rice being shot out of the cannons. Morley tried again. "Hey, Short, what happened?"

The Quaker cannons stopped booming. Shortpecker sat up and adjusted his glasses with his mangled right hand. Seeing Morley launched him into a familiar refrain. "You Betas are dumber than that moose. If the Dean sees what you've done, the House is going on social pro."

This time, Shortpecker had a point. Thanks to Professor Roller, the House was skating on the edge. Professor Roller had arrived one day in early May, compliments of the Town Highway Department. The Town had been repaving the road in front of Beta. It was a job any private contractor could have finished in a day, but after a week, the Town's crew still wasn't done. At quitting time on Friday, the foreman asked the Betas if he could park the Town's steamroller in the driveway for the weekend. That way, they wouldn't have to lug it all the way back to the yard. The Betas were only to happy to oblige.

The Town truck had hardly rounded the corner when the brothers had the steamroller cranked up and rolling. They soon began flattening bushes, bottles, and beer cans, but the more the brothers drank, the more they realized that they weren't maximizing the steamroller's full potential. Lenny the Lob solved that problem. He went over to Chi Phi and borrowed a lamp.

Physics I was a required course at Amherst, and by chance, the introductory physics text was authored by one Holton Roller. Physics I was a certified ball buster. Thanks to Professor Holton Roller, a number of brothers, including Morley, had been forced to retake it in summer school. Such being the case, it seemed only fitting that visiting Prof. Steam Roller should be asked to demonstrate how F (force) = M (mass) x A (acceleration). The subject would be the Chi Phi lamp.

The Professor's demonstration was a smashing success. The brothers stood mesmerized as they watched Professor Roller (M) accelerate (A) and apply a healthy dose of force (F) to the Chi Psi lamp. None of them had never seen such complete and wanton destruction. Their inquisitive minds demanded more.

Pledges were dispatched to scrounge an assortment of knickknacks from around the College. They filched a chair from DU, the companion lamp from Chi Phi, and a bicycle that Ken Bacon had carelessly left unlocked in front of the library. The Professor easily F'd them all, especially Bacon's bicycle. Word of his lecture spread across campus. Soon, the Beta parking lot was crowded with eager students, all shouting encouragement to Prof. Roller. The Psi U's showed up with another keg, which was quickly tapped, consumed and offered up to the Professor. Much to everyone's disappointment, the Psi U's keg resisted the M x A. It was too big and too round to be F'd.

It was then that Pigpen produced the President's trophy for the "Most Academically Improved Fraternity." The Betas had won it the previous year when, due to an unusually strong pledge class, they had climbed from 13th, and last, to a respectable 8th. The Professor had no trouble F'ing the trophy. Within seconds, it looked like the proverbial pancake.

That should have ended the class, but the Professor was on such a roll that he kept A'ing into a tree. The F of the impact broke his steering column. That marked the end of Prof. Steam Roller's lecture.

Breaking the Town's steamroller presented no problem. When the foreman of the Town's crew knocked on Beta's front door bright and early Monday morning, Brother Ruxin, President of Beta Theta Pi and by far the most eloquent member of the House, arose to greet him. Brother Ruxin sympathized with the Town's loss, and routinely blamed the damage on some blackguards from UMass. That was it for the steamroller.

F'ing the "Most Academically Improved Fraternity" trophy was different story. The trophy was over a hundred years old and had the name of each year's winning fraternity proudly inscribed into its once shiny, cylindrical surface. It had to be returned at the annual Awards Dinner, which was held near the end of each academic year. While the College might look the other way at a broken chair or flattened lamp, they would not condone the desecration of anything academic. The trophy had to be fixed.

Understandably, no jeweler would touch it. Pig Pen, who had F'ed the trophy, finally found an auto body shop in Holyoke that was willing to pound it out. Everyone assumed that the trophy would come back looking like new. It didn't. It came back looking like an old silver trophy that had been run over by a steamroller and pounded out by an auto body shop.

Morley always admired the way academics could launch into a spontaneous speech appropriate to any occasion. When Ruxin presented the refurbished trophy for "Most Academically Improved Fraternity" to President Plimpton, the President uncorked a beauty. He talked about the trophy's history. How his own fraternity, DKE, had won it when he was at Amherst, and now, for the first time in twenty-seven years, they had won it again. The President then went on about how much he had looked forward to this day, when he, as President of the College, could present this very same trophy to his old fraternity. But, thanks to the Betas' total disrespect for anything academic, that would not happen. Instead, the DKE's would get a mangled piece of metal that represented social irresponsibility, not academic improvement. Was nothing sacred?

In response to the President's question, Ruxin had fumbled through a plea for forgiveness. He blamed the destruction of the Trophy on some rowdies from Williams, and lamely apologized on behalf of the entire House. They should have known better than to trust anyone from Williams.

It was a noble but inadequate defense. The Administration wasn't buying it and now, thanks to Professor Roller, the House was in serious trouble. One more screw-up and they would be on social probation, which meant at least one semester during which no women or liquor would be allowed in the House. Social pro would mark the end of Beta. Everyone knew that the House couldn't last a semester without women and liquor. Broads and booze were the body and blood of Beta.

"Forget the Dean," Morley said to Shortpecker. "He's not coming over here. He's got enough problems just trying to get through graduation." Then he added, "Where the hell is Gootch?" Gootch was captain of the Amherst Rugby Football Club and one of the House's principal screw-offs. Everyone agreed that Gootch easily could have been on the Dean's good list if he'd applied himself, but Gootch preferred to be a Beta.

"Say, Morley," Shortpecker said, ignoring the whereabouts of Gootch, "where you been? Up banging that little honey from Smith?" Morley winced. Shortpecker always knew everything. "You oughta save your strength for the Old Blue. You Betas think more about your peckers than about winning."

Much to Shortpecker's delight, the brothers lying around the TV came back to life and began to rag Morley about getting laid before the game. Morley quickly retreated upstairs. He looked into Room Six. Half of the rugby team were laid out on mattresses that had been thrown on the floor. The room smelled of stale beer and fresh farts. It was obvious that the brothers were terribly hung over. That was not good. This was a big game. If Amherst could beat the Old Blue, it would have a legitimate claim to the national title, and with the big schools like Stanford and Michigan becoming serious about rugby, this could be Amherst's last shot at a national title.

Earl Smee, the King of Smut, was propped up on a cot in the corner, a cigarette in one hand, a beer in the other. The King of Smut was recounting the highlights of the previous evening. He didn't acknowledge Morley. Nobody interrupted the King of Smut.

Smee was starting a story about the Monk and Bailey. Any story about the Monk was bound to be good. The Monk was the funniest guy in Beta, and the King always caught him just right. "The Monk and Bailey are primed to play Williams today," the King began. He was talking about the lacrosse game.

"Williams is all that stands between them and an undefeated season and they don't want to blow it by getting shitfaced." Here Smee paused, then added, "Unlike the rugby team."

There was a collective moan from the mattresses. "Anyway." he continued, "the Monk and Bails head for Northampton trying to avoid the temptations of the Beta bar." Smee was getting into the story. Morley plopped down on a mattress.

"The Monk just wants to get a pizza, but you know Bailey, he likes talking to all the honeys. As luck would have it, the Bails picks off two Smithies at the next table. They're a couple of freshmen who've never been to Beta. Before you know it, the four of them show up at the Beta bar."

At this point, Smee stopped, took a swig of beer and lit up another cigarette. Rearmed and refueled, he continued. "Now these honeys aren't too bad, especially for the Monk and Bails." Everyone laughed. The Monk and Bails were not what you would call ass men. "After a couple of beers, it became obvious that we're talking drive-in material."

A knowing smile came to everyone's face. Drive-ins were a prominent part of Beta's social life. The roofs of the side porches to the House were just under the windows of the social rooms on the second floor. Since most of the brothers entertained their dates in the social rooms, any enterprising Beta could climb out onto the roofs and have his choice of live entertainment just by leering through the windows. These voyeuristic experiences, thanks in no small part to Smee's recaps, had become quite popular with the brothers.

"Of course, being freshmen," the King emphasized freshmen as if to highlight their naivete, "these honeys wanted to impress the Betas, so they drank far too much, far too quickly. Whereupon the Monk and Bails made their move."

Goopy Balderman sat up. Goopy didn't do too well socially, and even though it never seemed to help, he always paid careful attention to the details of every seduction.

"Bailey explained to the honeys that since he and Monk were big stars on the lacrosse team, it wouldn't be good if they were seen drinking before the Williams game. He suggested that they grab a few beers and head upstairs. The girls were very understanding. They didn't want to do anything to upset an undefeated season."

The King paused for another sip of beer. "As the Monk heads up the front stairs, he leans back and gives the brothers the high sign. Immediately, twenty guys head up the back stairs. The Monk goes into room four. Bailey maneuvers his honey into room five. The brothers pour out the window of room six."

At this point, Gootch interrupted. He wanted a rundown of all the brothers who had been at the drive-in. Amazingly, Smee remembered everyone. Smee's total recall was one of the reasons he was the King of Smut. He even gave a little summary of each brother's position. After setting the stage, he continued his story.

"Bailey, of course, is so preoccupied with the seduction that he forgets there are twenty guys driving-in on him. The lights are off and the curtains closed. In addition, he gets into one of his 'what is the meaning of Life?' discussions, which usually mean no action for the Bails. The Monk, on the other hand, is playing to the crowd. He arranges the curtains so everyone can see in and sets the lights so the honey can't see out. All the brothers immediately switch over to the Monk." Smee readjusted himself on the cot. He had come to the meat of his story.

"It's obvious that the beer is doing the job, because the Monk has moved into the seduction. After about 10 minutes, he's gotten the honey completely nude. Then he bogs down. She claims she's a virgin. Well, you know the Monk, he tells her that this would be his first time too, and he's never felt this way about any girl before, only he forgets her name." By now, all the brothers were sitting up. Although they were terribly hung over, Smee's story was bringing them back to life.

"Everyone would have stayed tuned to the Monk, but fortunately Fleas decided to check on Bailey. The 'Meaning of Life' speech usually marks a shutout for the Bails, but something's gone haywire. The speech is working for the first time in fifty tries. When Fleas looks in, Bailey and his honey are busy going at it, so Fleas just reaches in, opens the curtains, turns up the lights; and presto, we have the perfect drive-in."

At this point, Smee put on the same accent that Bailey used when he told one of his racial jokes. "Well Brother Bailey, he ain't too smooth. Instead of getting undressed, the boy just lifts up her skirt, and pulls down her panties. And he still has all his clothes on, including his Rebel Yell hat." Bradford Bailey was from Rock Hill, S.C., and Rebel Yell bourbon was his favorite drink. "I mean, it's no wonder the House has such a bad reputation." The King was on a roll.

"While we're watching the Bails' little ass bob up and down, who should come out on the porch but the Monk! He is totally naked except for his socks. We say to him, 'Monk, what are you doing? Where's your honey?' To which he replies, 'Ah, seriously, when you all drove out, I figured Bailey must be putting on one hellava show. Obviously, I made the right decision.'"

By this time, guys were rolling on the mattresses. Smee's stories were better than the real thing, especially when they featured the Monk.

When the laughter died down, Morley said, "Hey Gootch, how about it? We've got to get ready for the game."

Smee responded, "Hey Morley, where have you been? Up in your little room with Miss Margie." Before Morley could respond, the King put his nose in the air, like a dog smelling the wind. "Say, do I detect the smell of spermatozoa? Methinks you were drilling Miss Margie when you should have been studying the *History of Art*." Damn that Smee. He and Shortpecker could always tell when anybody got laid. Given the stench in room six, Morley knew that Smee couldn't smell a thing, but that didn't matter. Morley was guilty as charged.

Gootch was immediately pissed. "Come on Morley, how could you get laid before a game? You know the rules."

Rules, how could Gootch talk about rules. These guys had blown their brains out while he had gone to bed at eleven. He felt great. They looked like hell. Yet he was the one taking all the shit.

"Forget it, I'll drink an extra glass of milk. Let's get going. We have to eat and get taped."

"No problem," said Hondo, "lacrosse is away today. We'll have the gym to ourselves."

Gootch agreed. "Yeah. Come on, Smee, give us one more story."

Smee was only too happy to oblige. "What about the Ghurst mooning Boom Boom Harlow's housemother after he got her back an hour late?"

Everyone rolled back and started laughing. This was going to be a great story. The Ghurst had ended up in the Northampton jail.

III

They were late. The King of Smut had really done a job on the poor Ghurst. His account of the Ghurst's date with Boom Boom Harlow had all the makings of a Beta Classic. None of the brothers were willing to leave until the King had wrung out every sordid detail. Now they had to hustle to make the kickoff. It would be bad form to start the match without a full side. That was just the type of advantage the Old Blue loved to exploit.

Morley took a deep breath as he passed through the doors to the gym. He never fully relaxed until he was inside. The gym was the only place at Amherst where he felt comfortable. Inside the gym, he was free from professors, administrators, deans, abandoned dates, and screwballs like Elliot Ginsberg. The gym was his impregnable fortress; the only place where he was granted academic immunity. Academics meant nothing to the guys at the gym. Who cared if a ball dropped at 32 feet per second per second as long as you caught it.

Like Shortpecker, most of the guys who worked at the gym were disabled vets. Unlike Shortpecker, they didn't look disabled. Their scars were much deeper. They hadn't been wounded physically. They hadn't fallen on any grenades, they weren't missing a hand, a leg, an arm, or even part of their peckers. Their problem was that they had cracked under pressure. Like the soldier Patton had slapped and called a coward, they couldn't handle the stress of war. In many ways, their wounds were worse than Shortpecker's. Because they didn't look disabled, people didn't think of them as disabled.

31

Morley should have had some insight into their problems. His neighbor growing up had been Dr. Benjamin Simon, a well known psychiatrist who worked with mental cases during World War II. Dr. Simon had discovered that 90 percent of his patients were not true war casualties, that the stress of war had exposed some pre-existing, deep-rooted psychological problem.

Had they been properly tested and diagnosed beforehand, these men would never have been inducted into the armed services, and probably would have led relatively normal lives. But once their problems had surfaced, there was no turning back.

The Army was so impressed with Dr. Simon's work that they made a documentary film about it. The film was produced by John Huston and starred Dr. Simon. It was called "Let There Be Light." The Doc would show the movie at his party every New Year's Day just before the bowl games. The Doc was a football fanatic and liked the analogy between war and games. He claimed that war was really just the ultimate game. He was delighted when Morley made All-Scholastic, and offered to use his considerable influence to secure Morley an appointment to the U.S. Military Academy at West Point. "Good athletes make good soldiers," the Doc told Morley. "They can handle stress."

Morley had seen "Let There Be Light" a half dozen times, but he never made the connection with the guys down at the gym. He just thought they liked working with athletes. The reality was that this was the closest they could get to a battlefield. They were part of the war effort; they were the support system for Amherst's soldiers. When Amherst won, they won. They had done their jobs. They could go to the VFW with their heads held high.

Even if you lost, the guys at the gym would never desert you. They would just work harder to get you ready for the next match. They would make sure you that your uniform was clean, and laid out in a neat little pile; that your equipment was shined and in shape; and that you, their warrior, were properly taped and prepared to do battle.

After the game, it was more of the same. You came back to the gym all dirty and wounded. You eased out of your uniform, cut off your tape, slowly showered, and iced down your bruises. When you finally left the gym, it was a mess. Jocks, socks, shoes, shorts, pads, tape, and clumps of mud were strewn all over the place. The fortress looked like a pig pen.

When you came back the next day, everything was spic and span, and instead of saying, "I wish you slobs would stay the hell out of here," the guys down at the gym were genuinely glad to see you. Some days, Morley would just hang around the training room and do nothing. Nobody minded. The guys at the gym were better than mothers.

There was no time for lying around today. Morley went right to his locker and got undressed. It was the same locker he'd had for all four years. That was another thing he liked about the gym. Unlike professors, courses, and books, your lock and locker never changed. They were issued the first day you arrived at Amherst and were yours until you graduated, died, or got thrown out.

By his senior year, Morley couldn't even remember his combination. Those numbers had become part of his subconscious. Opening his locker had become a reflex, like getting a hard-on, which was the way Morley liked it. He didn't trust anyone, even himself, with the combination. His locker was his safe deposit box, the most private place he had in the world.

He opened the door slowly, carefully bracing it against his shoulder. Cleats, jerseys, jocks, socks, a bat, footballs, baseballs, squash balls, lacrosse balls, a rugby ball, knee pads, hip pads, mouthpieces, t-shirts, a squash racket, a duffle bag, and rolls upon rolls of tape all tried to tumble out. This collection of gear was Morley's inheritance from Amherst. It wasn't going anywhere until his Dad's station wagon was parked beside the gym ready to receive it.

As usual, the gym was spotless. No one was in Morley's row, but he could hear locker doors opening and slamming all around him. He took off his pants and socks. The cement floor was cold on his bare feet. He could feel himself beginning to sweat; the pre-game jitters had set in. It was time to meditate. Morley squeezed his cheeks together and headed for the hopper.

He found a free john and settled in. A euphony of bowels played around him. Someone checked into the next stall and dropped his shorts. Morley never dressed before he dumped. He had seen too many guys with pre-game jitters end up dribbling in their drawers or dangling their jerseys in the bowl.

His meditation was interrupted by a familiar voice. "Hey, Morley. Your voice might have changed, but your breath's still the same." It was Hondo.

"Yeah, Hondo, what's happening?" Morley said. Morley hated talking on the john, it always froze him up, but he had to talk to Hondo. Hondo was a Beta and the best athlete at Amherst.

"Did you see those bastards from Old Blue? They're sooo BIG." Hondo was in a talkative mood. Most guys had pre-game jitters, but not Hondo. Nothing bothered him. He was just a sophomore, but already a legend. He'd made his reputation as a flanker in football. He was All-Pro quick, had All-Pro hands, and was an All-Pro hotdog. Whenever they watched the game films, Hondo was the star of every play. It didn't make any difference whether or not he had the ball. If they weren't going to throw to him, Hondo would wave at the camera, point at the guy he was supposed to block, and then dance through his pass pattern. He was just so much better than anyone else that he could afford to be cocky.

Morley tried to cut him off. "They're big every year."

Hondo kept right on going. "I'm glad I'm not in the scrum. Not only are they big, they're mean. You guys are going to get killed."

Morley's bowels clamped shut. He was done.

"Thanks, Hondo, I appreciate that vote of confidence."

"No problem." It was no problem for Hondo. He was so quick, nobody would ever lay a hand on him.

Morley finished his paperwork and headed for the trainer's room. His feet plip-plopped on the cement. He could hear someone else's cleats clicking behind a row of lockers. You weren't supposed to wear cleats in the locker room. Walking on smooth cement in cleats was worse than walking on ice. Sooner or later you'd fall on your ass.

Morley entered the trainer's room and sat on a free table. The room was packed. Nobody was saying a word. The trainer's room before a game was like church. The sights, smells and sounds all helped you achieve the inner peace that you needed to play the game. The atmosphere was designed to convince you that you would be saved. The sight of the muscle chart, the smells of vaseline, iodine, rubbing alcohol and sweat, and the tunes from the radio that was older than Morley, mixed with the sounds of hundreds of yards of tape being stripped onto thighs, wrists, knees, ribs, and ankles, made you a believer. You might get wounded, but you weren't going to die. The guys from the gym had everything they needed to put you back together again.

Morley realized that this was the last time he would be called to the rail of the training table; the last time he would receive the communion of tape and vaseline, the last time he would be blessed by the hands of Winky Walt Szymanski. He was going to play this game, have Margie turn in the Asshole Theory, pass his comps, and graduate.

Anyone who ever played ball knows that a good trainer is equal parts physician, psychiatrist, fan, friend, and father confessor. Winky Walt was a good trainer. But if Winky shared the reverence of the moment, he failed to show it. He just kept taping and winking away.

The name "Winky," which was never used in front of Walt, came from a nervous disorder he had contracted during the War. According to Shortpecker, it was the damndest thing he'd ever seen. The new recruits had taken a bus from Amherst to the Springfield Armory. Walt had been doing just great, laughing, fooling around, having a good time. He'd passed his physical, was inducted, received his orders, and drew his uniform. Then when they handed him a rifle, Walt started winking. At first, everyone thought it was just a bit. The sergeant told him to stop winking, but Winky couldn't stop, so they sent him to the doctor. The doctor gave him the same Rx; he told Walt to stop winking. When he couldn't, they discharged him on the spot. Nobody could believe it. Most of the guys figured that Walt must have been faking it, but when they came home from the War, there was Walt, still winking, a disabled veteran.

Winky had just started to work on Dave Clapp's ankles as Morley entered. Clapp was a freshman and this was his first match with the "A" team. He was replacing Holmes Wilson at the right prop. Holmes had been Amherst's best prop and key jumper until he broke his wrist in a brawl after the Wesleyan game. Clapp was filling in for Holmes. At 6'3" and 225 pounds, he was plenty big enough, but everyone knew that the Old Blue was going to eat this big baby-faced kid alive. There was no way that a freshman could hold his own against the Old Blue. Morley decided he would do what he could to cover for Clapp. At least the kid had enough guts to show up.

Morley suddenly sensed that something was wrong. He realized that everyone was looking at him and smiling. Nobody was supposed to be smiling before a game. What was going on?

Winky finished with Clapp and signaled for Morley to get up on the table; it was his turn to take communion. But it wasn't his turn. Evan Maurer was next in line. No one argued with Walt, so Morley climbed up on the table and held out his right ankle, just as he had done a thousand times before. Winky didn't reach for a roll of tape. Instead, he got out a bottle of iodine and told Morley to roll over on his stomach. Then Morley figured it out. He never should have gotten Margie so excited. She had scratched his back pretty bad. Morley braced himself. He knew that he was about to pay for his sins.

Winky didn't waste any time. He started slapping on iodine like he was painting the side of a barn. Morley could feel it chewing into his back. He wanted to scream, but he didn't make a sound. He focused all of his attention on the radio. It was playing "Silver Threads and Golden Needles Cannot Mend This Heart of Mine." Damn that Margie, she was going to have to learn to control herself.

When Winky was through with his painting, Morley rolled over and put up his right ankle. He hoped no one would notice the tears in his eyes. If Winky saw the tears, he wasn't saying anything. He just kept winking and taping. They both knew that if you were stupid enough to get laid before a match, you had to pay the price.

Morley watched Walt's hands expertly wrap his ankles, his right thigh and his right wrist. He kept adding more yards of tape to the miles he already had logged onto Morley's body during the last four years. When he finished, he said the same thing he said before every game. "Go get 'em, Ed." Wink. Wink.

Morley limped from the trainer's room to the equipment room. At first it always felt like Winky had taped his ankles too tight, but by the time he got to the equipment room, the tape had started to loosen up. It would be perfect once the sweat worked its way through.

There was a line at the equipment window, but Morley, befitting a senior who had lettered in two sports, walked right through the door that said "No Admittance." Being allowed into the equipment room was like having a key to a bank vault. It was a license to steal, and that's exactly what the privileged few did. The bulk of Morley's wardrobe came from the gym. It was all part of being a soldier. Surely, those special few who were willing to go into battle for Amherst couldn't be denied an extra jock or T-shirt.

No one understood this unspoken right better than Eddie Martula. Eddie was the disabled vet who managed the equipment room. All Eddie said to most people was, "I ain't got any," but for Morley and a few other proven warriors, there was always plenty of everything. Morley appreciated Eddie's attention and often dropped by for a visit. He'd wander into the equipment room, lie back on a pile of sweats and start shooting the breeze with Eddie. Since one team or another was always buying new equipment, a constant stream of salesmen came through the supply room. If Morley happened to be there, Eddie would have him try on some of the new jerseys. Once a jersey was on, Morley never took it off, which was why he had the finest collection of jerseys in the Four College area.

Early in his senior year, Morley discovered that Eddie liked a shot of Scotch, so he kept a bottle of Cutty Sark in his locker.

After big games, when everyone else had cleared out and Eddie was left piled up to his neck in dirty equipment, Morley would go in and have a drink with him. Sometimes Eddie would space out. It wasn't anything serious. Eddie would just sit there in the middle of a mound of dirty socks and jocks with a strange look on his face. At first, Morley figured it was the booze, but then Shortpecker told him that Eddie suffered from shell shock. According to Shortpecker, Eddie had lost it during the Battle of the Bulge.

Like many jocks, Morley was intrigued with the idea of combat. Once when they were sitting in the equipment room having a drink, Morley mentioned to Eddie that he might have to go to Vietnam. He thought Eddie might loosen up and give him a few war stories. Instead, Eddie had given him an exceptionally strange look. The look said it all. There was no way that Eddie was ever going to talk about war. It was all right to ask Shortpecker about falling on the grenade. He could show you his scars. He was a hero. He marched at the head of the Memorial Day Parade. He didn't mind talking about "World War II, the big one." The guys down at the gym wouldn't even acknowledge its existence. The only wars that they wanted to talk about were the wars that Amherst played, season after season.

Morley limped into the equipment room. "Hey Eddie, what's happening?"

Eddie was too busy to answer. He was yelling, "I ain't got any!" to everyone who came to the window.

Morley walked over and picked up his pile. Only his jersey and shorts had ever been worn. The jock, socks, arm pad and T-shirt were all brand new. He put everything on but his cleats. He was about to walk out when he noticed that Eddie was gazing at the floor. "Hey, Eddie, aren't you going to wish me luck?"

That was enough to break the spell. Eddie looked up and smiled. It was probably the first time he had smiled all day. He said with his funny little Polish accent, "Morley, you come by and see me after the game. Your ol' buddy might have something for you."

"Yeah, Eddie, I'll be by. We'll have a drink."

Clapp came to the window. He looked nervous. "Eddie, can I have another sock? This one is ripped."

"I ain't got any!" said Eddie. He didn't even bother to turn around.

Morley grabbed a new pair of socks from the shelf and tossed them to Clapp. "Come on, Eddie, it's the kid's first match." As Clapp walked away, Morley added, "and we want him to look nice when they carry him out."

Eddie was not interested. He didn't care about a freshman like Clapp. "Yah, yah, yah. You see me after the game. Your friend may have something special for you."

Good old Eddie. At least he recognized that this was Morley's last game. He and Eddie were going to finish the whole bottle of Cutty Sark. By the time Old Blue had gotten through with him, Morley would need a few shots. Besides, the wardrobe he picked off today was going to have to last him for the rest of his life.

IV

It was almost two o'clock when Morley got to the field. The Old Blue had just finished warming up. They were standing around acting nonchalant. Morley despised the Old Blue. They were the dirtiest, most arrogant and unquestionably best rugby team in America. What's more, they knew it.

Most of the Old Blue lived in Manhattan and were out of school. Many were professionals; doctors, lawyers, and MBAs. They treated college teams as if they were little kids just learning the game. When they lost, which was rarely, it was never because they were beaten by a better side. It was because "our scrum half couldn't make it, he had to perform open heart surgery this morning," or "our best prop was called to the White House," or "this was the day that our fullback was scheduled to argue before the Supreme Court." No credit was ever given to the other side.

As soon as the hands of the chapel clock read two, the Old Blue began yelling at Neville, the ref, to start the match. They knew that three Amherst guys were still in the gym. They acted very annoyed when Neville politely informed them that "he was not yet prepared to blow the whistle." And for good reason. Neville was not only the ref, he was also Amherst's unofficial coach.

When Neville was sure that Amherst had a full side, he called the captains together to negotiate the length of the match. Thirty-minute halves were standard, but halves could be as short as twenty or as long as forty minutes. Morley was hoping for twenty-fives, certainly no more than thirties. It was too hot; he already was sweating and he'd hardly warmed up. Plus, it was

41

obvious that the Amherst RFC had had a rough night. Most of the side was resting on one knee. Clapp was the only Amherst guy on the field. He was practicing running dropkicks. Who in their right mind would ever try a running dropkick? Only the very best sides, like New Zealand's All Blacks or South Africa's Springboks, ever made a running dropkick. The Old Blue might try one, but only if they had a big lead, and even then, it was strictly for show. In the four years that he had been playing Rugby, Morley had never seen anyone score on a running dropkick.

He focused his attention on the guy Clapp would be up against in the lineouts. He was a big, stupid Irishman who had played on several international teams. Clapp was going to get hammered. He should have been praying rather than wasting his time practicing running dropkicks.

Morley looked around at the crowd. It was by far the largest of the season. At least five hundred people lined the field. Most of the fraternities had set up kegs. A bumper crop of tits and asses were basking in the warm spring sun. For the fans, this match was just one big party. For Morley, it was his last chance at a national championship.

Having stung his eyes, beads of sweat made their way down his nose and dropped onto the turf. His stomach had turned into its usual knot. Morley always felt sick before a kickoff. He wished they'd get the match started. He could see Gootch waving his hands and shaking his head. He must have been arguing about the time. He looked pissed. The Old Blue captain was probably some lawyer trying Gootch's nerves.

Morley glanced over at the Beta section. Smee had just finished setting up the keg and had drawn his first beer. His date's ample chest was straining against its skimpy halter. Morley could never figure out where Smee found these busty beauties, but he kept coming up with them. Seeing him there, a butt in one hand, a beer in the other, made it hard to believe that he could have been one of Amherst's greatest athletes.

As an incoming freshman, Smee had been billed as Amherst's quarterback of the future. He'd been a Parade Magazine high school All-American from New Jersey, but Smee had left his heart for organized sports back at high school, and for good reason. During the final game of his senior year, Smee's father, who had been his high school coach, had a heart attack and died on the sideline. After that, Smee had little desire to suit up. Put a keg on the side lawn of Beta and Smee would stand out there all day throwing pinpoint passes to anyone who came along. Ping, ping, ping, all perfect. Move the keg indoors, and that was the end of Smee. He'd wander in behind it, chuck the ball into the closet, and start thinking about how he was going to get laid.

There was no sign of Margie. Morley could only hope that she'd rallied. He caught sight of Professor Merrill. The Professor loved contact sports. He came to every football and rugby game. It seemed strange to Morley that the head of the Fine Arts Department would be hooked on football and rugby. He wished that he could have gotten closer to the Professor, but he knew that if he ever sat down and really talked with him, sooner or later the discussion would turn to the Fine Arts. That would be the end of Morley. It was much better just to keep his distance and play good ball. He didn't want to do anything that might upset Professor Merrill. The Professor was the key to his plan for graduation.

Morley began to feel sluggish. Thinking about the Fine Arts depressed him. Now he was tired. He never should have gotten laid. Next time, he'd keep his pecker in his pants, only there wasn't going to be a next time. This was it. Gootch was calling them together.

"Ok guys, suck it in, we're gonna go forty minute halves."

Everyone was stunned. "Gootch, you've got to be kidding," Morley said. "It's hot as hell, we're all hung over. Why the fuck didn't you go for twenty?"

"That touchhole pissed me off. Now let's go out and kick some ass." There was an audible groan from the Amherst RFC. Eighty minutes in this heat! Gootch had to be crazy.

The first twenty minutes were pure hell. The scrums were frequent and sloppy. Not only were the Old Blue big and mean, they were cunning. Being older, the Old Blue usually weren't in

43

as good shape as undergraduates, so they liked to start a match by unraveling their opponents. Surging before the throw-ins and wheeling the scrum were annoying, but the real key to the Old Blue's strategy was intimidation. Gouging, kicking, holding, and tripping were all part of their game. If they did it, it was just an accident. If you did it, it was poor sportsmanship, and they would stop the match to lecture you in their phony British accents.

It was all Old Blue bullshit, but it worked, especially against college teams. They were the best, so everyone played on their terms.

Everyone except for Clapp. During the first twenty minutes, it became clear that Clapp was a Jekyll and Hyde. Once the whistle blew, this cherubic kid turned into a monster. His face twisted into a permanent scowl and he looked like he hated both the Old Blue and Amherst. He became a third side.

This transformation started in the lineouts. Clapp was playing the number four position. That's where Amherst put its best jumper. Clapp was opposite the big Irish lock, the guy Morley had expected to kill him, only it wasn't working out that way. When the Old Blue kicked for touch, Amherst was awarded the throw-in. The Jeffs decided to start off throwing to Clapp, just to see what he could do. He did great. He came down with every jump, but more importantly, he wasn't just tapping the ball back. He was controlling it, bringing it down and holding it while the Amherst scrum packed around. That gave Amherst the time they needed to set up a play that would get the ball out to Hondo.

Hondo in the open field was like a cheetah on the prowl; he was both fast and dangerous. Hondo only had to touch the ball a couple of times before the Old Blue realized they had a problem. It was taking two people to mark him, a luxury even the Old Blue couldn't afford. Using an extra man to cover Hondo left a big hole in their line. It was just a matter of time before someone from Amherst was going to run through it. The Old Blue had to break the first link of the chain; they had to take Clapp out.

The big Irish lock tried elbowing Clapp in the groin when Clapp went up for a throw-in. Clapp came down, dropped the ball and started beating on the lock. The Old Blue scrum half, an exceptionally cunning little runt and world-class rugger, put on his most disgusted look and told Clapp, "grow up and play the game." Clapp stopped pounding on the lock, picked up the scrum half and dropped him on his head. When Gootch tried to intervene, Clapp knocked him down and went back to pounding on the Old Blue lock. By the time the Old Blue was able to spring their lock, his thick Irish head was a bloody pulp.

The Old Blue immediately demanded Clapp's ejection. That was a big loss of face for the Old Blue. Nobody ever wanted to admit that an opponent was too mean to play rugby. Neville emphasized that an ejection for unnecessary roughness was out of the question. He warned Clapp against any further fighting, but it was clear that a warning meant nothing to Clapp. No one was going to intimidate him.

Thanks to Clapp's domination of the lineouts, Amherst started kicking for touch, which gave the Old Blue the throw-ins. Due to Clapp, they couldn't throw to their number four man, so the Old Blue was just popping the ball into one of their props. This guy was playing the number two position opposite Beachball. Poor Beachball was having trouble just making the lineouts, let alone jumping. Beachball had never been the same after his forced sabbatical to Parris Island. He returned from the Marines a complete hedonist. Food, drink, and sex, all in excess, was his 'semper fidelis.' Now the Amherst R.F.C. was paying for it. The Old Blue began controlling the lineouts, but with Mr. Hyde bearing down on him, their number two man had no desire to hold the ball. He was dumping it back to the scrum half as quickly as possible.

Morley and Evan Maurer were playing the seventh and eighth positions in the lineouts. Knowing that Old Blue's prop wasn't going to hold the ball, they were busting through the line and waiting like two big cats to pounce on the scrum half. As soon as he touched the ball, they would maul the little bastard.

The seven and eight men from the Old Blue were trying everything they knew to block out Morley and Maurer. They both were small, quick, and dirty and had been around for years, but unless their prop was willing to hold the ball and be pummeled by Clapp, there wasn't much they could do.

The Old Blue's internationally-famous scrum half was taking a terrible beating. Playing Amherst was supposed to be a picnic in the country, and here he was getting creamed. On one lineout, Morley burst through and grabbed the scrum half as soon as he scooped up the ball. He had him wrapped up so tightly that the guy couldn't throw it or kick it. He couldn't even drop it. That made him fair game for anybody who could get a shot at him.

They didn't have to wait long. Maurer caught him with a stiff forearm to the side of the head. Morley could hear the crunch and felt the guy go limp in his arms. The Old Blue had to ask for "two minutes" while their scrum half returned from Disneyland. Knocking out Old Blue's star was a great psychological coup for Amherst.

Morley was loving it. He was so focused on the scrum half that when play resumed, the Old Blue was able to catch him flat-footed. They executed a play he had never seen before. As they came into the lineout, the Old Blue's seven and eight men bunched up tight. Morley and Maurer had to bunch up with them or they would be called offside. Then, just as the ball was about to be thrown in, their seven man, the one Morley should have been covering, broke to the back of the line. When Morley tried to break with him, it was too late. Their number six man had him by the shirt. By the time Morley got loose, the number seven man had caught the throw-in and was moving up the field unchecked.

The try was a thing of beauty. Amherst's inside wing had been forced to come up to mark the Old Blue's number seven man. That meant that Gootch had to move in a man, and that was all the Old Blue needed. They broke Amherst's line. Even Hondo couldn't catch him. The play went for 70 yards. As Morley watched the ball work its way down the field, he had to admit that these bastards were good.

Pat Thewlis, Amherst's fullback, had no choice but to concede the try. His only option was to force the Old Blue wing to touch the ball down in the corner of the end zone, which left the Old Blue's kicker with a terrible angle. He narrowly missed the kick, which held the score at 3–0, in favor of the Old Blue.

As the Amherst RFC huddled up for the kickoff, it was obvious that they had lost the momentum. Everyone was pissed. Gootch summed it up when he said, "Hey Morley, it's about the spermatozoa." What could he say? He had screwed up. All he could do was try and get it back.

Towards the end of the first half, the momentum started to swing back towards Amherst. Now the heat was taking its toll. The Old Blue was slowing down, while Amherst was sweating out its hangover. The Jeffs would have had a couple of tries were it not for the Old Blue's fullback. Every time Amherst got close, he would come up with the ball and boom it 40 yards back upfield. Amherst decided to drop back Morley and Maurer, its wing forwards. That would give them two more people to play these kicks.

This strategy paid off when the Old Blue fullback tried a short kick just before the half. Normally, the ball would have landed in the open field where the Old Blue scrum could have recovered it. Now, Morley, having moved back, was in good position to field the ball. He could hear Maurer yelling at him. "Take a mark, Morley. Take a mark."

Evan was right. The Old Blue scrum would be all over him if he tried to run. Morley punched his heel into the pitch, and shouted "MARK!" just as he caught the ball. It was a good mark, and should have given Amherst a free kick. Unfortunately, the heat had also gotten to Neville. He was out of position on the other side of the field and never blew the whistle. It shouldn't have mattered. Both sides stopped play when Morley called his mark.

Morley was taking a breather waiting for Neville to catch up with the play when one of the Old Blue's props bellowed, "the whistle never blew." He came rushing towards Morley. Morley turned around just in time to catch an elbow in the cheek. He wasn't prepared for the shot. It knocked him flat on his ass. A trickle of fresh blood wound its way from under his eye into the corner of his mouth. He was surprised that he still had the ball in his hands. It was then the whistle blew.

The play took place right next to the sideline and hundreds of people started booing. It was clearly a cheap shot, even for the Old Blue. The prop was all apologetic. In a loud, phony British accent, he immediately proclaimed, "Sorry, mate, but there was no whistle," and graciously extended his hand to help Morley up. Morley took the prop's hand. There was a burst of applause from the crowd. Everyone appreciated good sportsmanship. When he was on his feet, Morley said, "You want the fuckin ball? Here's the fuckin ball!" He proceeded to mash it into the prop's face. The ball flattened the guy's nose.

The entire Old Blue scrum was immediately all over him. There was nothing for Morley to do but cover his head and hope that he didn't get hurt too badly. Fortunately, everyone was packed in so tightly that nobody could get a shot at him. When he realized he wasn't getting hit, he opened his eyes. All he could see was the back of an Old Blue guy's head wedged in front of his face. Morley couldn't punch it, kick it, or bite it, so he tried to spit on it, but his mouth was bone dry, devoid of saliva.

People were shouting "get hold of Clapp," "by Jove, somebody stop that bastard," "OK Dave, knock it off." Morley felt himself being pulled out of the pile by his feet. While this type of exit was not unusual in rugby, he was surprised at who was doing the pulling. Hondo had one leg, Professor Merrill the other. Nobody could believe that Professor Merrill was in the middle of the melee. Even Clapp slowed down when he saw the Professor.

Neville was purple from blowing his whistle. Wisely, he called the half. Both teams grudgingly walked off to their respective end zones. Everyone gave Clapp a wide berth, but as soon as he left the field, he turned back into Dr. Jekyll. Were it not for the blood, sweat and dirt caked to his uniform, he could have been someone's younger brother helping pass out oranges at half-time.

The gash over Morley's eye needed stitches. Since there were no substitutions in rugby, there was no question in anybody's mind that Morley would keep playing. Mr. Brown, the Doctor, gave him a shot of Novocaine and began to sew him up. Dr. Brown, like most college physicians, received very little respect from his patients, which is why he was commonly referred to as "Mr. Brown, the Doctor." But Morley held him in high regard. Over the past four years, Mr. Brown, the Doctor, had treated Morley for a broken wrist, several concussions, a case of the clap, a broken nose, and numerous sprains and contusions. That Morley was still playing anything was a tribute to Mr. Brown's doctoring and Winky Walt's tape.

The cut took six stitches, which was a mere six flicks of the wrist for Mr. Brown. Winky was able to grease it and tape it well before the beginning of the second half. Thanks to the Novocaine, Morley didn't feel a thing.

By the start of the second half, the crowd had swelled to more than 700. Word had traveled back from Williams that the lacrosse team had won 9-7. Now the fans were drunk and happy. They knew that the next forty minutes of rugby would decide the national championship. Morley heard the whistle. He didn't feel like getting up. All he wanted to do was sleep. He sensed the sun had been blocked out, that someone was standing over him. He opened his eyes and saw a tall, lean man with short grey hair wearing a nice sport jacket and a little bow tie. It was Professor Merrill. He had a kind, calm look on his face. His eyes were confident. He held out his hand to help Morley up.

"Let's go, Edward, only forty more minutes. You're playing a great match."

Morley didn't feel the same confidence. All he could say was "Thanks, Professor, we'll get," but he wasn't sure he meant it. His legs felt dead and his body was so drained that it had stopped sweating. Mr. Brown must have gone overboard on the Novocaine. Morley couldn't feel half his head. The next thing he knew, he was receiving the ball.

The mayhem that had characterized the early part of the first half gave way to good rugby, not clean, but slower and more controlled. At the twenty-minute mark, Amherst finally scored their first try. It came from a beautiful scissor play off of a scrum. Gootch had pitched the ball to Hondo, who had cut back to the short side of the field. The Old Blue fullback was caught marking Hondo one-on-one. It was no contest. Hondo waltzed in for the try.

He placed the ball right in the middle of the end zone. Gootch's kick was perfect. Amherst had the Old Blue 5–3, with only twenty minutes to go. The Jeffs were now controlling both the scrums and the lineouts.

But the Old Blue were far from finished. Their play remained composed and professional. They weren't about to let a bunch of college kids wreck their picnic. A lot could happen in twenty minutes, and with twelve minutes to go, something did. Evan Maurer's skinny little legs could no longer support his massive upper body. For the third time in four years, something cracked. It was Evan's right tibia.

As Evan was carried off of the field, he pounded the stretcher in frustration. All his skinny little legs had to do was hold out for another twelve lousy minutes and he could have ended his athletic career with honor. Now Amherst would have to play the final twelve minutes with only fourteen men. They all knew that a seasoned side like the Old Blue would lock in on this advantage.

If things weren't bad enough, Beachball went into heat prostration while they were carrying Evan off the field. Mr. Brown immediately declared him through for the day. Now the Amherst side was down to thirteen men.

The match resumed with a scrum at the Amherst 20. The Old Blue forwards quickly capitalized on its two-man advantage by pushing Amherst off the ball, and keeping it in the scrum while they drove towards the end zone. Goopy Balderman, Amherst's lock, was suppose to control the scrum. Down two men, the scrum was out of control. Gootch was screaming at Goopy. "Wheel the scrum, Goopy! Goopy, wheel the fuckin scrum!"

Given the Old Blue's momentum, there was no way that Goopy could wheel it. The best he could do was collapse it. When the scrum finally collapsed at the ten yard line, the ball popped out the off side and rolled to the corner of the endzone. The Old Blue's scrum half was there waiting; he fell on it for an easy try. Once again, the Old Blue's kicker had a crappy angle, and by now, his legs must have felt like rubber. He missed. So with a little over ten minutes to go, the Old Blue led 6–5, and they carried a two man advantage. Things didn't look good for Amherst.

Amherst kicked for the sideline and managed to get the ball out of bounds on the Old Blue 32. Morley had to move up into Beachball's number two position on the lineouts while Hondo, the offside wing, had to come in and cover both the seven and eight positions. This new position in the lineout put Morley opposite the Old Blue prop who had cold-cocked him at the end of the first half. Looking at the prop revived Morley. The guy's eyes already were starting to go black, a sure sign that his nose had been broken. Morley knew that he probably didn't look much better. He wanted another shot at this bastard.

The Old Blue wasn't going to put the ball anywhere near Clapp or Hondo so they tried a high, soft throw-in to the number two position. As Morley went up, he felt his legs being kicked out from under him. The last thing he remembered was grabbing the ball.

V

The light hurt his eyes. He heard the radio playing "I Want to Hold Your Hand" and smelled a mixture of iodine, alcohol, vaseline, and sweat. He realized that he was in the trainer's room. Mr. Brown, the Doctor, was standing over him. Winky was at his side.

Mr. Brown, the Doctor, was looking into his eyes with a little flashlight that looked like a ball point pen. He clipped the light back into his shirt pocket and said to Winky. "He'll be all right. There's no concussion, but he must have taken a hell of a shot. There isn't much we can do about the teeth, they're just chipped. If they start to hurt, have him call Dr. Aarons." At this point, Mr. Brown gave Morley a jab on the shoulder. "Hey Morley, you played a hell of a game, we're going to miss you."

Mr. Brown walked out. Morley ran the tip of his tongue over his lower front teeth. The two middle ones were chipped. He couldn't tell how much of them was missing, but it couldn't be too bad. They didn't hurt. Walt started to remove the bandage from Morley's face. He was unusually careful. "Well, we finally beat the Old Blue."

Beat the Old Blue! What was Winky talking about?

Guys were drifting into the room, cutting tape from their wrists, knees, heads, thighs and ankles. Many were sucking down beers. Normally, Winky forbade beer in the trainer's room.

Morley was confused. "Walt, what happened? The last thing I remember is going up for a lineout."

"I told you he was out of it," Gootch said. "Morley, you won the game."

53

"What do you mean, I won the game? One minute you're giving me shit for getting laid, now you're telling me I won the game. What the hell is going on?"

"You're right," said Walt, winking. "He doesn't remember a thing."

"Morley," Gootch said, "Don't you remember getting knocked out?"

"Shit, I just told you, the last thing I remember is going up for the lineout."

"Yeah." Gootch said. "You went up for the ball, but some bastard cut your legs out from under you, and you ended up landing on your head. Everyone assumed you were through, but when you came to, you hopped up and said you were fine. Since Evan already had broken his leg and Beachball was blowing his gut, nobody argued with you." Gootch put down his beer and began cutting the tape from his ankles.

"Neville called for a new lineout," he said, peeling the tape from one ankle, then the other. "Clapp grabbed the throw in, but the Old Blue scrum was all over him, so he pitched the ball back to me. I was buried as soon as I touched it. The ball squirted free and that's when you broke from the pack, scooped it up, and headed towards the middle of the field."

"What happened then?" Morley said.

"Everyone assumed that you were going to work the ball out to Hondo, but instead, you faked the pitch and turned up field." Gootch picked up his beer and took a long drag, as if purposely delaying the best part of the story. "Then," he said, wiping his mouth with the back of his hand, "you tried a running dropkick."

"A running dropkick! You've gotta be shittin me. Why would I ever try a running dropkick?"

"Morley, you made it!" said Walt, winking happily.

"I made it! Come on, give me a break. Nobody ever makes a running dropkick."

"You did." Gootch said.

"It sailed through the uprights with ten yards to spare," Winky said. "And that was it for the Old Blue."

"Well, not quite." Gootch. said. "They tried to mount one last surge, but came unglued. Clapp was running around like a madman. We were all running around like madmen. I thought the damn match would never end. Finally, Neville blew the whistle and we'd won, 8–6. From now on, everyone gets laid before a match."

"At the end of the match, you don't say nothing to nobody," Winky said. "You just run off the field. Everybody figures you're still pissed because of the cheap shot. You didn't even clap 'em off."

That was poor form. Once the whistle blew, you always clapped off your opponent. It was part of the game. "When the Doc and me gets back to the gym," Winky continued, "there you was lying on the training table. The Doc thought that you might be passed out, but you was just asleep." Winky, unlike the students, appreciated Mr. Brown and always referred to him as the Doc.

Morley couldn't believe it. A running dropkick. Fuckin unbelievable! Rugby games weren't filmed, so he would never see the greatest moment of his athletic career. Winky finished taking off the bandage and gave Morley two salt tablets. "Take these, Ed, they'll make you feel better." Morley popped the pills into his mouth and lay back on the trainer's table. He could taste the salt mixing with his saliva. Guys were coming up to congratulate him, but he couldn't keep his eyes open. He was so tired. He fell back asleep.

When Winky woke him, almost everyone was gone. The party at Beta must have already started. It would be a blow-out, especially when the lacrosse team got back from Williams. Now that they had their undefeated season, those guys would be making up for two months of training.

Morley forced himself to sit up. The Four Tops were spinning "Bernadette" from Winky's radio. His body felt like one big bruise, but "Bernadette" helped get him moving. He slowly cut the tape from his ankles and limped to the showers. Clapp was the only guy there. He had his face buried under a showerhead, letting the water pour over his body. Morley was almost too tired to talk, but he managed to say, "Hey, nice going, you played a great game."

"Thanks, you didn't do too bad yourself," Clapp said, peeking out from under the stream. He was too shy to look Morley right in the eye. It was hard to believe that this was the same guy that had just decimated the Old Blue.

Morley left Clapp in the shower and dragged himself back to his locker. The gym crew already had cleaned up his mess. Morley automatically dialed his combination, removed his lock, and opened his locker. The bottle of Scotch was the first thing he saw. The Novocaine was wearing off; his face was starting to hurt even more than the rest of him. This was the toughest match he had ever played. He had destroyed his body. But so what, there was no reason to save it. He had just played his last game.

He grabbed the Cutty Sark, wrapped a towel around his waist, and hobbled over to the supply room. Eddie was delighted to see him. "Hey Morley, where you been. You look like hell. They say you won the game. You know, lacrosse won too. You Betas are going to have a big time tonight." He was talking non-stop. "The Old Blue and Williams all in one day, that's something, ain't it. Let's have a drink. You get some ice. Where did I put the cups?"

Eddie was more animated than Morley had ever seen him. He seemed nervous, like a little kid. Morley couldn't figure it out. "Say Morley, who I gonna drink with when you leave? How come you the only guy who come in and drink with me? What's a matter with them other guys? Don't they like old Eddie?"

So that was it. Eddie had realized he was about to lose his only friend. How was Morley going to explain this one to him? What was he going to say, "Eddie, the reason no one comes in to have a drink with you is because everyone—even the guys at the V.F.W.—thinks you're fuckin nuts?"

Morley grabbed some ice from a medical bag that was on the floor. "Eddie, give me some cups?"

56

"I ain't got any," Eddie said. Morley went over to the cabinet, got out two paper cups, filled them with ice, and poured two stiff drinks. Eddie was staring at the floor mumbling, "Who I gonna drink with when you go?"

Morley was about to tell him not to worry, that everything would be all right, when he heard someone at the window. It was Clapp. "Hey Eddie, here are those socks you lent me. Thanks."

Unbelievable, the kid was returning the socks. Nobody ever returned a new pair of socks. Morley had an idea. "Hey Clapp, come in here, I want to show you something."

Clapp hesitated. Freshmen just didn't come walking into the equipment room. "Come on in, it's OK." Morley reassured him. "Eddie, you know Clapp? He's only a freshman, but he's a good Beta."

Eddie looked up at Clapp. Clapp was a big bastard. "Sure, I know Clapp. Hey Clapp, you want a drink? Look what I'm giving Morley." Eddie pointed to a duffle bag in the corner. "They say you played a good game today. Mean as hell. That so? Here, you have a drink. Maybe you'll get a nice going-away present when you're a senior." Eddie belted down his drink.

Clapp was a quick learner. He looked around the supply room. Morley could see him calculating how much of Eddie's treasure he could squeeze into his locker. He was going to like drinking with Eddie.

Morley decided it was time to leave. He picked up the bag Eddie had given him and slipped out. When he looked back, Eddie was gazing at Clapp. Clapp was refilling their drinks.

Morley opened the bag as soon as he got to his locker. Good old Eddie had taken care of him. There were dozens of T-shirts, a couple of sweat suits, his Rydells, a rugby shirt, at least four pairs of shorts, a baseball cap and a football. He crammed the bag into his locker and got dressed. He would fight no more battles for Amherst.

Morley had to sit down when he reached the top of Memorial Hill. His legs were tired and he felt a little woozy. It might have been the booze, but he suspected it was the shots he had taken from the Old Blue. He lay back on the steps of the War Memorial. Late afternoon shadows were falling over the Holyoke Range. The new greens of spring were beginning to darken. Mount Nowatuck, named for the chief who once ruled the valley, pushed its rugged peak into a blue robin's-egg sky. At its base, a farmer was plowing his field. His little tractor left strings of brown lines as it wound its way back and forth across the landscape. It was amazing how straight the lines looked. Morley wondered how farmers did it. When he saw them at the V.F.W. or the Polish-America Club in Hadley, they were always shitfaced. Their fields should have looked like a Jackson Pollack painting, all twisted and bent, but what Morley saw below him was a quilt of neat little patches, the kind that Norman Rockwell painted for the cover of *The Saturday Evening Post*.

The breeze was sweet with the smell of freshly cut grass. Morley noticed a few guys lying on the hillside with their dates. Where was Margie? He didn't remember seeing her after the game. But then, he didn't remember seeing anybody. He sure as hell hoped she'd finished his paper. He felt the stitches under his eye, ran his tongue over his teeth, and thought about Margie. He reached down and readjusted his penis. Would she care if he looked like Frankenstein?

He leaned back and bumped his head on a stone. He turned around and saw that the word "Marianas" was engraved on its side. The next stone was labeled "Okinawa." The next "Midway." For the first time in his life, Morley took a good look at the War Memorial.

The War Memorial was nestled in a grove of pines between the quad and the gym. It was the boundary between academia and athletics. Granite steps led down to a small round flagstone terrace enclosed by a large chain that looped through granite posts. A circular monument of grey granite about two feet in height and ten in diameter anchored the center. Granite blocks like the one Morley'd just bumped his head on were placed around the edges of the terrace. Each stone commemorated a major battle of

World War II. Morley got up and walked over to the monument. Names were carved in concentric circles around its top. They were good Amherst names like Webster, King, Plimpton and Stow, hundreds of them. These were the Amherst men who had given their lives for their country. There weren't any Morleys, at least not yet, but if he didn't graduate, he could be joining these guys, and that was not how he wanted to be remembered at Amherst.

More grey granite steps led from the terrace down to the gym. Morley sat back down on them and looked out over the valley. He watched the little tractor finish the field. He could hear birds in the pines, chirping to one another. They probably were pairing off for the mating season. It was good to hear life surrounding this monument to death.

His mood was shattered by a grating nasal twang moving down the top set of steps. "Do you think we have enough room here, or should we move it to the Town Common?" Morley looked up. It was Elliot Ginsberg and a few of his screwball friends. Morley tried to tune them out, but there was no way you could tune out Elliot.

"No, we must have it here. The War Memorial is symbolic of what we're trying to accomplish." The speaker was a little creep that probably didn't even go to Amherst.

"Excellent point! How many more Amherst names will be carved into these stones by our criminally flawed policy in Vietnam?" a pear-shaped girl with hair down to her waist agreed.

Elliot was his usual argumentative self. "I disagree. This is a Memorial to war itself, not to the peace that we're trying to achieve. Just look at this inscription. 'Dedicated to Amherst men who in two great wars gallantly responded to their country's call.'

"Amherst people accept war, they think it's noble. The last thing they want is to question their country's call. Let's not kid ourselves. This Memorial does not mourn those who died, it glorifies them."

Some chubby bohemian seconded Elliot's point. "Elliot's right. We must stop these fascist pigs from their self-destructive and inane suicidal actions which dehumanize innocent victims and sacrifice them on the altar of the almighty dollar of capitalism." She paused, then added. "Besides, all the action's on the Common. That's where they line up for the parade, and they've chosen Memorial Day to plant the new trees. I say we move to the Common."

Morley could just see Shortpecker and the boys from the Club when these nuts showed up. The Memorial Day Parade was the biggest day of the year for the V.F.W., and the Town was making a big deal out of replacing all the trees that had died on the Common. The chubby bohemian was right. Moving the protest to the Common would sure enough get the Town's attention.

Elliot's twang faded as he and his gang moved back up the stairs. Well, if that's how Elliot wanted to waste his time, so be it. Lacrosse had just beaten Williams; Rugby had just beaten the Old Blue. It was a beautiful day, the birds were singing, Spring was in the air, and if Margie had come through with "Discovering Himself," he was almost home free. He knew that he should go back to his room in North and study for his comps, but he decided to stop by the House for just one beer.

He struggled to his feet and took a last long look at the vista. The little tractor was gone, the farmer done for the day. Morley could feel the breeze getting cooler. It was time for him to move on. He limped up the stairs and headed for Beta.

VI

"I don't want to join the Army
I don't want to go to war
I'd rather hang around Piccadilly Underground
Living off the earnings of a high-born lady

I don't want a bullet up me arsehole
I don't want me buttocks shot away
I'd rather stay in England, merry merry England
And fornicate me fooken life away.

Ohhh . . . on Monday I touched her on the ankle
On Tuesday I touched her on the knee
On Wednesday, I confess, I lifted up her dress,
On Thursday I put me hand a-higher, higher,
Friday I put me hand upon it
Saturday she gave me balls a tweak
And on Sunday after supper
I rammed me fooker up her
And now I'm paying four and twenty a week.

Oh Blimey, I don't want to join the Army
I don't want to go to war
I'd rather hang around Piccadilly Underground
Living off the earnings of a high-born lady

I don't want a bullet up me arsehole
I don't want me buttock shot away
I'd rather stay in England, merry merry England
And fornicate me fooken life away."

As Morley came in the back door of the House, he could hear the singing coming up the stairs from the Beta bar. He couldn't help but appreciate the irony of the song. He didn't want to join the Army; he didn't want to go to war; he didn't want a bullet up his arsehole; and he didn't want his buttocks shot away. He'd rather stay at Amherst, merry merry Amherst, and fornicate his fooken life away.

Morley glanced at the sign over the stairs to the bar. It said "Facilis Descensus Averno." The Descent to Hell was Easy. The bar was packed. Morley loved the way everyone waved their cups, clamoring for a refill. They sounded like baby birds chirping for something to eat. Not to worry, no one would go hungry tonight, not after Amherst had beaten the Old Blue.

The King of Smut was manning the tap. He had it running wide open. A cigarette was dangling from his lips. Smee was trying to smoke, drink, and pour a steady stream of beer all at the same time. His honey was sitting next to him, setting up the cups. Her halter did little to conceal its treasures. She provided the crowd with a great shot every time she bent over for a new cup. Smee was rolling his eyes and smacking his lips. After a few more beers, it would be time for a King of Smut drive-in movie. With a little luck, this simple barmaid might soon become a starlet. *The Orgy*, Hogarth, Scene III from *The Rake's Progress*, circa 1734, popped into Morley's mind. It was one of the many paintings Morley had taped to his wall. It showed a young wastrel over-indulging in wine and women. If Hogarth had used the King of Smut as his rake, he'd still be painting.

Morley could feel some tension as he entered the bar. Any animosity between the two sides should have been left on Memorial Field, but Morley hadn't clapped the Old Blue off, which was highly irregular. For all the Old Blue knew, he still might be pissed about the cheap shot. Morley looked at the Old Blue prop whose nose he'd mashed. His face was a mess. Judging from his raccoon eyes, his nose was broken. But then, Morley wasn't going to win any beauty contest, either. His bottom teeth were chipped, and Mr. Brown, the Doctor, hadn't bothered to trim his stitches. They were hanging down his cheek like little spider legs.

The crowd parted as best it could while Morley pushed his way to the tap. He ended up standing beside the prop. The prop broke the ice. "Say, mate, buy you a beer."

Morley recoiled at the word "mate." This guy was probably from Brooklyn. But what the hell, none of that phony crap meant anything now. Amherst had won.

"I don't know if I want a beer from anyone as ugly as you." Morley said with a chuckle.

"With your looks," the prop bellowed in a loud English accent, "You'd bloody well better take a beer wherever you can get it. Haw, haw."

He handed Morley the beer that Smee had placed in front of them. Morley sipped off the head. It tasted wonderful. He was just thinking that the first beer was always the best, when the prop pointed at him and crooned:

> "We call upon Morley to sing us a song,
>   So sing, you bastard, sing!"

Morley struggled for a song. He had a tin ear, and he always had trouble memorizing songs. But at least he could crank out the first verse of "Four and Twenty Virgins":

> "Four and twenty virgins
>   Came down from Inverness
>   And when the ball was over
>   There were four and twenty less . . . "

The whole bar chimed in with the Chorus:

> "Singing, balls to your partner,
>   Backs against the wall!
>   If you never get laid on a Saturday night
>   You'll never get laid at all."

Other individuals picked up the lead. Morley had done his job. Now he was free to sit back and enjoy the singing.

"Oh, the village cripple, he was there,
He was just too much
He lined the ladies against the wall
And stuffed them with his crutch,

(Chorus) Singing, balls to your partner,
Backs against the wall!
If you never get laid on a Saturday night
You'll never get laid at all."

The verses kept coming. The real fun of playing a team like the Old Blue was that they always had dozens of new verses.

"Oh, the village grandmother, she was there,
Sitting by the fire
Knitting contraceptives
Out of India rubber tires,

(Chorus)

"Oh, the village farmer, he was there,
Sickle in his hand,
And every time he dosie doed
He circumcised the band,

(Chorus. . . .)

Morley finished his beer. He knew he should leave, but this was turning into a great party, and the lacrosse team hadn't even shown up yet. It wouldn't be right not to wait for them. He held up his cup for a refill, and then remembered Smee's honey. "How bout a new cup," he yelled. The bar was well rewarded as she obligingly bent over.

When the Old Blue finally finished with Four and Twenty Virgins, there wasn't a sexual fantasy that had escaped the young maidens from Inverness. Gootch, as Captain of the Amherst RFC, was the next to be sung into service. There was no question as to what he would sing. "Sweet Cecille" was his favorite. Gootch was so smitten with sweet Cecille that he had actually visited Leominster Square when he was in London.

Gootch had a squeaky little voice that got squeakier when he sang. He reminded Morley of Alfalfa in "Spanky and Our Gang," but that didn't stop Gootch, especially when he was going to sing "Sweet Cecille."

> "Oh, my name it is Sweet Cecille
> I live in Leominster Square
> I wear an open-toed sandal,
> A rosebud in my hair,
> I went for a ride on the chug chug
> So crowded that I could not stand
> A little boy offered me his seat
> So I felt for it with my hand.

The bar enthusiastically picked up the chorus. Gootch was very pleased with this show of support for "Sweet Cecille."

> (Chorus) "Oh, we're all queers together
> Excuse us while we go upstairs
> Oh, we're all queers together
> And nobody bloody well cares."

Gootch launched into the second verse. He was on a roll.

> "Oh, the sexual life of a camel
> Is stranger than anyone thinks
> At the height of the mating season
> He attempts to bugger the Sphinx
> But the Sphinx's sexual orifice
> Is clogged by the sands of the Nile
> Which accounts for the humps on the camel
> And the Sphinx's inscrutable smile.
> (Chorus) "Oh, we're all queers together
> Excuse us while we go upstairs
> Oh, we're all queers together
> And nobody bloody well cares . . . "

Gootch kept the versus coming until he had run through what he assumed was all of "Sweet Cecille, but much to Gootch's

65

delight, the Old Blue offered some new additions. Sweet Cecille was postponing Smee's drive-in, but everyone was having such a good time, nobody, least of all the King of Smut, seemed to mind. The beer was going down easy. Morley was feeling very relaxed. His body no longer hurt and his head had stopped throbbing. He looked around and saw that the bar was loaded with good looking women. Besides the usual Beta Honeys, there were some genuine classic beauties. Many looked like mannequins. These were the New York models that traveled with the Old Blue. In the past, they had been off limits to college kids, but now that Amherst had beaten the Old Blue, Morley wondered if they were part of the spoils. The Old Blue had never been shy about picking off Beta Honeys, and besides, in four days Morley would no longer be a college kid. Maybe it was time to make a move.

Then he remembered Margie. Where was she, and what about his paper? He worked his way through the crowd and found the Harts. The Harts knew everything. "Hey Harts, you seen Margie?"

"Morley, my boy, I have not only seen her, I have applauded her." Harts only called people 'my boy' when he was shitfaced.

"Applauded her, what are you talking about?"

"Very simple, my boy, were it not for Miss Margie's send-off, you would never have played the game of your life, and we never would have beaten the Old Blue. Thus we accorded Margie a standing ovation at the end of the match."

"Oh, great, she must have appreciated the recognition."

"Actually, she didn't stick around." Harts said. "The last we saw of Margie, she was leaving the field with some guy in a Yale jersey. She told me to tell you not to worry, that your paper was done and delivered. She'll call you next week."

Some guy in a Yale Jersey. That must have been her old warhorse. Now Morley was pissed. Here he plays the game of his life and Margie leaves him for some stiff from Yale. He held up his cup. "Hey Smee, here's your help."

The Old Blue's scrum half was offering a song. It was "Rhodine School," one of Morley's favorites.

"Oh, we are from Rhodine, good girls are we,
We take pride in our virginity
We take all precautions against all abortions
'Cause we are from Rhodine School."

As the keg got lighter, the singing got louder.

(Chorus) "Up school, up school, up school
Hey up school
Hey!
Laah-la la-la la la la la la
Hey!
Laah-la la-la la la la la la . . . "

Obviously, Margie would never make it at Rhodine school.
She apparently had little pride in her virginity. Imagine leaving
Morley for some stiff from Yale.

"We have a curate here at our school
He has a little teeny weeny tool
It's all right for key holes
And little girls' pee holes
But no good for Rhodine School.

(Chorus)

That Yalie's little tool would be just right for Margie. "Smee, fill
me up."

"We have a vicar here at our school
He has a very prodigious tool
It's all right for tunnels
And the Queen Mary's funnels
And super for Rhodine School."

(Chorus)

The beer was going right to Morley's head. Screw Margie,
who needed her when the Beta Bar was loaded with honeys.

"We have a new girl, her name is Flo
Nobody thought she'd ever go
But she went with the vicar
A bloody sight quicker
Than anyone at Rhodine School."

(Chorus)

Margie was another 'Flo.' She took off with this guy from Yale a bloody sight quicker than anyone at Rhodine School.

"We have a new girl, her name is Jane
She likes to do it now and again
And again, and again, and again. . . . "

The exploits of the girls from Rhodine School were interrupted by a ruckus upstairs. There was much singing, and it didn't sound like it was coming from the Mormon Tabernacle Choir.

"Oh the girls take their pants off to us
(Boom boom boom)
We are the people, so they say
Live on the shady side of Easy Street
And this is our night to shine,
(Boom boom boom)

"We are the people, people,
We are the people, people,
We are the people, so they say,
We are the people, people,
We are the people, people,
We are the people, so they say.

"Oh you must be a Beta Theta Pi
Or you won't go to Wooglin when you die
When you die, when you die,
Or you won't go to Wooglin when you die."

It was the lacrosse team. As they stumbled down the stairs, there was no question that they had made a few stops on the way back from Williams. All eyes focused on Smee's honey as she bent over to set up a new round of cups. When everyone was reloaded, Brother Bailey grabbed Morley by the chin and said in a loud voice, "Brother, you done look BAD."

Morley fed back the line that Bails wanted. "But Doctor, I feel GOOD."

With that, the Betas began chanting, "Looks bad, feels good. Looks bad, feels good." Bailey raised his hands and said, with his black accent, "It done become apparent that you niggers be lookin for a joke." There were few blacks at Amherst, and none at the Beta Bar. The national charter of Beta Theta Pi discouraged the acceptance of blacks.

The chant continued. "Looks bad, feels good. Looks BAD, feels GOOD." The Old Blue contingent didn't know what was going on, but they could tell whatever it was, it was going to be good.

Bailey signaled for quiet. He then assumed the Drill Instructor pose he'd picked up during his forced sabbatical to Parris Island. When it was quiet, he started his story. "Well Leroy, he done get up one mornin and he be feelin GOOD."

To which the crowd responded, "Yeah brother, we hear ya, Leroy, he be feelin good."

"In fact, Leroy, he done be feelin SO GOOD that he done corn row his head and put on his best duds, the big platform shoes with the goldfish swimmin in the heels, the leopard skin pants, the suede leather vest, lots of gold chains, and his big black fedora with the ostrich feather in the hatband. I mean, this dude, he not only be feelin good, he be lookin GOOD! . . . "

"Yeah brother, we hear ya."

" . . . so Leroy, he done head downtown. Well, he be struttin along when who should come by but Marylou. Now Leroy, he be tryin to score on this fox, so he say jus as sweet as he can, 'Why, hello, Marylou, how are you?'

"But instead of gettin all warm and friendly like, Marylou, she jus look at Leroy and say, 'Why Leroy, what done happen to you boy, you look BAD!'

"Well with that, Marylou, she done walk off. Leroy, he can't figger what be wrong so he keep on walkin, and pretty soon he see Ruby comin in his direction. Now Ruby, she be another chick he done wanna pluck, so he puff hisself up like a big cock and say, 'Good mornin Ruby, how are you?'

"But Ruby, she done get the same look Marylou had, and she say, 'Leroy, you look BAD. What you been doin to yoself, boy.' And she done walk off.

"Well Leroy, he ain't feel so good no more. These two gals, they done deflate him. I mean, his ass be startin to drag. Before he have time to regain his composure, Minnie she be comen down the road. Now he already be puttin Minnie away, so he figger he be in for a warm reception.

"Only Minnie, when she done see him, she fly off the handle. 'Leroy!' she done yell. 'What you been doin to yoself, boy? You done look like you been tomcattin all night. I mean you look BAD!'

"Well, that be it for Leroy. Now he be totally deflated. His ostrich feather be all droopin, and the goldfish in his heels, they gone belly up. But he still feel GOOD. So he walk into the One-Two Club and right away all the brothers done get on his case. 'What wrong with you, Leroy, you look like you 'bout to DIE.'

"Finally Raspus done tell him, Leroy, if I be you, I done get my black ass up to the Doctor.' So Leroy, he done get his black ass up to the Doctor.

"Well the Doctor's office, it be packed with some real sick-lookin brethren, but Leroy he still feelin GOOD. Finally the Doctor, he done stick his head out and say, 'who be nex?' but when he see Leroy he say, 'Leroy, you be at the head of the line. I don't want no nigger dyin in my waitin room. Son, you done look BAD!'

At this point in the story, Bails always came up with a big pair of glasses which he put on to play the Doctor. With the glasses on, he looked exactly like Algonquin J. Calhoun from the Amos & Andy show. It was a great bit.

"So the Doctor, he done be fussin over Leroy like the boy bout to die, and he say, 'Leroy, what be the matter with you?'

"But all Leroy can say is, 'Doc, I feel GOOD.'

Now Bailey took off the glasses, and began strutting around, rubbing his chin. "Hmm, looks BAD, feels GOOD. This be a most unusual case. What we need here is some research."

Whereupon Smee handed Bailey a big book from behind the bar. Bails held the book up like a preacher and moved the glasses down to the end of his nose. He started leafing through the book, mumbling "Hmmm, looks bad, feels bad. No, that ain't you," and then, "Hmmmm, feels bad, looks good, no, that ain't you neither."

When he had played the crowd just long enough, Bailey stopped, jabbed his finger into the book and said, "Ah HAH, here you be, Leroy. Looks BAD, feels GOOD."

Then looking up over the rims of the glasses, Bailey shook his head and said, "Leroy, I got bad news for you, boy, you done be a VAGINA."

The Beta Bar went wild. Anyone with a vagina certainly had cause to be offended, but nobody was. The mannequins were flashing their pearly whites like they were posing for *Vogue,* and several members of the Old Blue had crowded around Bails and were asking him to repeat the story. It was a safe bet that before too long, Leroy was going to be visiting merry, merry England.

Smee's date was laughing so hard that her jugs were bouncing up and down like two boats in a hurricane. It would have been a new benchmark for Leroy if he could have flopped one of those beauties out of its halter, but much to the bar's regret, they kept hanging in there. The keg kicked and there was a pause in the festivities while Harts helped Smee tap another. It would have been the perfect time for Morley to leave, but how could he ever leave this place? Where else was he going to find guys like this, not to mention the honeys? The hell with his comps, this party was just starting, and with Margie gone, he was free to concentrate on some new talent. He might look BAD, but he felt GOOD.

There was a cheer as a new stream of cold brew started flowing from the tap. Morley's cup was one of the first refilled. It was time for another song.

Beachball: "And in this cage, ladies and gentlemen, we have the Chief of the Fugawi!"

Bar Group: "The Chief of the Fugawi?"

Beachball: "Yes, the Chief of the Fugawi."

Bar Group: "Fan-tastic! In-credible! Totally unbelievable!"

Beachball: "Yes, ladies and gentlemen, the Chief of the Fugawi is one of the most unique animals in the Animal Kingdom, in that the Fugawi's are only 4'1" tall. Yet, the grass where they live in darkest Africa is 4'6" tall. Hence, as they wander through their native habitat, the Chief is heard to cry, 'We're the Fugawi! We're the Fugawi!'"

(Chorus:) "We're off to see the Wild West show
The animals and the kangaroo-oo-ooo-s
Never mind the weather
As long as we're together
We're off to see the Wild West show."

VII

The rumbling of a passing truck shook Morley's mind into a state of semi-consciousness. His head began to throb, his whole body ached. His tongue started to explore the dryness in his mouth, but stopped when it reached the chips in his teeth. He tried opening his eyes. The right one wasn't cooperating. It was then that he remembered the stitches in his cheek. He had no idea where he was.

The room gradually came into focus, like watching a Polaroid develop. Colors emerged and stuck to forms. Morley blinked his eyes as bouquets of tulips sprouted around him. Their bright yellow blossoms immediately marked his location. This wallpaper belonged to the Majestic Motel, the garden spot of Rte. 5. He knew he wasn't alone. Over the last four years, he'd spent many nights at the Majestic, and he never woke up alone.

Morley listened for the other breath. It came deep and somnolent. Scenes from the previous evening began to flash through his mind. He focused on a frame where he was asking one of the Old Blue's mannequins if she wanted to rack it. Her eyes sparkled at him, her mouth, the most beautiful he'd ever seen, glistened. The lips, the teeth, all just perfect. He moved a hand under the sheets and softly fingered the warm flesh next to him. It was surprisingly corpulent.

Morley rolled over, eagerly anticipating the sight of this unblemished beauty. He jerked his hand back. A beam of sunlight, falling from a hole in the curtain, illuminated a big fat girl with long, stringy black hair. Her face was streaked with mascara, her mouth smeared with iridescent white lipstick. Her teeth, or at least the ones that he could see, were crooked and stained. She smelled like a used cigarette. Where had THIS come from?

His head started to pulsate. He frantically tried to remember leaving the Beta Bar, but his mind was in full denial. It would not acknowledge meeting THIS. Where was the smiling mannequin?

The fat girl rolled over. She plopped a pudgy paw onto his unit, purred, and snuggled closer. Morley's early morning hardon wilted. How was he going to get out of this mess? He had to escape, the sooner the better. The girl must have driven them. Morley didn't have a car, and nobody would've been stupid enough to lend him one. He had to have been knee-walking drunk when he left Beta. THIS was probably the only broad big enough to carry him out.

He sat upright and very still until he was sure that she had sunk back into a deep sleep. Then slowly, ever so slowly, he eased himself out of the bed onto the floor. His head was pounding. His stomach felt like it had turned upside down. He was determined not to lose his lunch. He had to escape. Even his hangover wasn't as bad as waking up to THIS.

Once on the floor, Morley started to grope for his cloths. Except for the one wayward sunbeam, the room was still dark. He had no idea of what he had been wearing. He found a shoe, then another, a sock, a T-shirt and his jeans. That was enough. He waited for a truck, a real room rattler, to lumber by before he opened the door and slipped out into the parking lot. An elderly couple was loading their car. It was a big Olds 88 with Minnesota plates. The couple stopped packing and stared at Morley's bare ass, their mouths pursed in disapproval like *American Gothic.*

He struggled into his jeans, wedged his feet into his shoes, and hopped down to the highway. He took a pee in the gutter, and stuck out his thumb. He wondered what Christian was going to pick up a half-dressed, unshaven, unshowered, stitched up sinner on a Sunday morning. Much to his relief, the third car screeched to a stop. It was a red convertible with the top up. As Morley opened the door, an effeminate voice greeted him. "Hey, big fella, need a ride?"

A thick gold bracelet accentuated a form fitting shirt that was open to the navel. A gold necklace, neatly trimmed mustache, and bleached blond hair fit the profile. This guy was as sweet as a chocolate-covered cherry.

Morley looked across to the parking lot. He could see the fat girl talking with the couple from Minnesota. They were pointing at him. While Morley didn't want to encourage the queer, what choice did he have? He hopped in.

His not so good samaritan came right to the point. "You know," he said, before Morley had even slammed the door, "I was going the other way when I saw you."

Oh boyoboyoboy! thought Morley, here it comes. "Well, it sure was nice of you to turn around."

"Yes, I saw you standing there and I said to myself, 'Now there's a guy who could use a blowjob." He turned in his seat and stared right at Morley. "WOULD you like a blowjob?"

"Gee, I never really thought about it, it being Sunday and all." He could see the fat girl waddling down the driveway. "I've got to get back to Amherst, but once we're there, who knows." The guy floored the convertible. To Morley's great relief, the Majestic disappeared in the plastic that served as a rear window. For the next ten miles, the queer gave Morley a very upbeat sermon on the pleasures of oral sex. There was no question that he was a true believer. He had himself drooling by the time they reached the light at the Common. That's when Morley jumped out.

"Hey," he shouted, entirely too loud. "What about your blowjob?" A couple of Psi U's were standing on the corner, waiting for the light to change. They gave Morley an odd look. He offered no explanation, but made a dash for the Library. He planned to hide in the reference room until he was sure that his saviour had given up on him. The last thing he wanted was some sweetie following him into Beta, especially after last night. Imagine what the brothers would think. He leaves with THIS and returns with a chocolate-covered cherry. Even a shot in the head from the Old Blue couldn't explain anything that bizarre.

When he was sure that the coast was clear, Morley snuck out of the Library and scurried across to Beta. By now, the King of Smut would be starting his recap. Morley undoubtedly had won top billing. He was going to take a lot of abuse.

As he approached the House, he noticed Elliot Ginsberg and his gang parading around the Common. They were carrying signs protesting the war. Elliot's little group had grown to a couple of dozen. Morley was surprised that some of the demonstrators actually looked normal, even refined. It appeared that Elliot might have tapped into a few parishioners of the Grace Episcopal Church, a gray stone edifice that fronted on the Common. Recruiting some main-line Episcopalians was a quantum leap for Elliot. His strategy to move the protest off campus might have been a good idea.

But then again, maybe not. Two Town cops were sitting in a squad car monitoring the demonstration. They didn't look too happy. The Amherst police were all members of the VFW, and most of the other townspeople, if they thought about it at all, probably supported the war in Vietnam. It was safe to assume that the Town wasn't too pleased at having their Common occupied by protestors and malcontents. Elliot would have to be careful. The Town wasn't as easy going as the College, and the Amherst police were a lot less tolerant than the campus cops.

Morley opened the door to Beta. He was surprised to find over a hundred people crammed into the main hallway. Then he remembered. Today was the Final of the eighth annual Beta Masters, one of the biggest events of the Spring. The winner would be crowned the Master-Beta and presented with a green jacket, compliments of some drunk from Dartmouth, class of '58. A group of guys was gathered around the Greek, placing their bets. Elliot would have been pissed that most students at Amherst were more interested in the Beta Masters than the war in Vietnam. But then, you couldn't bet on the war. The match was about to start, which was a break for Morley. Nobody paid any attention to him.

This year's final had come down to Robert "Hondo" Bryant versus Lowell "The Gator" Cabot. Not surprisingly, Hondo was the odds-on favorite. While Hondo was the best athlete at Amherst, the Gator looked one of its worst. This skinny, bespectacled, six foot-three bookworm never should have been a Beta. The House had pledged him that spring "from the pool."

Amherst, like every institution, recognized that it harbored a handful of individuals who were socially unacceptable. For that reason, the College had a policy that every freshman who went through rushing had to receive at least one bid. This rule meant that at the end of rushing, there was always a few losers that had been rejected by every house and were thrown into a pool. Each house, in turn, was required to dip in and pull someone out of the pool until it was empty. In fairness to the system, some of Beta's most interesting brothers had been plucked from the pool.

You had to look real hard to find anything interesting about Lowell Cabot. The most significant thing about him was that somehow he was related to both the Lowells and the Cabots, and had received an automatic legacy admission to Harvard. Why he had chosen Amherst was still unclear, even to the Gator. He once mumbled something about searching for his identity, which was found for him when Evan Maurer came back from spring break in Fort Lauderdale with a little alligator. The gator bore such an amazing resemblance to Lowell that the brothers immediately tabbed the gator "Lowell," and Lowell, "The Gator."

Lowell never commented on his newfound identity, but no one much cared. Nobody ever saw him. The Beta Masters was the first time that he had ever participated in any House activity. Many brothers didn't even recognize his name when it showed up in the pairings. The Gator was just as surprised. He hadn't signed up for the tournament. Peeps Pole, his pledge father, had entered him. Peeps was hoping that the Beta Masters might give the Gator some exposure. Now, much to everyone's amazement, he was vying for the green jacket.

The Gator's improbable road to the finals had been marked by a series of fortuitous events. He received a bye in the first round when Chan North, his initial opponent, was unexpectedly told by the Dean to take a sabbatical. Chan had been done in by Professor Holton Roller. Chan claimed that he couldn't find his Physics book, and that's why he had taken a zero on the midterm. The Dean was not swayed by this argument. He suggested that Chan might take better care of his textbooks after a stint at Parris Island.

Just the luck of the draw, the brothers figured. The Gator would be history when he met Moose MacNaughton in the second round. The Moose had gone all the way to the final four the year before. He was one of the tournament's early favorites. But the Gator caught the Moose on a bad day.

The clubs used in the Masters were spindles taken from the Beta bannister. They came in two sizes, tall and short. The Moose, who was 6'5", favored the tall, but The Gator, due to the fact that he had already paid his bar bill, had first dibs on the clubs. At 6'3", he naturally chose the long spindle. Seeing that the bannister was about to give way, Shortpecker forbade the removal of any more spindles. The short spindle was too much for the Moose. He couldn't buy a putt, and the Gator moved to the round of eight. Now the whole house knew his name. Peeps Pole was very pleased.

The Gator's next opponent was an independent who was participating by invitation. Independents in the Beta Masters were the equivalent of amateurs in the real Masters. Nobody ever expected them to win, but they added another dimension to the tournament.

No independent had ever reached the Final Four. With the honor of the House riding on his thin, wimpy shoulders, all of the brothers were pulling for the Gator. He didn't let them down. The Gator eliminated the independent in a four down, three to go rout. As a member of the Final Four, the Gator was becoming somewhat of a celebrity. Peeps Pole encouraged him to come by the House more often, which The Gator did. But it didn't help. The Gator was still pretty awkward. He didn't date, he didn't play any sports, and he didn't have any good stories. When he came over, he just sat around. The Gator was not in the mainstream of fraternity life.

The semifinals pitted The Gator against the King of Smut. Smart money was on the King. The only variable was whether the King would show up sober, or even moderately sober. He didn't. He arrived at the first tee totally shitfaced, and The Gator walked away with a lopsided six up, five to go victory. Now the Gator was pitted against Hondo for the championship. Unlike Smee, you could bet that Hondo wouldn't show up shitfaced. Hondo took every game seriously. He was the defending champion. The Greek was taking no action on the match itself. The only betting was on when Hondo would win.

The general consensus was that the Gator would be fortunate to take a hole, especially since they would be playing on the Championship Course. The Greens Committee had been working on the Championship Course all spring. They had tested and retested every possible shot and angle. They did not quit until they were satisfied that they had created the most demanding course in the history of the Beta Masters.

The match was just about to start. The King of Smut was getting ready to make the introductions. The Greek was closing his book. Morley didn't want to attract any attention, so he squeezed in next to Mr. Dunster.

Mr. Dunster was Scrounge's father. Scrounge was another weirdo fished from the pool. He lived next to the boiler room in what had once been the coal bin. He'd furnished his room with junk so pathetic that even the Betas had discarded it. Scrounge seldom came out during the day and was most visible late at night when he emerged from his bin looking for cold pizza and leftover women. Mr. Dunster was dropping off Scrounge's laundry, which was always good for a laugh since the Scrounge never changed his clothes. Mr. Dunster must have gotten sucked into watching the tournament.

Smee had stationed himself in the middle of the hall. The King of Smut was dressed like a real announcer. He was wearing a blazer and tie and had a microphone. When he moved, you could see that the mike's cord wasn't attached to anything, but that didn't deter the King. He swished what was left of the cord around as though he were trying to get it out of the crowd's way. It was a nice touch.

The Gator was beside him. There was no sign of Hondo. Lowell was very nervous. He kept twisting the Moose's favorite spindle around in his hands. The King considered giving the Gator a word of encouragement, but then thought better of it. It was time to get going. "Gentlemen," the King said, "on behalf of every Mastur-Bator, it is my pleasure to welcome you to the finals of the Beta Masters." There was a very polite applause, the kind that you would find at a real golf match. "Thank you. Thank you very much. Now it gives me great pleasure to introduce the contestants. This year's final pits Lowell 'the Gator' Cabot against the defending champion, Robert 'Hondo' Bryant."

There was a tremendous boo at the mention of Hondo's name, even though Hondo was nowhere to be seen. The crowd was getting worked up. Smee put his arm around the Gator. "Gator, before we start, would you like to say a few words to your many fans, both here and those watching you on the tube?"

The Gator looked like he was about to fudge his undies. In all his life, he'd never gotten this much attention. Smee tried to hand him the mike, but the Gator refused to touch it. Peeps Pole jumped to his defense. He grabbed the mike from Smee and shouted into it, "My man is going to kick Hondo's ass. Let's hear it for the Gator." Peeps' pep talk produced only a few sporadic claps. There was no ground swell of support for the Gator.

"Please Peeps, try to restrain yourself." Smee said in all seriousness. "This is the Masters, and we expect the brothers to show the proper decorum, especially in front of so many quests." It was true, golf etiquette was a big part of the Beta Masters. Pushing, shoving and any other form of raucous behavior was frowned upon. When one hole was finished, the crowd was expected to move courteously to the next, and naturally, all talking was prohibited during any shot. Having admonished Peeps, Smee continued with the introductions. "And now, gentlemen, if you would be so kind as to make room, let me introduce the defending champion of the Beta Masters, Robert 'Hondo' Bryant."

There was a loud boo as all eyes turned to Room 4. The door swung open, and there stood Hondo wearing a multicolored golf cap, which was offset by a cheap black Ban Lon shirt, black levis, black socks, and real black golf shoes. To top it off, he had painted on a Simon Legree mustache. That was the end of Beta's new found decorum. Cries of "Pimp," "Hondo, you hot dog," "Give it a rest, Hondo," and "Hang it up, you turkey" greeted Hondo as he took the mike. It was just the response he was looking for. "To all of my loyal fans," he said, with total insincerity, "I just want to say that I appreciate your support, and even though the Gator looks hungry, I promise he won't eat my lunch."

More catcalls. Even if the match stunk, Hondo always put on a good show. Smee reclaimed the mike. He started outlining the course and explaining the rules. The crowd was hushed with anticipation. They knew it was going to be a very difficult course, and, sure enough, what Smee described was a killer.

The first hole started in the middle of the third floor hallway and went to a green located in a remote corner of Room 1. From there the finalists would wind in and out of the bedrooms on the third floor until they headed to the seventh green which was in the middle of the hallway on the second floor. That meant on seven, they'd have to play down the stairs.

Holes 8 through 12 were played around the second floor. The thirteenth hole, like the seventh, went down the stairs, but the thirteenth green was precariously placed at the very front of the landing between the first and second floors. Any player who overshot this green would continue down the stairs to the first floor and almost certainly lose the hole.

Once on the first floor, the course snaked through the living room, the TV room, the library, and finally into the main hallway. The eighteenth green was smack in the middle of the main hallway. The course was set up so that a seat on the main stairs would provide an excellent view of the final green. Robert Trent Jones could not have designed a better hole for watching golf. Regretfully, everyone knew that the 18th hole, the ultimate spectator hole of the Beta Masters, would be wasted. Lowell "the Gator" Cabot would never get to hear the roar of the crowd as he strolled down the main hallway. He undoubtedly would be headed for the showers long before he reached the eighteenth.

Crowd control was always a problem. There were too many people to follow the golfers through the upstairs bedrooms, so the King's play-by-play would be critical. If he could excite the crowd's imagination, everything would be all right. If not, they would be crawling all over the place trying to see what was actually happening. Fortunately, everyone, including the participants, usually preferred the King's description of the match to the match itself. The King could spice up the simplest shot by adding just the right amount of smut.

After the introductions, Morley and Mr. Dunster moved with the crowd as they followed the contestants and the King of Smut up to the third floor. As defending champion, Hondo had the honors. Hondo's tee shot was a thing of beauty. It ricocheted off the leg of the radiator and caromed straight into Room 1. The Gator, immediately feeling the pressure, shanked his drive under the radiator. Smee was doing his best to make things sound exciting. According to the King, Hondo squeaked out a win on the first hole when the Gator had to "claw his way out from under the radiator." In reality, the Gator had used up a stroke removing his ball from an unplayable lie, while Hondo simply tapped his second shot into the hole. Anyone who could see what was really happening could tell that the match was going to be a rout. Even Smee was going to have a tough time trying to keep this match interesting.

The Gator managed to halve the second hole, but then lost number three badly when he fell victim to another radiator. Morley kept moving right along with Mr. Dunster. Having reared the Scrounge, he didn't seem to notice that Morley hadn't showered or shaved and was only half dressed.

Holes 4, 5 and 6 were all halved, but the Gator was in way over his head. He was scrambling for his life. Everyone figured that Hondo would rip him up on the seventh, a transition hole that moved the match from the third floor to the second floor. There was no way that the Gator could handle the stairs.

As the King was quick to explain, the key to the seventh was coming down the stairs at the right speed. There was nothing at the bottom but a banister, whose spindles now seemed very far apart. If your ball came down the stairs too fast, your only hope was to hit a spindle because if it rolled through the banister, it was "hello first floor, goodbye seventh hole."

Morley and Mr. Dunster had moved back down to the second floor where they had a good view of the green and the stairs. They were counting on Smee's commentary to carry them through the first part of the seventh. According to Smee, both Hondo and the Gator had excellent tee shots, but who could believe Smee? Hondo must have played well off the tee because his second shot came rolling down the stairs at just the right velocity. There was a polite applause as all ears tuned to Smee's description of the Gator. If the Gator blew this shot, he might as well head for the showers; there was no way he could come back from three down after seven, especially against Hondo.

"The Gator is addressing his ball. 'Hello, ball.'" Smee must have been running out of material if he had to pull out that old chestnut. A moan went up from the spectators on the third floor. "Oh Boy!" Smee reported. "The Gator has blown it. He hit it too hard! This could be the match!"

The Gator's ball came bounding down the stairs. It had first floor written all over it. Bonk. The ball hit a spindle dead center and trickled to within sixteen inches of the cup. There was a tremendous roar as the crowd was pressed around the Gator, pounding him on the back and congratulating him on his good luck. Nobody could believe it. Those kind of breaks usually were reserved for Hondo. The Gator smiled sheepishly and mumbled, "Gee, thanks, guys."

Despite all the attention, the Gator managed to tap in his putt. He was now only one down with eleven to play. He had become the darling of the gallery.

If Hondo was shaken, he didn't show it. He took the 8th with a spectacular birdie, and they had halved the 9th, 10th, and 11th holes, leaving Gator two down.

The Gator wouldn't quit. He won the 12th when he whacked his ball out of Room 5, off the corridor wall, and back into Room 6. It had been a daring shot, but the Gator knew he had to gamble. The fans were beginning to appreciate the kid's spunk. Mr. Dunster clapped so hard that he dropped the Scrounge's laundry bag.

By virtue of his win on twelve, the Gator had the honor on thirteen, another transition hole. Unlike seven, thirteen didn't go all the way down the stairs. There was a landing between the second and first floor and this is where the Greens Committee had placed the cup. Having the cup on the landing presented an interesting option. You could play it safe and approach the cup in two or bank your shot off of the back wall and try to get close enough for a birdie. The only problem with banking the ball off of the back wall was that the cup was placed at the very edge of the landing and if you hit your tee shot too hard, the ball would roll past the cup and down the stairs. The spectators were buzzing. With the exception of Mr. Dunster, who wasn't familiar with the intricacies of the course, everyone realized that the Gator had to make a decision. Some were yelling "Go for it, Gator! Go for it!" while others were pleading for him to "Play it safe."

Mr. Dunster was wedged against the wall next to Morley. He looked confused. He asked Morley what was going on. Morley gave him as brief an explanation as possible, whereupon Mr. Dunster started yelling, "Go for it, Gator, go for it!" Morley was surprised. It was tough to picture anyone holding Scrounge's laundry as a high roller.

The Gator walked back and forth several times studying the angles of the stairwell and decided to play it safe. He had defied gravity on the seventh. Why push his luck? He was only one down and there were better places to gamble once they reached the first floor. The thirteenth was halved with unspectacular pars.

The fourteenth hole was a double dogleg. It started on the

backside of the landing, took a right turn down the lower half of the stairs to the main hallway, and then made a left through either of two archways leading into the living room. The cup was at the far end of the living room. The 14th was the longest hole on the course, a par five, and a difficult one at that. The trick was to come across the landing in one, go down the stairs with the second shot and have the ball end up in front of one of the two archways.

If you tapped your second shot and trickled it down the stairs, hopefully it would stop in front of the near archway. From there, a player had three shots to get across the living room and down for a par five. A better approach was to try and hit your second shot hard enough so that it stopped in front of the second archway. From there, you had a shot at an eagle three.

The problem with going for the second archway was the couch in the front hall. Getting the ball to roll under the couch was no small feat. The couch, in its prime, only cleared the floor by a few inches. Now, thanks to Shortpecker's daily siestas and notable girth, there was a pronounced sag in the middle. If a ball were bouncing too much coming off of the stairs, it would never make it under.

Both players hit solid drives to the top of the stairs. The Gator was away. To the delight of the gallery, he went for broke. The crowd oohed and aahed as his second shot zipped down the stairs and went cleanly under the couch. When it finally rolled to a stop in front of the far archway, they burst into a spontaneous chant of "Gator, Gator, Gator!"

Now the pressure was on Hondo. He was a picture of pure concentration, his stroke flawless. The ball looked right on the money as it headed underneath the couch, but then something happened. It never came out. The gallery went nuts. What had happened to Hondo's ball? It wasn't bouncing, and it couldn't have hit a leg. It wasn't that far off line.

The crowd surged towards the couch, but Bunnsie, the Chairman of the Greens Committee, jumped onto the couch and ordered everyone to "stand back." Bunnsie took his job very seriously. Smee jumped up onto the couch next to him. The King of Smut looked very much like Dan Rather on the day President Kennedy was shot. It was obvious that he smelled a story.

"Gentlemen! Gentlemen, please control yourselves!" Smee said. He put his arm around Bunnsie and waved the mike signaling for silence. "Gentlemen, please, if you will control yourselves, I have here with me Paul Axtell Bunn, the head of the Greens Committee for the Beta Masters." Smee shoved the mike into Bunnsie's face and began to interview him. "Fetal Pig—if I may be so bold as to address you by your nickname?" Bunnsie was known as Fetal Pig because he had no earlobes. "Do you have any idea what happened?"

Bunnsie was confused. He didn't know what was going on. He looked like some startled eyewitness being interviewed at the scene of an accident. Then he remembered his duty. "No, but if you all will get out of the way, I'll take a look."

Smee had positioned himself perfectly. Holding the mike in one hand, he waved his arms, motioning the crowd back from the couch. "Yes, by all means," he was saying, "the fans must move back so that Fetal Pig may make a proper investigation of this most unusual situation." Somewhat reluctantly, the gallery moved back so that Bunnsie could get on his hands and knees and peer under the couch.

Smee kept up a running commentary. First to the crowd: "As you can see, Bunnsie has now assumed the fetal position and is about to look under the couch. This has to be one of the most exciting moments in the history of sports. Can anyone answer the riddle as to why Hondo is ball-less?"

Smee held the mike to Bunnsie's ass: "Tell us, Fetal Pig, have you gotten to the bottom of it?"

Bunnsie mumbled something inaudible. Smee repeated his words to the crowd. "He said, 'Shit, it hit a book.'"

"Who the hell left this book under the couch?" Bunnsie was screaming.

Smee dutifully repeated, "Fetal Pig says, 'Who the hell left this book under the couch?'"

Bunnsie stood up on the couch and grabbed the mike from Smee. He could hardly contain himself. Something good was coming. "You won't believe it. This book is *Introductory Physics* by Professor Holton Roller."

The crowd immediately broke into the chant, "Steam Roller, Steam Roller," but Bunnsie wasn't through. He had the cover open and was now jumping up and down in pure glee. "Wait a minute, wait a minute! Guess who it belonged to! Channing North!"

Guys were buckling onto the floor. Tears of laughter were streaming down Bunnsie's face. It couldn't have been more perfect. Chan North's missing Physics book, written by Professor Holton Roller, stops Hondo Bryant's go-for-broke shot in the Beta Masters, evening the match.

But being blocked by Chan's book didn't derail Hondo. He came right back to win the 15th. They halved the 16th and 17th. Time was running out for the Gator. He was one down with one to go.

The eighteenth was a simple par three. Hondo had the honors, and with a one-hole advantage he played for a conservative par. If the Gator had any mettle under that thin skin, it was time for him to show it. And that's just what he did. He put together two super shots for a birdie and a win. As unbelievable as it might seem, the match was tied after eighteen. It was on to extra holes.

Play had been going on for more than two hours. The gallery had swelled as word of the match spread over campus. Everybody, especially Smee, was eager to get to the tap. Morley was surprised that Mr. Dunster was still following the match. His wife would kill him when he got home. After all, how long does it take to drop off your kid's laundry?

Since everyone wanted to start drinking, Bunnsie proposed that they create a super hole. The longer and more complicated the hole, the less chance that Gator and Hondo would halve it. The Greens Committee unanimously endorsed this proposal. The extra hole would start on the third floor and finish in the middle of the first floor hallway. Technically it was classified as a par four, but they would need considerable luck to make par, especially since they had to come down two flights of stairs.

As Hondo and the Gator headed upstairs, the crowd fanned out all over the House. The Greek was sitting at the foot of the main stairway, reworking a bunch of bets. The odds were now dead even. The Gator, as the sentimental favorite, had picked up a large contingent of supporters. But most of them were betting their hearts, not their heads. Nobody who thought about it would ever bet against Hondo.

Smee was barking out a crisp commentary from the third floor. Like everyone else, he was extremely excited.

The Gator and Hondo both had good tee shots, but then the Gator got lucky again. As on the seventh hole, he hit his shot hard down the third floor stairs, but this time the ball did not hit a spindle at the bottom. It went right through the banister and dropped onto the first floor hallway about twelve feet from the cup.

The House went bonkers. Hondo was unperturbed. He hit what looked to be a perfect shot down the stairs, but when it reached the second-floor bannister, Hondo's luck turned sour. His ball hit a spindle and failed to fall into the first-floor hallway.

That was it for Hondo. Everybody knew that they were witnessing the end of an era. Amherst's greatest athlete was about to be beaten by a "from the pool" pledge. The crowd, in a display of very poor sportsmanship, started chanting "Goodbye Hondo." Morley and Mr. Dunster had stationed themselves on the first floor, right by the hole. They could hear Smee delivering Hondo's epitaph from up above.

"Apparently, this is it for Hondo," Smee said, above the buzz coming from the huge crowd. "It is going to take him at least three more shots to get down, and from what we see of the Gator, he should be home in two." Then Smee added, noticing that some people were starting to head for the bar, "Please, hold your positions. We will not go on tap until the match is over."

Hondo was taking his time analyzing his situation. He had a lousy lie. His ball had bounced off the spindle to the far end of the second floor hall. Even if he could get his next shot through the bannister, it wouldn't drop anywhere near the hole; the angles were all wrong.

Without the slightest warning, Hondo hacked at the ball as if he were trying to beat it into the rug. Amazingly, the ball bounced straight up and over the railing, ricocheted off a wall, flew back over the bannister, bounced off a spectator, and ended up a mere two feet from the cup. It was, without question, the greatest shot in the history of the Beta Masters.

If the House had rocked after the Gator's shot, it felt like it was going to collapse now. The crowd was falling all over itself trying to congratulate Hondo. Smee had lost his voice. He was talking into the mike but no sound was coming out.

For his part, Hondo strolled down the stairs acting as if nothing had happened. Conceivably, Hondo had gotten so accustomed to pulling off the impossible that he honestly failed to understand why other people thought it unusual. He was one of those rare individuals who was so talented that he considered exceptional feats to be ordinary. He always came through when it counted.

The Gator was devastated. Even though he only lay two, and Hondo three, Hondo's shot had put him on the defensive. You could see the Cabot confidence draining away.

The crowd winced as he stabbed at his first putt. Under the circumstances, it was a creditable effort. It rolled up towards the hole and stopped about two feet away from the beer cup. When Bunnsie measured the balls, he determined that the Gator was still away. Now the pressure was really on. Smee motioned for absolute silence. The Gator stood over his ball.

He looked like death. It rimmed the cup and stopped an inch away. The Gator tapped it in for a respectable bogey and received a very warm ovation.

Now it was Hondo's turn. If he made this putt, he would win the Beta Masters. A hush fell over the House as he approached the ball. Then, to everyone's amazement, Hondo straddled the ball and prepared to hit it with the spindle behind his back. The crowd immediately began shouting, "Hot dog! Hot dog!," but before they could work into a full-fledged chant, Hondo stroked the ball. Plop! In it went. The match was over. Hondo was the Master Beta.

VIII

Mr. Dunster prompted a new round of cheers when he announced that the next keg was on him. There would be hell to pay when he got home. Mrs. Dunster was not a Beta Honey.

Morley reluctantly struggled against the flow of fans heading to the Beta Bar. It would have been easy to let himself go, to be swept down the stairs, but he resisted. He knew he had to get back to his room in North. It was time to implement the next phase of his plan for graduation.

As he walked outside, he was not surprised to see that Elliot was still holding his ground on the Common. His troops had been reduced to a half dozen regulars. The Episcopalians from Grace Church were gone. They must have figured that they had done their good deed for the day, and, flushed with self-righteousness, retreated to respectability. They didn't realize that marching with Elliot was a full time job. If only Elliot were Hondo, or even the Gator, he would have drawn more support. But Elliot would never hold a crowd. Even if he were right about the war, most guys thought Elliot was an asshole.

The hot water pummeled over Morley's bruised and battered body. He could feel his muscles loosening. He took a long, long shower. Suddenly his bed looked very inviting. He put on the Glee Club record, set the switch to automatic replay, and lay down for a minute.

"*Strang-ers once, we came to dwell to-geth-er, sons of a moth-er wise and true, Now we're bound by ties that can-not sev-er, All our whole life thro'.*"

91

The sound of the Glee Club singing the Senior Song filled the room. The Senior Song had unexpectedly become a big part of his plan for graduating.

Morley had flunked his comps in April. He knew then that he could never learn enough about the Fine Arts to pass the make-up exam. How could he squeeze four years of work into four weeks? There had to be another way.

Harts had found it. It was a notice in the *Amherst Student* announcing the election of the Class Officers. By tradition, each of the six class officers picked one member of the faculty as an honorary member of the class. According to Shortpecker, being named an honorary member was a big deal. It was the ultimate affirmation of a faculty member's teaching skills.

"Morley, why don't you become a class officer and name Professor Merrill as your honorary member?" Harts had said. "How could the Professor flunk his sponsor?"

Bingo! Just like that, Harts had it. Professor Merrill was all the help Morley needed. He was the key to graduating. "Come on, Harts," Morley had said, "let's go sign up for a class office."

Unfortunately, when they looked at the slate, the field was pretty well covered. Some of Morley's best friends were running for President, Vice President, Secretary, Treasurer, and Marshall. There was only one office left open, the Class Choregus. Harvey Hayden was the sole candidate. Harvey was President of the Glee Club, an independent, and Morley hardly knew him. There would be no problem taking on Harvey.

"Hey, Harts," Morley had said, "what's the Class Choregus?"

"I'm not sure." Harts said, "I think it's the guy who carries the flag around. But what do you care? Any office will do."

Harts was right again. What did Morley care. He'd be Class Garbage Collector if it gave him the right to sponsor Professor Merrill as an honorary member of the class. What could be simpler. Win the Class Choregus, sponsor Professor Merrill, pass his comps, carry the flag, and graduate. That was his plan.

Morley had thrown his hat into the Choregus ring, and thanks to a strong turnout by the fraternities, was an easy winner.

At the first and only meeting of the class officers, he had named Professor Charles H. Merrill as one of the six honorary members of the Class. Their induction would take place at the Senior Chapel. Without missing a beat, Morley had left the meeting of the class officers and double-timed it over to the Mead Art Building, where he scheduled his makeup exam for the day after the Senior Chapel. So far, his plan was right on track.

Then, came a glitch.

Three weeks before the Senior Chapel, Morley had been at Beta, studying the pictures in the latest *Playboy,* when he had gotten a call from Professor Bruce Crumpett. Professor Crumpett was the Faculty Adviser to the Glee Club. "Mr. Morley," the Professor had said, "I suggest we get together to go over your duties at the Senior Chapel."

"I don't understand, Professor," Morley told him, scrutinizing Miss May, "I have no duties at the Senior Chapel."

"Are you not the Class Choregus?" Professor Crumpett asked, somewhat testily.

"Oh yeah. I guess I have to carry the flag."

"Carry the flag?" the Professor said, confused. "Mr. Morley, the Class Choregus doesn't carry the flag. He leads the College in song."

"He does WHAT!" Morley dropped Miss May.

"Leads the College in song. I strongly suggest you come see me immediately."

Morley had run downstairs. Harts was lying on the couch in the TV room with Shortpecker. They were watching "The Guiding Light."

"Harts, I just got a call from Professor Crumpett. He says the Class Choregus is responsible for leading the College in song. You said the Choregus carries the flag. What's going on?"

"Oh, I meant to tell you," Harts said, not bothering to turn from "The Guiding Light," "It's the Class Marshall who carries the flag. I got a little confused."

"A little confused! Harts, you know I can't sing."

Harts had looked up. "Morley, take it easy. Go see Crumpett

and find out what you have to do before you get all upset. There's no way they're going to make you sing all by yourself. You'll probably just have to stand in front of the Glee Club and wave your arms for awhile. Don't worry about it. Professor Merrill's going to be an honorary member of the class. That's the important thing."

Morley calmed down. As usual, Harts was right. They wouldn't make him sing by himself. There were at least eighty guys in the Glee Club. If all he had to stand there and wave his arms, that was okay. Just so long as Professor Merrill got his honorary class membership.

The clanging of the bells returned Morley's mind to the record. The Glee Club was singing To The Fairest College, the other song that was part of Morley's plan.

"To the fair-est col-lege of them all, We will sing with heart-y will. Till the ech-oes from each clas-sic hall, Fill our hearts with an-swering thrill."

Morley rolled over. He peered out his window at the hands on the clock. They confirmed what the bells already had told him, it was 4 o'clock. The Senior Chapel wasn't until 7:30, so he could catch a few winks. If he got up by five, he'd still have two hours to rehearse his singing.

Morley closed his eyes. He thought back to his meeting with Professor Crumpett, three weeks earlier.

* * *

The Professor's office was tucked away in the Octagon, the little yellow building that was the home of the music department. In his four years at Amherst, Morley had never before entered its eight sides. Now he grasped the big brass knob and read the small gold letters on the solid green door. They said, "OCTAGON, 1848."

The interior of the Octagon was dark and smelled like 1848. Crumpett's door was open. His office was nothing more than a cubbyhole, littered with sheets of music. A short rotund figure was hunched over the desk. Morley knocked on the frame. Professor Crumpett turned around.

"Ah, Mr. Morley," he said curtly. "Our Class Choregus."

"You got him," Morley said with a touch of sarcasm. He wasn't about to suck up to Crumpett. To him, Crumpett meant nothing. He was just another one of those tweedy little twerps who was always fluttering around the faculty lounge.

"Well, Mr. Morley," Crumpett had said, "Having bested the President of the Glee Club for the office of Choregus, I now assume that you are prepared to lead the College in song." Crumpett obviously was peeved that Morley had beaten his boy, Harvey Hayden.

"I'm not prepared to do anything," Morley told him. He moved into Crumpett's cubbyhole. Crumpett was not used to dealing with jocks. He began to act like Morley was a large dog who suddenly might bite him. He slid his chair back against the wall. His tone became conciliatory. "I'm sorry, there doesn't seem to be much room, Mr. Morley. Here, let me find you a chair."

"Look, Professor," Morley said, "I don't need a chair. Just tell me what I have to do, and I'll get out of your hair." The thought of getting out of Crumpett's hair amused Morley. The Professor was bald on top, but tried to cover his pate by combing hair up from the sides. Morley looked down at the long stringy strands that curled across the Professor's cranium. This up and over side sweep only accentuated Crumpett's shiny dome.

"What you have to do is sing, Mr. Morley." Crumpett said, as he patted his frizzled wave. "Have you done much singing?"

"No, but that shouldn't be a problem. I can handle 'Lord Jeffrey Amherst,' at least the first verse."

Professor Crumpett sat up in his chair. "My dear Mr. Morley, 'Lord Jeffrey Amherst' is not sung at the Senior Chapel."

"No? Then what is?"

Crumpett wasn't ready to tell him. Instead, he wanted to make a point. "Surely, Mr. Morley, you realize that the Senior Chapel is not for the Seniors. No, Mr. Morley, at Amherst, we sing for our supper. This ceremony is for the life's blood of the College. It is for the Alumni!"

Uh, oh. That was trouble. No one messed with the Alumni Office. Those guys were like the Mafia. All they cared about was money. If you screwed up one of their deals, you were dead.

"That's not good, Professor," Morley said. "Maybe I will have a seat." He pulled up a chair. "So. Just what does the Class Choregus have to do at the Senior Chapel?"

The Professor jumped to his feet. "Sing, Mr. Morley! Sing!"

Morley slid his chair back to give the Professor some more room. "Sing WHAT, Professor?"

"The two songs that form the backbone of the College's musical tradition." Crumpett grabbed a book from the shelf behind his desk, and presented it to Morley. "I don't suppose that you've ever seen this fine publication?"

The title of this fine publication was *Amherst College Sings*. It was, indeed, the first time that Morley had ever seen it. He leafed through the pages. There must have been a hundred songs, all about Amherst. Most of them had been written by students and alumni before the turn of the century. At least half of them were in Latin. With the exception of the first verse of *Lord Jeffrey Amherst,* Morley didn't know any of them. There were titles like *All Hail Sabrina Dear, The Soul of Old Amherst, Ubi Bene, Ibi Patria,* and *Juba Hallelujah.*

"I think now that you can see why the office of Class Choregus traditionally has been filled by the President of the Glee Club," Crumpett said superciliously. "You do read music, don't you, Mr. Morley?"

"Not a note, Professor. I'm afraid we've got a problem."

The Professor looked confused. "I beg your pardon, Mr. Morley? I have no problem. I know all these songs."

"Yes sir, but you seem to forget that it is I who has to do the singing. When I open my mouth, it won't sound too good for the Music Department." Here, Morley paused. He knew he had the Professor by the short hairs, and not the ones on his head. "Professor, the Alumni Office is going to think that you dropped the ball."

Crumpett collapsed back into his chair. He raised his hands.

"No mas, Mr. Morley, No mas." His tone changed. "Unfortunately, you are quite correct. The Alumni Office has determined that there is a direct correlation between the ambience of the Senior Chapel and alumni giving. That is why it must be done properly."

"I can see that, Professor, but once again, what is it I have to do?"

Crumpett put on a dreamy look. He was into the Senior Chapel. "The lights are turned low, the organ fills the old Chapel with 'A Mighty Fortress Is Our God.' The faculty, the Administration, and the senior class march in bedecked in their caps and gowns. The President gives his opening remarks. The Dean presents the class awards. Six faculty members are inducted as honorary members of the class. Then, the Class rises and the Choregus leads them in the 'Senior Song.'"

"The 'Senior Song?'" Morley said. "What's the 'Senior Song?'"

Crumpett ignored him. He wasn't finished with the Senior Chapel. "After the 'Senior Song,' both verses I might add, the principal speaker gives his talk. When he's finished, the Class Choregus leads the assembly in 'To The Fairest College,' during which the procession marches out. Once the Chapel is empty, the Alumni Office starts sweeping up the checks and that's it." The Professor sat back in his chair.

"Professor, if I've got it right, what you're telling me is that I just have to learn two songs, the 'Senior Song' and 'To The Fairest College.'"

"Yes, Mr. Morley, but with feeling," the Professor said emphatically. "You must sing these songs with feeling." He paused before delivering the next note of bad news. "Unfortunately, you cannot rely on your classmates for much help. It used to be that everyone knew all the songs. Today, it's only the Glee Club that sings, and I'm afraid that after beating Hayden, you can't count on them for much support."

Screw the Glee Club, Morley thought. Any idiot can learn two songs, even me. Plus, the Alumni would add their voices. Those old farts loved to sing. Some of them probably would belt it out in Latin. "So, Professor," Morley said, "how do I go about learning the 'Senior Song' and 'To The Fairest College?'"

"Well, since you don't read music, the best I can do is lend you this Glee Club record." He handed Morley an album titled 'Amherst Sings.'"You'll have to pick the songs up by listening to the record. This is a particularly fine recording, so please, try not to scratch it." Morley had taken the record, and, while having to learn the two songs was an unexpected inconvenience, it was no big deal. Or so he'd thought.

Then, came a bigger glitch.

On May 16, just two weeks before the Senior Chapel, the Trustees of Amherst College announced that Robert Strange McNamara would be receiving an honorary degree at graduation.

John J. McCloy '16, former Assistant Secretary of War under Secretary Henry L. Stinson, former President of the World Bank, former U.S. High Commissioner for Germany, former Chairman of the Chase Manhattan Bank, former Chairman of the Ford Foundation, current Chairman of the Council on Foreign Relations, and current Chairman of the Board of Trustees of Amherst College, had unilaterally decided that Amherst should show its support for America's efforts to defend democracy in Southeast Asia. It was John J. McCloy '16 who had nominated Robert S. McNamara, Secretary of Defense and principal architect of the war in Vietnam, for the honorary degree, and when John J. McCloy '16 made a nomination, it was usually accepted, especially by the Trustees of Amherst College.

Not everyone at Amherst felt as strongly about Robert Strange McNamara as John J. McCloy '16. It was rumored that the faculty and administration were divided on the issue of awarding an honorary degree to McNamara. Even those members of the college community who supported America's role in Vietnam thought it inappropriate for the Trustees to make such a controversial decision, but not surprisingly, it was Elliot Ginsberg who had taken the first action. Elliot began circulating a petition opposing McNamara's honorary degree. The petition described McNamara as the "embodiment of the Vietnam war" and the "architect of death and destruction." As usual, Elliot did not draw much support. Most students, faculty members, and administrators weren't about to sign a petition drafted by Elliot Ginsberg denouncing John J. McCloy's selection for an honorary degree. Nobody in their right mind wanted John J. McCloy to see their name on Elliot's petition. John J. McCloy might have made a mistake, but who was going to tell him?

Then, came the biggest glitch.

On Saturday morning, while Morley was distracting Margie from "Discovering Himself," *The Amherst Student* for May 28, 1966 announced in big, bold, and defiant, headlines that Henry Steele Commager, Professor of American Studies and without question the world's most renowned scholar of American history, would be the speaker at Senior Chapel. Just a month earlier, Commager had publicly characterized America's Vietnam policy as "legally untenable and morally unsound." It generally was assumed that his speech at the Senior Chapel would be critical of both the war and McNamara, and that Henry Steele Commager would tell John J. McCloy that he had made a mistake. If Henry Steele Commager were speaking, the Chapel was sure to be packed.

The Amherst Student, which was run by a group of guys almost as far out as Elliot, didn't help matters any when it ran an editorial billing Commager's speech as a potential benchmark in American history, and condemning the United States' actions in Southeast Asia. The *Student* was the first newspaper in the country to come out against the war. It suspected that McNamara was vulnerable to a direct hit.

On May 18, the Secretary had given a speech in Montreal during which he noted the inadequacy of guns and bombs as instruments of economic and social development. "Who is man?" he had asked. "All the evidence of history suggests that man is a rational animal—but with a nearly infinite capacity for folly. His history seems largely a halting, but persistent, effort to raise his reason above his animality. He draws blueprints for Utopia, but never quite gets it built. In the end he plugs away obstinately with the only building material really ever at his hand: his own part-comic, part-tragic, part-cussed but part-glorious nature." After that performance, some of the press began to suspect that McNamara was losing his military marbles.

A week later, speaking at his daughter Kathleen's graduation from Chatham College in Pittsburgh, the Architect of Death and Destruction did it again: " . . . the ambivalence of technology grows with its own complexity," he said. "The real question, clearly, is not whether we should have tools, but whether we are becoming tools."

By the time of the Senior Chapel, rumors of Commager's upcoming speech had reached the *Springfield Union,* the *Boston Globe,* and even the *New York Times.* The press was flocking into Amherst. If Henry Steele Commager teed off on McNamara, Amherst could very well to establish itself in the vanguard of organized dissent against the war in Vietnam. The Alumni Office was fighting a rear guard action. What the hell would their big givers think? Most of them were probably cut from the same cloth as John J. McCloy '16. Thanks to McNamara's honorary degree, Morley's plan had gotten out of hand. If ever the Alumni Office needed a Choregus with the voice of a nightingale, or at least a Harvey Hayden, it was now. What they had was Morley.

* * *

The bells shook Morley to his senses. "For we have yet a little while, to linger, youth and you and I, in College days." The record player was automatically replaying the "Senior Song." He leaned back and looked up at the clock. He'd overslept. It was seven o'clock. The Senior Chapel would be starting in half an hour. He couldn't linger any longer. He got up and turned off the record. It was covered with scratches. Crumpett wouldn't like it, but too bad for Crumpett. For all he cared, Crumpett could sit on his record and rotate.

Morley put on his cap and gown and stood in front of the mirror. He looked surprisingly academic, even smart. He fiddled with his tassel, but couldn't remember on what side it was suppose to hang. No matter, he had bigger problems. It was Game Time. All of Amherst would be exhorting Morley to "Sing, you bastard, sing!"

IX

A swarm of parents, alumni, protestors, and reporters were trying to get into Johnson Chapel. Many carried signs, either for or against the war. Some students were wearing white armbands. Morley saw Elliot Ginsberg wrangling with some big, stupid looking Irishman who was waving a sign that said, "Nuke the Gooks." How could Elliot waste his time arguing with anybody dumb enough to walk around waving a sign that said, "Nuke the Gooks?" This guy had to be some Southie from UMass auditioning for a career in Boston politics.

Morley hiked up his gown and skirted to the back of the Chapel where the Class was assembling. At first, he couldn't recognize anyone. The Class looked totally different in their caps and gowns. It was like walking into a costume party. Then he heard Lawrence Myers Mudd, III's, deep voice. It had been four years, almost twenty percent of Morley's life, since Professor Kinsey had ground Mudd under his shoes at the opening History lecture. He wondered what Slosher would have thought of all this academic pomp and preening. He probably would have labeled everyone an asshole.

Harts grabbed his arm. "Morley my boy, you look like a veritable canary." His breath smelled like beer. Harts must have spent the last three hours at the 19th hole of the Beta Masters.

"Harts," Morley said, "don't give me any crap. If it weren't for you, I wouldn't be in this mess. Do you know either one of these songs?"

"Will you stop worrying about those damn songs," Harts said. "Nobody cares about the songs. They're all wetting their pants over Commager's speech. Just mouth the words and let the Alumni do the singing."

"Yeah, right, only you're not the one who has to stand up in front of all of these people looking like an asshole."

Morley worked his way inside the door to the bottom of the stairs where the other class officers had assembled. He pulled Charlie Firestone under the stairwell. Charlie was the Class Marshall. He was holding the American flag. "Look, Charlie, I've got a little problem," he said. "Maybe you can help me out."

Charlie wasn't one of Morley's close friends, but he was a good guy. "Yeah, what can I do for you?" Charlie said as he readjusted the flag so that it stuck out from under the stairwell.

"I might be a little shaky on these songs," Morley said, reaching under his gown for a piece of paper. "Here's a copy of the words. If I run into any trouble, how about cuing me?."

"Sure, no problem." Charlie said, studying the piece of paper. "Geez, where'd you get these? I've never heard either one of them."

Great! Wasn't there anybody who knew these damn songs? Morley's bowels began to churn. He shuffled to the men's room, claimed a stall, and carefully lifted his gown. He didn't want it dangling in the bowl. Anybody who had ever played ball knew how easy it was to dangle the tail of your jersey in the bowl. It happened to every rookie. He sat down and tried to remember the songs, but he couldn't concentrate. The guy in the next stall was grunting, groaning and breaking wind. He sounded like he was about to DIE.

Morley completed his paperwork, inspected his gown, and started to wash his hands. The toilet next to him flushed. The stall door opened and in the mirror, Morley saw Henry Steele Commager. Morley didn't know what to say, but he felt he had to say something. "Hey, Professor," he said into the mirror, "how's it going?"

The Professor smiled. "A lot better now, thank you." The Professor was wearing a crimson hood over his gown. The hood was laced with ribbons of all different colors. He looked like a peacock.

As Morley chucked his paper towel into the basket, he noticed a piece of toilet paper hanging from the bottom of the Professor's gown. "Excuse me, Professor," he said, "but I think you might have dropped your robe in the bowl."

The Professor looked down in disgust. "Damn, it happens every year. You'd think I'd learn." As Morley walked out, the Professor was standing in front of the sink, rinsing his gown like a rookie.

The line was forming up behind John J. McCloy '16, President Plimpton and the Dean. Morley was reminded of Raphael's *Pope Leo X With His Nephews, Cardinal Giulio de' Medici and Luigi de' Rossi.* In his cap and gown, John J. McCloy '16 bore an uncanny resemblance to Pope Leo X, and the faculty, adorned in their academic finery, could easily have passed for the College of Cardinals. Morley spied Professor Merrill and moved in next to him. "Evening, Professor."

"Good evening, Edward. How's the eye?" the Professor said, studying Morley's stitches.

"The eye's fine. It's my voice I'm worried about."

"Nonsense. You'll do just fine." The line started to move.

As the procession marched around to the front of the Chapel, John J. McCloy '16 raised his hand to the overflowing crowd and nodded piously as it parted before him. He ascended the steps of the Chapel, and strode purposefully through the big green doors.

When John J. McCloy '16 crossed the threshold, the organ erupted into Martin Luther's most famous hymn. *"A might-y fortress is our God, A bul-wark nev-er fail-ing."* Morley had never heard the hymn sung with such vigor. The Alumni Office must have been very pleased. Vigorous singing meant hearty checks.

"His king-dom is for-ev-er. A-men." By the time the congregation reached the last verse, the hymn had carried the entire procession to their assigned seats.

As the *A-men* faded into the rafters, Charlie Firestone, the Class Marshall, stepped forward and carefully placed his flag in its holder next to the podium. He turned to the Class. Charlie was a little guy, but standing there in his cap and gown next to the American flag, he seemed much larger than he was in real life. His voice assumed a similar stature. He commanded the Class, "Remove Your Caps." There was a rustle as everyone removed their caps. Then Charlie directed the congregation to "Take Your Seats." Everyone sat down, only there weren't nearly enough seats. Much of the congregation was left standing in the aisles.

President Plimpton took the podium. He seemed perfectly calm, even amused.

"I can't possibly understand why this ceremony has drawn so much interest," he said with a mock naivete, "but if those of you who are standing in the aisles would care to sit on the floor, I trust that the fire marshall might grant us a one time dispensation." He began his remarks as soon as everyone had settled down.

"To you, the Class of '66, I shall not try to create a sentimental nostalgia, for that would be looking backward. We are here to look ahead." A long-haired creep with a scuzzy-looking girl had plopped themselves on the floor next to Morley. Morley immediately noticed that the girl wasn't wearing a bra, and that when she leaned forward, he could see down her blouse. He was rewarded with a full view of her left breast, and while it wasn't any Rubens, it was enough to keep his attention.

Cal was saying something about keys, how everything in our society was locked up, and how being a college president was like being a janitor. Morley wasn't really listening and missed the analogy. He was trying to study the songs that he'd Scotch taped to the inside of his mortarboard, but due to the hippie girl's left breast, he was having trouble concentrating.

"Gath-er clos-er, hand to hand, The time draws near when we must part." Morley shut his eyes and repeated the line. He thought he had most of the *Senior Song*.

"I hadn't been the head janitor at Amherst for more than a few minutes when I learned that the keys of education are to open up, and not to lock in, or lock out," Cal said. The hippie girl nodded her head. Her boob bobbed agreeably. Morley lost another line. He started over. *"Strang-ers once, we came to dwell to-geth-er."*

"How much will you let a key unlock you, and how much will you use your key to unlock?" Cal challenged the class. The hippie girl leaned back, stretching her blue denim work shirt shut. That was the end of Morley's free shot. He peered back inside his hat. *Now we're bound by ties that can-not sev-er, All our whole life thro'.*

"Can you decide how much you are here to change society, and how much society is here to change you?" Cal had taken on a Socratic tone, which was a bad sign. In academia, that usually meant that the speaker was about to wrap it up. "No one knows these proportions, but it would be my hope that Amherst encouraged you to venture, and dared you to change." Cal paused, looked over the Class, and delivered his finale, "May Amherst continue to be your key!"

There was polite applause as Cal turned the podium over to the Dean. Morley kept memorizing the *Senior Song* as the Dean started recognizing the Best This and the Best That. Morley knew that his name would not be called. These were the Bests for academics and citizenship. Athletics were ignored whenever the College donned its cap and gown.

Morley didn't look up until Cal had resumed his position at the podium. This was the part of the ceremony that Morley had been waiting for. He listened intently as the President began to announce the six faculty members that had been chosen as honorary members of the Class of '66. Here was the key to his education, the one that would unlock the door to his comps.

"If they will please come forward as their names are read, we will now induct these gentlemen into the Class of 1966." The fifth name read was "Charles Hill Merrill, Professor of Fine Arts."

You were supposed to hold your applause until all six of honorary members of the Class had come forward and received their medallions, but Morley didn't wait. He began his applause as soon as the President tied the purple and white ribbon around Professor Merrill's neck. If there was any question who had nominated Professor Merrill for the Class of '66, Morley made sure that it was answered.

Morley was still gazing at Professor Merrill when he realized that everyone else was staring at him. According to the program, it was time for the Class Choregus to lead the assembly in both versus of the *Senior Song*, by J. S. Hamilton '06.

Morley got up. His knees were knocking. He felt like a midget compared to Charlie Firestone. He heard himself say, "Please rise." He was surprised that his voice sounded so much in control. He took out the little pitchpipe that Professor Crumpett had given him. The note he was supposed to blow was clearly marked, but Morley missed the mark. He blew blindly into the first hole that hit his lips. By the look on Crumpett's face, he knew he'd delivered the wrong note. Unfazed, he raised his arms, and after the customary pregnant pause, brought them down with a great flourish and squeaked, *"Strang-ers once, we came to dwell to-gether, Sons of a moth-er, wise and true."*

The congregation recoiled as if Morley had just scraped his fingernails across a blackboard. Even Morley was repulsed by the squeal, but kept pushing through the first verse. *"Still the love of col-lege days will lin-ger Ev-er in each heart."*

By the end of the first verse, Morley had heard enough. Ignoring the program, he touched the fingers of his right hand to his left palm signaling for a Time Out, and ordered the congregation to "Take Your Seats!" Most of the congregation did as they were told, but the organist, whose back was to the audience, stuck to the program and launched into the second verse. There was some confusion until Professor Crumpett ran over and cut the organist off. An embarrassing stream of truncated notes drooled from the pipes that ran up the back wall of the Chapel.

President Plimpton, who obviously had been expecting both verses, scrambled back to the podium. He gave Morley a puzzled look, as if to ask, "What happened?" Morley shrugged his shoulders, as if to answer, "So I dropped the ball. No big deal, just pick it up and keep moving."

That's just what Cal did. He began his introduction for Professor Henry Steele Commager. This was the moment that most everyone had been waiting for. The mention of Henry Steele Commager started flashbulbs popping and cameras grinding. There was an anticipatory creak as people sat up in their pews. Reporters moved up the aisles to the front of the Chapel. Morley did his best to ignore the commotion, and focused on the paper taped to the inside of his cap. He had to learn this second song. If the *Senior Song* had been bad, *To The Fairest College* was going to be worse. He hadn't given it equal time, and he knew the Alumni Office would go bananas if he blew this one.

The Chapel rose to its feet in a standing ovation as Henry Steele Commager approached the podium. The Professor fiddled with his notes while he waited for the assemblage to settle down. The hippie girl leaned forward with anticipation. Morley's eyes shifted from his cap to a new view of her left breast. Commager began.

"President Plimpton, Trustees of the College, members of the faculty, honored guests, families, and friends of the Class of 1966: I am grateful for the opportunity to address you on this occasion. Throughout my professional life I have been deeply involved with Amherst, and I am proud to have played a part in preparing its graduates to deal with the complex and important problems which face our nation. In the process I have gained a most profound respect for the value of an Amherst education."

The girl strained forward. On the inside of her left breast, nipple high, Morley spied a little tattoo. Monk had once taken him to the Block in Baltimore where he'd seen a stripper with "hot" on one hooter and "cold" on the other. He was sure this message would be more temperate. He leaned over for a closer look, but the girl sat back. Commager was getting into the meat of his address.

"No other war in which we have been engaged, except possibly the Civil War, poses so many or such difficult problems to the student of history as does our

109

war in Southeast Asia. With all the other wars the causes have seemed comprehensible, the objectives plausible. The Vietnam war alone seems to be the product of willful folly, hysteria, and paranoia, lacking in logic, purpose or objective, and waged with insensate fury against victims with whom we had no quarrel and who are incapable of doing us any harm. Americans are now bombing rural hamlets and villages indiscriminately, that is the meaning of a 'free fire zone,' dropping napalm and 'daisycutter' bombs whose only use is the killing or maiming of civilians, using defoliants and herbicides guaranteed to impair the ecology for a century, and destroying Vietnam with an overkill prohibited by the laws of war which we ourselves prescribed at Nuremberg. The story is becoming so familiar and so painful that many Americans prefer to ignore it or forget it or pretend that it somehow is not really happening. And yet it is happening, and for reasons which no one in an official position has ever been able to make clear. Rarely before in history has a great nation drifted so mindlessly into catastrophe."

Commager's delivery was continually interrupted by scattered applause and cries of "Murderers!" and "Stop the war!" Any euphoria the Alumni Office might have experienced during "A Mighty Fortress Is Our God" was quickly evaporating. Commager's address was not what the Alumni Office and John J. McCloy '16, wanted to hear. How could Amherst be so stupid as to award an honorary degree to the mindless architect of an immoral war?

"At some point during the last twenty years, our government has somehow become committed to the conviction that the United States has vital interests in mainland Asia and is therefore destined to be an Asian power. Once committed to this notion, we have found ourselves inexorably caught up in a war not only against the Chinese Communists—who have had an awkward habit of winning victories—but against Communism everywhere in Asia.

"Many scholars have examined the assumptions which lie behind our Asian policy, and have found them wholly lacking in credibility or logic. Why did American statesmen ever suppose that we had either the right or the competence to be an Asian power? We would, after all, consider any Chinese statesman who thought that China should be an American power bereft of his senses. But no matter. Our government has rejected the conclusions of the scholars and has even punished them for arriving at such conclusions."

Whenever the hippie girl stopped clapping, she would lean forward trying to absorb all of what Henry Steele was preaching. Each time she leaned forward, Morley bent over to get a better peek at her tattoo.

"After 1945, a war psychology took command of America. We had always thought of ourselves as the most successful of nations; now the pressures of the Cold War required us to be Number One in a very hard sense, not only as against any other nation but as against any other combination of nations. The psychology of war shifted our center of gravity from the State Department to the Pentagon, perhaps from the Congress to the Pentagon, possibly even from the White House to the Pentagon."

Commager had said the magic word, "Pentagon." It was if Groucho Marx's duck had dropped down with a hundred dollar bill in its beak. People were hollering and booing. Morley saw his opening. He dropped his pen next to the girl. When Commager started up again, he reached over to get it. True to form, the girl bent forward at just the right moment. For an instant, Morley's face was inches from her breast. His eyes focused on the tattoo. It was a blue dove, exactly like the one on Elliot's PEACE sign.

"When Washington became President, the United States Army consisted of fewer than 1,000 men and officers. Now ours is the largest and most powerful military establishment in the world. It absorbs one-third of the budget, maintains its own foreign-affairs policy, and even instigates wars and supports revolutions without the knowledge of the Congress to whom is assigned the authority to declare war.

"To take care of all this there has emerged a new security bureaucracy, made up of the most distinguished men, recruited from the most distinguished universities, the most successful law firms, the richest banks, the most powerful corporations. Men who, for all their education and their sophistication, their high sense of personal integrity and personal honor, have uncritically adopted the war psychology. They have lent their great talents not to devising ways of reducing tensions and avoiding war, but to ways of exacerbating tensions and preparing for war. And—when it didn't come fast enough—making war. With so much going for war, it inevitably came. And thus the bureaucracy has been triumphantly vindicated in its apprehensions and its prophecies."

Commager was in complete control. Morley couldn't believe that this was the same befuddled guy he had seen rinsing toilet paper from his robe like a rookie. At the podium, Commager was All-Pro.

"It is a sad fact of modern business and of modern politics that the most immoral acts are committed not by hardened criminals, but by the gentlemen of impeccable academic and social credentials who preside affably over great institutions, and who sin impersonally and at a great remove in time, in space—and in law—from the consequences of their crimes."

Now, Henry Steele Commager was criticizing more than just McNamara and the architects of the war. He was denouncing

John J. McCloy '16 and anyone else who supported, or even condoned, the war. Like Martin Luther, he was taking on the establishment. The Alumni Office must have been going apoplectic. Here was the start of a new reformation.

"In 1907, E.A. Ross propounded this thesis in a brilliant but neglected book entitled *Sin and Society*—which in light of recent events has proven to be remarkably prophetic. Ross said: 'Those responsible for these crimes never think of themselves as criminals, nor are they ever punished, even by public disapproval. On the contrary, they sit on the boards of foundations and accept honorary degrees from universities, they are welcomed into the best clubs and the most fashionable churches.'"

For those opposed to the war, this was too good to be true. Henry Steele Commager was a genius. He had the right forum, the right material, and the reputation to speak with impunity.

"The managers who have prepared for war and then embraced it, are not conscious war mongers. They are the leaders of a bureaucracy which operates impersonally, almost mechanically, and which in the end achieves a life of its own. That is the way we have fought our war in Southeast Asia, impersonally and mechanically. Never before in history has a nation been systematically destroyed, as Vietnam is being destroyed, by high-minded gentlemen who appear more animated by sorrow than by anger as they direct their computerized technology to deliver their surgical strikes."

Morley figured that he had about three minutes left to master *To The Fairest College*. He looked into his cap one last time. *We will sing of man-y a vic-to-ry, on dia-mond, field and track, Midst the gold-en haze of col-lege days, Our hearts to thee turn back.*

"And so we find ourselves trapped by bureaucracy in a pattern of synthetic politics and synthetic morals, appropriate only to a war fought with impersonal technology over issues that no one can explain, supported by arguments that are spurious and by rhetoric that is canting and unctuous. The most conspicuous feature of the Vietnam landscape today is not the millions of craters which make the land look like the surface of the moon, but the fog of deception and lies that hangs over it. Indeed, nothing about this war is genuine or honest or real except the death and devastation we have poured into Vietnam: that is real.

"This is a war that we not only cannot win, but must not win. Some wars are so deeply immoral that they must be lost if we are to survive morally. I believe that the war in Vietnam is such a war, and that the truest patriots are those who resist it!"

Johnson Chapel erupted. Anyone who might have felt that the war in Vietnam was wrong now had both the historical and moral justification to oppose it. Thanks to Henry Steele Commager, the anti-war movement had just become legitimate. There was no way that McNamara could fail to respond to this broadside. When the greatest living American historian calls you "an impersonal machine of death and destruction" and maintains that the truest patriots are those who resist your war, you've got to say something.

For most, the Chapel was over. All the crowd wanted to do was get out and discuss Commager's speech. But the Chapel wasn't over. There was still one item left on the program. The Class Choregus had to lead the College in the singing of *To The Fairest College* by D. C. Bartlett '03.

Morley's mistake with the *Senior Song* had been actually trying to sing. The Harts was right; better just to fake it. This time he would mouth the words and let the Glee Clubbers carry it. No one would ever know.

When the uproar caused by Commager had settled down, Morley rose. Again, in a loud, clear voice, he commanded the congregation to "Please Rise." He took out his pitchpipe, this time remembering to look for the mark. There were two marks, one for the *Senior Song,* the other *To The Fairest College.* He'd forgotten which was which. He had a fifty-fifty chance; he picked a hole and gave it a toot. Once again the scowl on Professor Crumpett's face told him he'd blown it.

Morley raised his hands high and wide, as if offering thanks to some unseen god above the Chapel. When he was certain that he had everyone's attention, he brought them down with an exaggerated flourish and mouthed the words, *"To the Fairest College of them all, we will sing with hearty will."*

There wasn't a sound, not one peep. The faculty, administration, students, parents, friends, guests, protestors, and reporters all stared at Morley. The organist, after being abandoned on the second verse of the *Senior Song,* turned around wondering when to start.

The awkward silence was broken by a stage whisper: *"To the fairest College of them all, We will sing with hearty will."* It was Charlie Firestone cuing Morley with a suspiration that reverberated throughout the Chapel. Not that it mattered, Morley was beyond help. He just stood there, his arms locked in the air in front of his chest. Charlie, loyal to the end, kept trying: *"Till the echoes from each classic hall fill our hearts with answering thrill."*

Some Betas began to laugh. This had to be singularly the most embarrassing moment in Morley's young life. There was nothing he could do but gut it out. He re-raised his arms over his head, brought them down with a somewhat deflated flourish, opened his mouth, and spit out the words Charlie had just fed him. *"To the fair-est col-lege of them all, we will sing with hearty will."*

Fortunately, before he could croak the second line, Professor Crumpett pointed to Harvey Hayden who immediately hummed a note. That note activated the organist, the glee clubbers, and most of the Alumni. Much to the Alumni Office's great relief, *To The Fairest College* was finally joined with a hearty will.

Morley just stood there, flapping his arms like a mute nightingale, while the procession began to file out. But Morley wasn't the only one who'd had a tough evening. Thanks to Henry Steele Commager's broadside, John J. McCloy '16 now looked more like Judas Iscariot than Pope Leo X. The Dean also was quite upset. "For Christ's sake," he snapped at Morley as he strode by, "you think you could've at least learned the songs."

Other members of the faculty and administration muttered the same complaint, but Morley just smiled and kept flapping his arms at Harvey Hayden. Fuck'em. There was only one person who mattered to Morley, and that was Professor Merrill. When he walked by, he was all smiles and motioned for Morley to join him in line.

Together, Morley and Professor Merrill marched out of Johnson Chapel. There was still hope. *"Hail Al-ma Ma-ter, our well loved Mo-ther, Old Am-herst, here's to thee. We'll love thee ev-er, all boys to-geth-er and ev-er faith-ful be!"*

X

Morley stood naked in front of the congregation. Hundreds of people in black robes were clamoring for him to "sing, you bastard, sing!" He opened his mouth, but nothing came out. He looked up. Robert Strange McNamara was leaning over the balcony, wearing a crimson robe with a big block "H" on it. It reminded Morley of the Harvard drum. In one hand, the Secretary of Defense was holding a bullhorn; in the other, his teeny weeny tool. He began whispering the words to the *Senior Song* into the bullhorn and started to pee on Morley.

Voices from within the black robes yelled at Morley, "Sing, you bastard, sing!" Again, Morley opened his mouth. Again, nothing came out. Black robes started to rush towards him. He began to see faces. They looked like the Old Blue scrum. Professor Crumpett was urging them on with a pitchpipe that sounded like a gong. Everyone was shouting at Morley. "Sing, you bastard, sing!" Professor Merrill was at his side trying to pull him away. The stream of pee from Robert Strange McNamara moved closer. Morley took a deep breath and opened his mouth. It was his own scream that woke him up.

He was lying naked in his bed at North, his body soaked in sweat. The bell from Johnson Chapel vibrated through the room. Morley heard a commotion below his window, leaned over, and looked out. He was surprised at the size of the crowd in front of the Chapel. Hundreds of people were milling around. Many were waving signs that said things like MCNAMARA SUCKS, STOP THE WAR, NOW! and HO, HO, HO CHI MINH/THE N.L.F. IS GONNA WIN. Some creep that Morley had never seen before was addressing the crowd with a bullhorn. Morley couldn't hear what the guy was saying, but the crowd kept exhorting him on.

Elliot Ginsberg was standing next to the speaker holding his PEACE sign. The dove hovering over the word "Peace" looked like it had flown straight from the hippie girl's left breast. Maybe Elliot wasn't wasting his time at these rallies; maybe he was getting something.

The bells said it was nine o'clock; Morley had been conked out for eleven hours. His mind, trying to catch up on its sleep, had forgotten his bladder. He had to take a wicked piss. The metal dormitory bed squeaked as he rolled to his feet. The sleep had helped, but he was still stiff and sore. He slipped on a pair of gym shorts and hobbled down the hall to the head. He was almost fully relieved when a dapper little guy in a madras shirt and white Bermuda shorts sidled up to the urinal next to him. Morley recognized him but couldn't remember his name.

Morley grunted a "hello." The little guy acknowledged his grunt with a Chiclet smile and a mellifluous "good morning." Morley began to suspect that this guy might be in the Glee Club. His suspicion was confirmed when the guy started humming a tune. Only a glee clubber would sing and pee at the same time. The tune sounded familiar, but Morley couldn't quite place it. On the way back to his room, the words finally came to him: *To the fairest College of them all, we will sing with hearty will.* That little twerp had been ragging him, and he didn't even know it. Trumped again by another glee clubber. How bad was that.

But then, how bad was his performance at the Senior Chapel. Morley hadn't stayed around to collect any plaudits. When the recessional had reached the front door of the Chapel, he'd said good night to Professor Merrill and run straight to his room in North. He didn't want to see anybody. With his comps today, the last thing he needed was a bunch of guys giving him crap about his singing. The only memory he wanted from the Senior Chapel was Professor Merrill walking beside him as an honorary member of the Class of '66.

Morley flopped back onto his bed. He tried memorizing some

pictures, but he couldn't concentrate. The bullhorn blared through his window. Now he was getting annoyed. Didn't these people have anything better to do? None of them had to worry about their comps. It was a beautiful day. Why didn't they just walk over to Memorial Hill, lie down, and enjoy the view? Did they really expect that demonstrating in front of the Chapel was going to stop a war 12,000 miles away? The bed squeaked again as he got up to shut the window.

The fanatic with the bullhorn was whipping the crowd into a frenzy, screaming with such passion that the vein in his forehead looked ready to burst. Despite the distortion of the bullhorn, Morley began to catch a few words: "Profits" "Capitalism" "Oppression" "Massacre." Leaning his head out the window, Morley picked up phrases: "Millions of innocent people are being slaughtered by capitalism" "We are seeing the dawn of another Hitler and his henchmen" "People continue to starve while we pour billions into the weapons of death." Listening carefully, Morley was able to hear it all.

"When William James said, 'Damn the absolute,' he was speaking for most of his countrymen," the speaker shouted into the bullhorn. "All through our history we have practiced the axiom 'theory may mislead us, experience must be our guide.' The one major departure from it, the state sovereignty theories of the ante-bellum South, led to disaster. But the entire logic of the Vietnam war is the product of absolutes that have no basis in reality. They are theories shrouded in peace and honor that in fact have no peace or honor."

What the hell was this guy talking about? "Damn the absolute"? "The state sovereignty theories of the ante-bellum South"? How could this mumbo-jumbo get people so excited? What were they hearing that Morley wasn't? It must have been good because Elliot looked like he was about to shoot his wad as he stood there pumping his PEACE sign up and down.

Morley slammed the window and went back to his bed. *The Last Supper*, Leonardo da Vinci, c. 1495–98. Mural. Santa Maria della Grazie, Milan, was the first painting to catch his eye. It

119

reminded him that he hadn't eaten for almost a day. How could he study on an empty stomach? Time for a break. He got up and headed for the snack bar.

On his way out of North, Morley stopped to study the crowd in front of Johnson Chapel. Elliot's scruffy group of hippies was evolving into a microcosm of the college community. There were some professors, real students, and other normal people you'd see around town. They all were listening intently to a fat, middle-aged lady with disheveled grey hair who had seized the bullhorn. She was clamoring that "the same forces that have enslaved women for all these generations are perpetrating an illegal war on women, children, and millions of innocent peasants." The crowd roared its approval.

Mid-morning was always a busy time at the snack bar, but now that classes had ended, it was more crowded than usual. Morley was hoping to find an empty table, but he could see right away that every table was taken. Fortunately, a quick scan of the room produced no Betas. It was still too early for the brothers, which was just fine with Morley. He had no desire to hear a recap of his performance at the Senior Chapel. The King of Smut could make a career out of that story.

Morley got in line and ordered eggs, bacon, an English muffin and a large chocolate milk shake. He loved to wash down a big breakfast with a chocolate shake. It was a little treat he gave himself every now and then, and right now, he needed a little treat. He paid his bill and spied a table in the back that looked almost empty. As he got closer, he could see that Clapp was sitting there all by himself.

"Hey Clapp, how ya doing." Clapp looked up with his deceptive choir boy smile.

"I really appreciate your introducing me to Eddie," Clapp said. "He's a great guy."

"Yeah, I thought you two might get along. Just don't talk to him about the war. That really spaces him out."

"Which war?"

"Any war, they're all the same with Eddie."

Clapp was reading the College's newspaper, *The Amherst Student*. Morley noticed a picture of Monk under a headline on the back page. He was blocking a shot against Williams. The photo caption read "Stuart Cooke '68 Shuts Down Williams." Under the photograph of Monk, there was a long article about how lacrosse had gone undefeated. The write-up of the rugby game would be on the inside of the back page. Even though the Amherst R.F.C. had just won the national championship, lacrosse still got the back page because it was an official college sport.

"Mind if I look at that when you're through?" Morley said.

The Amherst Student was distributed free, so there were plenty of copies lying around, if you wanted to get up and hunt for one. Clapp wasn't the kind of guy who went hunting. "Here." he said, leaning over to the next table. He grabbed a paper that was sitting there. The table was full of Phi Gams. It wasn't clear that they were through with the paper, but no one objected.

The front page coverage was divided between Commager and John J. McCloy '16. A complete text of Commager's speech and several commentaries, pro and con, were carried on page 6. The editorial condemned both the war and McNamara's upcoming honorary degree. Before Morley could get to the rugby write-up, an article on page 8 stopped him. It was a feature on Elliot Ginsberg. The headline read "Ginsberg says 'Pampered Amherst Liberalized by Vietnam Conflict.'" There was a picture of Elliot holding his PEACE sign. Morley spread some jam on his English muffin and started reading the article.

> The radical movement at Amherst is a comparatively recent phenomenon tracing its origins to the activities of Amherst Students in the South in the early sixties. Although membership of the Amherst Students for a Democratic Society (SDS) is only about 20, the influence of these and other members of the New Left seems to be growing . . .

Judging from the crowd in front of the Chapel, it was really growing. With all this McNamara bullshit, Amherst might be overrun by radicals. Morley carefully arranged a strip of bacon on his English muffin and took a big bite.

"Amherst, like most prestige colleges, is turning out people more interested in their own careers and their own successes than any political commitment." That's how Elliot Ginsberg '66 characterizes what he thinks is wrong with American education today. Ginsberg, who founded the Amherst chapter of Students for a Democratic Society 16 months ago, represents a minority of students on campus who are very dissatisfied with their experience here.

As Morley loaded up the other half of his English muffin, he wondered what Elliot's parents thought about their son, the protestor.

"The system places values on getting ahead," Ginsberg explains, "and most students, since they are under pressure to do well, play it safe and take the easy path that will lead them to a safe job, a nice car, and their box in the suburbs."

What was wrong with having a safe job, nice car, and a box in the suburbs? That's why Morley wanted his diploma. Having a safe job, a nice car, and a box in the suburbs sure as hell beat going to Vietnam and getting a bullet up his asshole.

According to Ginsberg, "A paternalistic Administration, in treating students as pampered children, destroys any sense that students are citizens who have a right to make decisions about the future of the community."

Paternalistic? Okay. Amherst kept an eye on its *Sons of a mother Wise and true.* But pampered? How could Elliot possibly think they were pampered? Morley didn't feel pampered. The administration had been threatening to throw his ass out for four years. What type of pampering was that? And what about Elliot? The Dean was always hauling him onto the carpet for disrupting the college community and for bringing outside agitators into Amherst. No, the Administration might be paternalistic, but they sure as hell didn't do too much pampering. Morley finished his English muffin and began to work on his eggs.

> While the number of committed radicals has stayed small, Ginsberg believes there has been a "general liberalization of student opinion at Amherst" during his four years here. He attributes this change in part to the war in Vietnam which, because it is "senseless to any moral person," has made many students less hostile to the radical's point of view.

More than likely, people had just gotten used to Elliot and accepted the fact that he was a screwball. After four years, most people had learned to ignore him.

> In its first year and a half, SDS has sponsored a program of speeches on Vietnam at the First Lutheran Church, run a march in Northampton to protest the resumption of U.S. bombing of the North, and brought several leading community organizers here to speak. But Ginsberg wishes that more could have been done. He wants SDS to become the organization that will mobilize organized dissent through direct action and protests.

Morley put down the paper, finished his eggs, took a taste of his milkshake. "Hey Clapp, did you read this article on Elliot Ginsberg?" he said.

"Yeah, he's a pretty interesting guy," Clapp said, not bothering to look up from the sports page.

"Don't you think he's a little out in left field?" Morley said.

Now Clapp looked up. He studied Morley for a moment, then said simply, "No. I think he's absolutely right."

Morley never would have expected Clapp to agree with Elliot. He figured that Clapp, like every good Beta, would automatically label Elliot an asshole. But then, who could figure out Clapp? Certainly not Morley. Clapp got up to leave. "Well, I've got to be going. Best of luck on your comps. You'll break the Greek if you pass them."

Morley sucked some more of his shake. "Thanks. Put a few bucks on me. I've got a plan."

"I hope it works," Clapp said as he walked out. As Morley leaned back to savor the rest of his shake, he noticed Elliot standing at the cash register. He was alone, searching the room for a seat. He started to make his way to Morley's table. "Mind if I join you?" he said. "This seems to be the only place to sit."

"Sure, make yourself at home."

Elliot sat down. His tray was loaded with a Shitburger, which was officially known as a Truckburger and consisted of a bacon cheeseburger with lettuce, tomato, fried onions, and pickles, topped with a fried egg. He also had a shake and a double order of French Fries. Pumping that PEACE sign must have burned up some calories. Morley held up the paper. "I see you got some ink."

Elliot clasped his Shitburger with both hands. He obviously took eating as seriously as protesting. "I'm surprised you took the time to read it," he said, getting ready to take a bite.

"Well, there's a lot going on with Commager attacking McNamara and all that stuff. Judging from the crowd outside of the Chapel, it looks like you've picked up some real support."

"I must admit, it doesn't hurt having Henry Steele Commager in your corner. In fact, I had to sneak away for awhile, I'm not used to such a crowd."

Morley turned to the article on the rugby match while Elliot wrapped his mouth around his Shitburger. He was hoping that *The Amherst Student* might have gotten a picture of his running drop kick, but the photo they ran showed Hondo breaking loose for his long run. The photographer for the *Student* might not have known much about rugby, but he had learned long ago to keep his camera trained on Hondo. Elliot's Shitburger was gone by the time Morley had fully digested the write up of the Old Blue match.

"Now that you've read it, what do you think?" Elliot said, delving into his fries.

"They give a good description of my kick, but I would have loved to have seen a picture of it." Morley said, his mind still on the Old Blue.

"No, I mean now that you've read the article on me, what do you think?"

"Oh, that, well to be honest, Elliot, I'm not sure I understand your problem. After all, McNamara is the Secretary of Defense. You ought to show him some respect."

Elliot finished his first order of fries. Now that he was refueled, he was ready to start debating. He wiped his mouth and asked Morley. "Do you respect the Dean?"

"Of course not, but that's not the same thing. You can't compare the Dean with the Secretary of Defense."

"Why not? They're both positions of authority. If you blindly respect one, you should blindly respect the other. If you think the Dean's wrong, why can't I think the same thing about McNamara? Didn't you hear Commager's speech? McNamara is wrong!"

"Look Elliot, the Dean's just a regular guy. McNamara's got the CIA and all these other people telling him what's going on. He knows what he's doing. I didn't hear you complaining when the National Guard was covering your ass down in Mississippi. Seems to me you only support the system when it does things your way."

"Morley, you miss the point. I'm not against the system. I'm against people who refuse to question the system. We have an obligation to be politically active. If we think the government's wrong, we have an obligation to protest. Mobilizing dissent is a legitimate part of the system. By my standards, you're the one who's wrong, because you refuse to become involved. Didn't you listen to Commager? 'Immoral acts are committed not by hardened criminals, but by gentlemen of impeccable academic and social credentials.' Our government is been taken over by immoral people, and this war is an immoral act being committed by men like McNamara." Elliot paused, stuffed a couple of fries into his mouth, then added, "Considering it might very well kill you, how can you afford not to protest it?"

125

With the mention of Vietnam, Morley was reminded of his immediate concern, his comps. It was time to go. "Elliot, all I have to do to stay out of Vietnam is to pass my comps in Fine Arts. If I can get my diploma, I can forget about the war." He emptied his milkshake, put it back on his tray, and picked up his copy of the *Student*. Staring at him was a picture of John J. McCloy '16 in his cap and gown. "Say, did you ever notice how much John J. McCloy looks like Pope Leo X?"

"What!?"

"Yeah. Look at this picture of McCloy. He looks just like *Pope Leo X* by Raphael."

Elliot looked at the picture of John J. McCloy '16. "You know, Morley, I never took any Fine Arts, but it's funny you should make that comparison. Do you remember reading *Young Man Luther* when we were freshman?"

"No."

"Leo X was the Pope that excommunicated Martin Luther. One of the reasons that Luther was excommunicated was because he opposed the system of indulgences."

"Indulgences?"

"Yeah. Indulgences were part of the system set up by the Catholic Church that allowed privileged people to buy their way out of their obligations. For example, the privileged didn't have to go on pilgrimages, and that's why this war isn't important to you. Amherst is your indulgence. You graduate, you get a safe job, and you avoid going to Vietnam."

"You got it. If I can graduate, my ass is saved."

"That's my point. Luther rebelled because he thought the practice of selling indulgences weakened the Church. I rebel because I think the kind of self-centered elitism fostered by Amherst weakens our society. So what if you flunk your comps? What does it matter? You don't give a shit about Fine Arts. Forget your comps. Come picket the Town's Memorial Day Parade with me. It will make you feel good, like you're really doing something."

Morley stood up. "Elliot, that's the stupidest thing I've ever heard. I can just see me telling my father that I flunked out because I skipped my comps to protest the Memorial Day Parade. He'd have me committed."

Elliot wasn't finished. "You know, Morley, you're wasting a great talent. If you were to approach some cause with the same creativity and energy you apply to sports, your social life, and avoiding anything academic, you could make a difference."

It was hard for Morley to believe that Elliot had just paid him a compliment. He had always assumed that Elliot resented the fact that he played sports, was a member of a fraternity, and spent so much of his time getting drunk and laid. Now he sounded almost envious. Maybe Clapp was right. Elliot might be an asshole, but he was an interesting asshole. Like Luther.

Morley was about to follow up on Elliot's comment when he saw Bailey, Beachball, Maurer and the King of Smut come walking into the snack bar. "Thanks, but right now, the only difference I'm gonna make is on my comps." He started for the side door, then added, "Hey Elliot, watch yourself down on the Common. In case you haven't noticed, the Town cops don't like you."

There were still a few protestors milling around in front of the Chapel, but the bulk of the crowd was gone. Like Elliot, they must have been getting ready to picket the Town's Memorial Day Parade. The *Student* had announced that after the picket of the Parade there would be an all-night workshop at the library to determine the best way to protest McNamara's honorary degree. It was going to be a busy time for Elliot. Commager's speech had moved him to center stage.

Morley saw the girl with the dove on her left tit walking hand-in-hand with a sleazeball. He was not the same guy she had been sitting with at the Senior Chapel. Morley couldn't believe that Elliot wasn't boffing some of these hippie honeys. For most of them, SDS meant Sex, Drugs, and more Sex.

As he trudged up the stairs, Morley heard the chapel bells strike ten. He had just four more hours to learn four years' worth of Fine Arts. It wasn't going to be easy, but if he could pull this one off, he would have earned his license to practice self-centered elitism. He would have paid for his indulgence.

He was surprised to see a note taped to the outside of his door. It was "From the Desk of Al Most." Al was the Alumni Secretary. "Ed, come see me ASAP. Al" was all it said. Morley knew that it must have something to do with his singing, or lack of it. Al didn't like it when things got messed up. He was the epitome of the paternalistic system. Once you'd obtained your safe job, nice car, and box in the suburbs, guys like Al were always coming around offering some indulgence. Give us lots of money and we'll grant you an honorary degree. Give us lots of money and we'll take your kid. Give us lots of money and we'll put your name on a building. That's the way the system had always worked, at least up until now. John J. McCloy '16's decision to indulge Robert Strange McNamara could be the start of a new reformation, and to think, it was happening at Amherst. Al must have been shitting his drawers.

Morley crumpled the note into a little ball and chucked it down the stairwell. Up your ASAP, Al. If I don't pass my comps, neither one of us will have to worry about my singing.

XI

At quarter to two, Morley got off his bed, put on a clean white shirt, his Amherst tie and his "A" blazer. He checked himself out in the mirror. The swelling in his eye had gone down but, Mr. Brown, the Doctor, hadn't trimmed his stitches very well. They dangled over Morley's cheekbone, a nice reminder of what he had given, and taken, for Amherst.

He took one last look at the collage of pictures scattered around his room, locked his door, and plodded down the stairs out onto the Quad. The spring leaves flittered in the breeze, their chlorophyll still pale with adolescence. In a few days, they would mature to a dark green, but Morley wouldn't be there to see them. One way or another, he'd be gone. He thought of all the touch football and stickball games he had played under this canopy. Now all those games were over. AT&T wasn't big on stickball, and if he didn't pass his comps, the Viet Cong would be chucking grenades, not footballs, at him.

A painting kept flashing through his mind. *The Last Judgment,* Hubert and/or Jan Van Eyck. The top half of *The Last Judgment* consisted of a dour congregation piously sitting in straight-backed pews having a righteously miserable time. That was Heaven. Naked bodies interspersed with rats, bats, and all types of monsters were strewn all over the bottom half of the picture. They reminded Morley of Sunday morning at Beta. That was Hell.

Morley had his own version of Heaven and Hell. Heaven was Amherst without all of the academic bullshit; Hell was all the academic bullshit. Right now he felt like he was heading towards the deepest depths of Hell.

129

He trudged through the courtyard behind James and Stearns, the freshmen dormitories. He didn't stop until he got to the steps of the Mead Art Building. Mead was a funny place. It was built on the former site of Stearns Church. When the College razed the Church in 1948, it couldn't bear to do away with the solid stone steeple, so it was left standing, complete with carillon, next to the front door. When Morley first saw it, he thought it looked out of place. Now, after four years, he couldn't picture the entrance to Mead without it.

He took a deep breath, opened the door and entered the Mead Art Building. Dick Chamura and Stanley Jimanski were in the corridor, changing a light bulb.

Stanley and Dick were the custodians at Mead. They had been there since WWII. Like most of the guys who worked at the College, they were strong supporters of Amherst athletics. Dick was up on the ladder fiddling with the bulb. Stanley was at the bottom, holding a copy of Janson.

When Morley became a Fine Arts major, he'd signed up for a part-time job manning the front desk at the gallery. He'd hoped to absorb some of the Fine Arts by osmosis. In the process, he'd gotten to know Dick and Stanley. The friendship had turned out to be much more valuable than osmosis.

One of Stanley's and Dick's jobs was to set up the slide shows for Professor Merrill's tests. These tests were based on the hundreds of slides of painting, sculpture and architecture that Professor Merrill showed during his lectures. After each lecture, Dick and Stanley posted photographs of the slides on the walls of the basement. A few days before each test, the basement would be mobbed with guys studying the pictures. Morley didn't like looking at the pictures when other people were around. It made him feel stupid. The real Fine Arts majors would analyze, dissect, expound upon and critique every picture, while Morley was struggling just to memorize the titles. He much preferred studying the pictures alone, after the building closed.

That's when Dick and Stanley came in so handy. They would give him hints about what slides would be on the next test. The routine was always the same. Morley would be looking at the pictures, and after a while Stanley and Dick would come by. Completely ignoring Morley, they would stop and scan the walls. After a while, Dick would say something like, "Gee, Stanley, dat Homer sure did like pumpkins." Then they would both crack up as Morley frantically scurried around the basement, clutching his Janson, trying to find something related to pumpkins.

Pumpkin Patch, Winslow Homer, 1878, watercolor and pencil on paper. Homer went to France in 1866 and 1867 and absorbed the French interest in broken, changing light. His watercolors of the 1870's, including *Pumpkin Patch,* show a looseness of handling and brilliance of color which few of his contemporaries achieved.

And so it went. By playing this game, Morley usually was able to squeeze three or four pictures out of Stanley and Dick. They were infallible. If Dick and Stanley gave him a hint, he could be certain it would appear on the test.

"Hey, what are you guys doing here?" Morley said. "It's Memorial Day. Why aren't you down at the V.F.W. getting sloshed with all the other vets before the parade?"

They ignored him and went into their routine. Only this time, there were no hints. "Hey Stanley, Twachtman sure do like *David* by Donatello," Dick said, fiddling with the bulb.

"Yah," Stanley said, reading from Janson. *"David,* by Donatello. 1430–1432, bronze. Da first lifesize nude statue since antiquity dat is wholly free standing."

"Yah," Dick said, "Donatello's *David* is as queer as a three dollar bill, just the way Twachtman likes 'em."

"Dick. How uncouth. Da correct term is *contrapposto.* Da fact dat Donatello chose to model a adolescent boy, rather dan a full grown youth with swelling muscles, makes da body of David speak to us more eloquently dan da face."

"Stanley. Enuffa Donatello. Tell me about Michelangelo's *Da Creation of Adam.*"

Stanley licked his thumb and flipped forward in his Janson. "Fresco, Sistine Chapel, 1508–1512. Shows not da physical molding of Adam's body but da passage of da divine spark—da soul—and dus achieves a dramatic juxtaposition of Man and God unrivaled by any udda artist."

"But Twachtman, he just likes da way Adam's dick is hangin over his leg."

They went into gales of laughter. Stanley closed his Janson. That was it. Stanley and Dick had just given him ten big points. Morley nodded and headed for Professor Merrill's office.

It was exactly two when Morley checked in with Miss Malle, Professor Merrill's long-time secretary. Miss Malle was her usual curt self. She looked and acted like a librarian: thin, colorless, and prim, with thick glasses. She only smiled when Professor Merrill was around.

"Good afternoon, Miss Malle. I'm here for my hanging."

Miss Malle saw no humor in Morley's greeting. "The Professor is running a little behind, Edward, he'll be with you in a few minutes."

Morley started to sit down but just then, Associate Professor Alan Twachtman arrived. "Thanks, I'll wait outside. Just give me a call when the Professor's ready." Morley had no desire to be in the same room with Twachtman. If it weren't for Twachtman, he wouldn't be in this predicament.

It was Twachtman who had prepared the Department's comprehensive exam, which all the Fine Arts majors had taken together. Even the real Fine Arts majors felt it was a ballbuster. Four hours, sixty slides, four minutes to analyze each slide. Morley had received a 38, which was fine with Twachtman.

Alan Twachtman really didn't want to be at Amherst. He resented being stuck in a minor department at a small country college. He made it clear to anyone who cared to listen that he was just marking time until he could return to New York City. He was openly contemptuous of jocks and would never dream of attending a rugby match. He much preferred entertaining selected students at his *pied a terre* in the butler's cottage behind the

132

Emily Dickinson House where he served them caviar and cham-pagne. Morley had never been invited to Associate Professor Twachtman's. To Twachtman, Morley was a grub that had some-how infested the world of Fine Arts.

Morley stood in the lobby looking at the bust of Augustus P. Mead. The funds for the museum came from a bequest by Augus-tus P. Mead, one of the founders of the architectural firm McKim, Mead and White. For the first time, he noticed an inscription carved on the wall of the foyer next to the bust. It read:

> I hope for such a study of Art at Amherst as may take
> the subject out of the realm of pedantry into the realm
> of actual life and keep it there as something that every
> educated man should follow with feeling, with emotion,
> with love.

Apparently that was Mead's intention for his bequest. It was amazing the bullshit you could spout if you had a few bucks. If some guy from the V.F.W. came up with that line, they'd laugh him out of the Club.

"Edward, the Professor will see you now," Miss Malle called from the office.

Professor Merrill sprang to his feet as Morley entered. "Come in, Edward, come in. It is so good to see you." The medallion signifying his honorary membership in the Class of '66 was dan-gling from the purple and white ribbon around his neck. At first glance, it seemed like an extension of his crisp little purple and white bow tie.

"Thank you, Professor. I see you're still wearing your medal-lion."

The Professor was pleased that Morley had noticed. "Of course. It's quite an honor to be part of the Class of '66. Wouldn't you agree, Alan?"

Twachtman was standing next to the slide projector. He was not enjoying this banter between Morley and Professor Merrill. "Professor Merrill, I have a busy schedule," he said testily. "I suggest that we get on with Mr. Morley's exam."

"Relax, Alan, we must give Edward his due," the Professor said, eyeing Morley's stitches. "In his own way, he's contributed a lot to the College."

"Professor, I am well aware of Mr. Morley's contributions to the College. May we please start the exam?"

"Are you ready, Edward?" the Professor said.

Twachtman sat down and picked up the clicker to the slide projector. His thin, pointed face, slicked-down hair, beady eyes and skinny little body made him look like a caricature of a weasel. Morley felt his stomach turn into the same knot he always got before a kickoff. "Yessir, I guess it's *The Third of May.*" he said.

The Professor looked confused. *"The Third of May?"*

"Yes sir, Goya's painting, *The Third of May.* You know, the one with the guy standing in front of the firing squad?"

"Of course, of course," the Professor chuckled. "Isn't that good, Alan. *The Third of May.* I'm sure you'll dodge our bullets, Edward." Twachtman cracked a grim little smile. He must have liked the analogy.

"Well, Edward, we will stick to the same format that Associate Professor Twachtman used for the Department's exam, but this time we'll do it orally." Morley liked the way that Professor Merrill referred to Twachtman as an Associate Professor, leaving no question as to who was in charge. "Let's try to spend no more than a minute and a half on each slide. A half hour should give us enough time to see what you know about the Fine Arts. Twenty slides, each slide is worth five points. One point for identifying the painting, sculpture, or building in question; one point for the artist; one point for the period; two points for explaining its style, medium, and significance. A minimum of sixty points is required to pass. Associate Professor Twachtman has selected the first ten slides, I have chosen the last ten. Relax, take your time, and I'm sure you'll do fine. Are there any questions?"

"No questions, sir, but since I must pass this test to graduate and accept the job I've been offered by New England Tel and Tel, may I make a statement before we begin."

"A statement?" the Professor said, obviously taken aback. "I don't believe that anyone has ever made a statement, but by all means, please proceed. Don't you agree, Alan?"

Twachtman slumped into his chair. "Pleeease, Professor Merrill, can't we get on with this."

"No, no, we must hear Edward's statement. Surely we don't want a Fine Arts major to feel that he was denied a fair shake on his final exam, especially when he could turn off our phones. Ha. Ha." Twachtman had been overruled. "By all means, let's hear your statement, Edward."

"Thank you sir. I would just like to say, I not only hope for such a study of Art at Amherst as may take the subject out of the realm of pedantry into the realm of actual life and keep it there as something that every educated man should follow with feeling, with emotion, with love, but also . . . " and now Morley stared right through Twachtman, " . . . that those who teach the study of Art at Amherst will rise above the pedants, those narrow-minded teachers who insist on exact adherence to the rules, and welcome the spirit of free expression which is the very foundation of the Arts."

It was a quick kick, executed to perfection. The Professor loved it. "Excellent, Edward. Excellent. Very well said, don't you think, Alan? We must remember that. Rise above the pedants, welcome a spirit of free expression. Very good, Edward. Very good."

Twachtman offered no response. The lights went out. There was a moment of darkness before the first slide flashed onto the screen. It was some broken-down temple that Morley had never seen before. There was an embarrassing silence as Morley said nothing for a full minute and a half. Twachtman was grinning from ear to ear. He had taken the first round.

The ruins were followed by Donatello's *David*. Thanks to Dick and Stanley, Morley had *David* by the balls. He was tempted to immediately regurgitate everything Dick and Stanley had told him about Donatello's *David*, but instead, he decided to hold it for awhile. Twachtman was looking at his watch. Professor Merrill began toying nervously with his medallion. "Any thoughts on this one, Edward?"

"*Contrapposto,* Professor Merrill," Morley said matter-of-factly. "*David,* by Donatello. 1430–1432, bronze. This is the first lifesize nude statue since antiquity that is wholly free standing. The fact that Donatello chose to model a adolescent boy, rather than a full grown youth with swelling muscles, makes the body of David speak to us more eloquently than the face."

"Full score! Good show! Wouldn't you say so, Alan?" Professor Merrill said, throwing his hands in the air as if Morley had just scored a touchdown. Twachtman pursed his lips and pushed the clicker. *David* was succeeded by *The Creation of Adam.* Dick and Stanley had saved him again.

"*The Creation of Adam,* by Michelangelo. Fresco, the Sistine Chapel, 1508–1512. Its significance is not in the physical molding of Adam's body but in the passage of the divine spark—the soul. It thus achieves a dramatic juxtaposition of Man and God unrivaled by any other artist."

Professor Merrill could not contain himself. "Excellent, Edward. That was just perfect. Janson himself couldn't have put it any more eloquently."

The next slide was a painting of nude little boys splashing around a wooded pool. It was followed by a mangled scrap of metal that could have been created by Professor Roller. Morley was forced to take two standing eight-counts, but thanks to Stanley and Dick's ten points, there was no way that Twachtman could knock him out.

Still, Morley would need some more luck. It finally came on the sixth slide, *Waterside Scene,* a watercolor by John H..Twachtman, 1853–1902. John H. Twachtman was Associate Professor Twachtman's great-uncle. Morley had been burned by a Twachtman on the first exam, and was pretty sure that Alan would use his great-uncle to trip him up again. But Morley had it covered. He came out swinging. "*Waterside Scene,* by John H. Twachtman, 1853–1902. A watercolor and gouache on cardboard. I believe this piece is part of Amherst's permanent collection."

"Quite so," Professor Merrill agreed. "I think Edward's nailed this one cold."

Twachtman challenged the Professor. "I suggest that we give Mr. Morley three points on this slide. He obviously knows nothing about the painting."

"Not true!" Morley protested. "I'm not through with Twachtman. I'm prepared to go for full credit, but I thought that you were in a hurry."

"Quite right," Professor Merrill agreed. "Alan, you did say you had a busy schedule. But I guess you can always make time for Uncle John. Ha, ha, ha. Please proceed, Edward."

"Thank you, Professor. John H. Twachtman studied in Munich and Venice in the late 1870's, and in 1883, he went to Paris where he lightened his palette. By the time he returned to Cos Cob, Connecticut in 1888, he was a respected impressionist and soon became a member of the Ten, who exhibited together from 1898 through 1917. Twachtman's association with the Ten is most interesting in that . . . "

"Professor Merrill, pleeease," Alan whined. "I, more than anyone, am well aware of the life of John H. Twachtman. Will Mr. Morley cease this obfuscation and kindly tell us something about the work."

"Alan, I'm surprised that you're not more impressed with Edward's knowledge of Twachtman. After all, he is one of the lesser known impressionists. If I were you, I would be flattered with Edward's obvious admiration for your, ah, great-uncle, isn't it?"

"Professor, I'm flattered to pieces, but now, Mr. Morley, let's hear something about the painting."

There wasn't much to *Waterside Scene*. It looked as if Great-Uncle John had gone to lunch in the middle of this piece. Fortunately, Alan had prepared a description of *Waterside Scene* that hung in the gallery next to the watercolor. Morley countered perfectly. "Here with only the sparsest, basically two-dimensional design, Twachtman has managed to convey light, water and atmosphere." Morley looked at Associate Professor Twachtman. "Anything else you would like to know about Twachtman, or should we move on?"

Morley clearly had won this round. Alan gave him a prissy look and, with a peevish flick of his wrist, pressed the clicker. Morley was able to pick up six more points by weaving and bobbing his way around Rembrandt's *The Blinding of Samson*, Michelangelo's *The Last Judgment,* and Mantegna's *Saint Sebastian.* Now, going into the tenth slide, Morley had 21 points. Twachtman had never expected Morley to do so well. He'd doubted that Morley would be in double figures when he delivered his coup de grace, *The Expulsion from Eden.*

Morley, correctly figuring that Twachtman would go heavy on the symbolism of blindings, crucifixions and expulsions, had focused his attention on works of doom and gloom. He was able to nail Massaccio's *The Expulsion from Eden* for four points. At the end of ten slides, it was Morley 25, Twachtman 25. Not only had Twachtman not knocked him out, Morley had actually stayed even.

Professor Merrill took control of the clicker. His face looked kind and calm, the same as when he helped Morley up for the second half against the Old Blue. His eyes were confident. "Let's go Edward, only ten more slides. You're doing fine."

"Yes, sir."

The Professor's first slide flashed onto the screen. Twachtman moaned in disgust. It was *Whistler's Mother.*

"*Whistler's Mother,* by Whistler." If he had ever known it, Morley had forgotten Whistler's first name. " . . . 1870's. This picture illustrates the French influence on American painting. It also is interesting in that it shows the artist's respect for his mother. Next slide, please." Professor Merrill prepared to punch the clicker.

"Wait a minute. Wait a minute!" Twachtman was on his feet. "Surely, Professor Merrill, you're not giving full credit for that slide?"

"Which slide, Alan?"

"James Whistler's *Arrangement in Black and Grey: The Artist's Mother,* 1871."

"Why, I thought that Edward knew it cold."

"Knew it cold?" Twachtman whined, assuming the *contrapposto* position. "Well. First he got the title wrong, then he didn't even know Whistler's first name."

"That's not so," Morley interrupted. "It's James. I was just trying to speed things up because of your busy schedule."

"That's very considerate of you, Edward," Professor Merrill said. "Yes, I believe you deserve four points. Let's move on to the next slide."

Twachtman wasn't giving up. "The painting was completed in 1871, not 'the 1870's,' and most importantly, Whistler would be dismayed to hear his painting portrayed as a symbol of our latter-day 'mother cult.' He, more than anyone else, wanted the canvas to be appreciated for its formal qualities."

"Please, Alan, let's not nitpick. If it makes you feel any better, we'll knock off another point." He paused and looked at Morley. "Edward, despite Associate Professor Twachtman's limited time, I'm afraid that we will have to go into more detail." Morley knew that the Professor was giving him every close call, but even then, it might not be enough. Losing another point here hurt. He needed to average 3½ points per slide, which, even with Professor's Merrill's help, wasn't going to be easy. Twachtman was coming after him on every slide.

"Certainly, sir."

"Good. If you're ready, let's move onto some architecture." Mrs. Whistler was replaced by the Empire State Building.

"The Empire State Building." Morley said confidently. "So named because the State of New York is often referred to as the Empire State. I believe that this nickname comes from New York's illusion that it is an empire unto itself. We see this attitude reflected in teams from New York, like the Old Blue."

"Excellent point," Professor Merrill chortled. "I've never thought about that. The Empire State, very interesting, don't you agree, Alan?"

Twachtman was totally frustrated. He looked like he was about to cry. "Pleeease, Professor Merrill, I have no interest in

Mr. Morley's theories on the nicknames of states. Will he please elaborate on the architecture of the building."

"Alan, you must make up your mind. One minute you want more detail, the next, you want to speed things up. Please proceed, Edward."

Morley was almost starting to enjoy this exam. With Professor Merrill on his side, he felt like he was gaining control. "The Empire State building was opened during the Depression, and is the world's tallest structure."

"False! False!" Twachtman was on his feet again. "It is not the world's tallest structure. It is the world's tallest building! I demand that we subtract two points!"

Professor Merrill decided to take the three points and run. "You're absolutely correct, Alan, I'm afraid we can only give you three points on that one, Edward."

"That's fine, Professor. You know me, I never question an official's call."

"May we have the next slide," Twachtman demanded, pleased with his apparent victory. Twachtman thought that he had screwed Morley out of two points, but in reality, Morley had just knicked him for one. Thanks to the Professor's superb block, Morley never had to mention the architects or anything else about the Empire State Building.

The Empire State Building disappeared and was replaced by *The Thinker*. "Now we'll test you on some sculpture," the Professor said. "Show him no mercy, eh, Alan?"

"*The Thinker*, by Rodin."

"Right again." the Professor said. "It's obvious you're well prepared for this exam." He paused and clicked the button. *The Thinker* became a memory. "Let's see what you know about the Ash Can School."

"Wait, wait, wait!" Twachtman protested. "What about the time, the style, the significance of *The Thinker?*

"Oh, good point, Alan. Edward's been so quick lately that I almost forgot. What can you tell us about *The Thinker*, Edward?"

Twachtman had him, and he knew it. His ferret face assumed

its thin little grin. He had broken Morley's momentum.

"I'm afraid you've got me, sir. Sculpture is not one of my strong suits."

"Yes. I'm aware of that. Well, two points is better than none."

Stag at Sharkey's. It was one of Morley's very favorite pictures, and George Bellows was one of the few painters with whom Morley could identify. Bellows was a big, easy going guy who came from Ohio to New York in the early 1900's. Sharkey's, a local bar that became a "members only" club on fight nights, was right across the street from his studio. Bellows loved the fights, and was one of those guys that could mix easily with all levels of society. Morley knew all of these facts, and for one and a half minutes he actually sounded like a Fine Arts major. He had forgotten about the Ash Can School, but thanks to Professor Merrill's introduction, he managed to work it in. When Morley finished with *Stag at Sharkey's,* even Twachtman couldn't mark him down.

"Any questions on this slide, Alan?" Professor Merrill asked. "If not, let's move on." There were no questions. *Stag at Sharkey's* had knocked the grin off Twachtman's ferret face.

American Gothic. Morley had seen this painting a thousand times, simply because it hung in the head at Beta. He looked directly at *American Gothic* every time he took a pee. He knew those faces by heart. Unfortunately, he didn't know much about the painting. He thought that it was done by some guy named Grant and remembered Professor Merrill mentioning something about the pitchfork being a phallic symbol. Morley pitched enough bullshit for two points. As the room went dark, he did some quick mental arithmetic. He had 40 points with only five slides to go. It was going to be close.

"I know that this is not your strong suit, Edward, but I am afraid that we are going to have to go back to sculpture," Professor Merrill warned him. "We want our graduates to be conversant in all the Fine Arts. Isn't that right, Alan."

Morley gave a sign of relief when Michelangelo's *David* flashed onto the screen. "Ah, the real *David,*" he said. "By Michelangelo, 1501–1504." Professor Merrill was an avid fan of Michelangelo's and had devoted a whole lecture on his *David*. Morley looked over at the Professor. He was aglow. Morley poured it on. "Nowhere are the unique qualities of Michelangelo's art more evident than in the *David*. Unlike Donatello's soft little boys," Morley said, smiling at Twachtman, "Michelangelo's *David* shows the beauty, power, and swelling volume of a real man. This *David* not only became characteristic of Michelangelo's style, but through him it became the style of Renaissance Art in general. Next slide, please."

"Very good, Edward. Very good. Full credit, correct, Alan? Now, let's look at a painting from the same period."

This time, David was succeeded by the *Mona Lisa*. Thanks to the Professor's help with the period, Morley was assured of three points, but that wasn't enough, he needed at least four. Morley had to say something significant about the *Mona Lisa*. The problem was that he couldn't remember anything significant about the *Mona Lisa*. Professor Merrill began playing with his medallion while Twachtman started to break into his beady little grin.

Then Morley remembered that Rocky and His Pals had just featured the *Mona Lisa* in one of their Fractured Fairy Tales. According to the Fractured Fairy Tale, Leonardo had started to paint the *Mona Lisa,* but then, for some unknown reason, she went into a state of depression. She wouldn't smile. It turned out that she was having trouble with her boyfriend. Once Leonardo fixed that up, the *Mona Lisa* turned aglow.

"Obviously the most intriguing characteristic about the *Mona Lisa* is her smile," Morley said. Professor Merrill let go of his medallion. Twachtman's face reverted to a scowl. "We look at her and are beguiled by her personality. What is going through her mind? What thoughts produce this smile? Is it merely the echo of a momentary mood, or is it the timeless quality of maternal tenderness? Maybe she is thinking about her boyfriend. Whatever, it is the way in which da Vinci has captured this smile which is the key to the *Mona Lisa*."

Morley had his four points. "Thinking of her boyfriend," the Professor said. "That's an interesting observation. Obviously you've been doing some research, Edward."

"Actually, sir, I got that point from a recent TV special on the *Mona Lisa.*"

"Oh, really? I missed it. Did you happen to see it, Alan?"

Twachtman ignored the question. He was looking at the next slide. It was a large stone church. Morley started to panic. He had seen it before, but he couldn't remember where.

"Back to some architecture, Edward," the Professor said. "Judging from your Boston accent, you'll be quick to recognize this one."

Of course. It was Trinity Church in Copley Square, by Henry Hobson Richardson. Morley had walked past it a hundred times on his way to Fenway Park. But he didn't know the date. The most obvious characteristic of Richardson's work was his use of heavy stone. Morley remembered that it had something to do with the Roman style, so he decided to throw in a little jargon and hope for another point.

"Trinity Church is a good example of Richardson's use of masonry to effect a neo-Romanesque style. Notice the symmetry and the massiveness of the building." Professor Merrill tried to cut him off before he could go any farther, but it was too late. "One is reminded of the aqueducts of ancient Rome," Morley concluded. Twachtman pounced on him.

Morley sensed right away that he had screwed up. He had gotten his three points, he should have shut up. If he kept things superficial, Twachtman couldn't touch him. The minute Morley mentioned the aqueducts, he had given Twachtman a specific, and specifics meant more names, dates, styles, and other comparisons.

"You say that Trinity Church is reminiscent of the Roman aqueducts, Mr. Morley. That is an interesting point. Would you care to elaborate on it?" The light from the projector showed that the weasel had caught his prey.

Morley looked to his corner for help. "Well, if you know what an aqueduct looks like, the resemblance is obvious. Wouldn't you agree, Professor Merrill?"

"Yes, of course, I think that the aqueducts are a fine example of the Romanesque style, let's move on."

Twachtman had him, and he wouldn't let go. "Since Mr. Morley brought up the Romanesque comparison, perhaps he would be so kind as to comment on how Richardson's contact with Labrouste also influenced his design."

That was it, he had just bitten Morley for another point, and they all knew it. "Sorry, time's up, we'll have to move on." the Professor said as he changed the slide. "I'm afraid we can only give you two points for Trinity Church.""

Wind From the Sea covered the screen. If you didn't know *Wind From the Sea,* you didn't know anything about the Fine Arts. Professor Merrill owned *Wind From the Sea,* and displayed it at a special lecture he gave at his home once year. Due to the picture, and lots of wine and cheese, nobody ever cut this special lecture on Wyeth.

"*Wind From the Sea,* by Andrew Wyeth, presently owned by Professor and Mrs. Charles H. Merrill, Amherst, Massachusetts."

The Professor smiled and gave Morley a look of encouragement.

"Wyeth painted *Wind From the Sea,* a tempera, in 1947. It is one of his Maine series. The room is in the Olson house, which he used as the object of a number of other paintings. It is interesting to look at the curtains and see the flower that has been painted into the lace. Apparently, Wyeth painted over another painting when he did *Wind From the Sea* and incorporated the flower into the curtains."

Morley stopped and looked at Professor Merrill. "Is that all right, sir? I could go on."

"Splendid, Edward. Splendid. Full credit, correct, Alan?" Twachtman was silent. "If my calculations are correct, you have 56 points going into the final slide. Of course, you need 60, so we hope you'll finish up strong."

"Yes sir, I'll try." Morley could feel the sweat rising on his brow. This was it. One more lousy side. He looked at the screen. *Wind From the Sea* was blown away. In its place sat an old friend—Lord Jeffery Amherst.

Morley's mind jammed. During the last four years, he had seen this picture of Lord Jeffery Amherst more than any other painting. It was on book covers, T-shirts, sweat shirts, the sign in front of The Lord Jeffery Inn, and, most notably, on every beer cup from Russell's. Morley had spent half of his time at Amherst looking at this portrait of Lord Jeffrey. Now, for the life of him, he couldn't remember a single thing about it. He was screwed. He remembered seeing the original somewhere. But where?

Suddenly, the lights went on. He heard Professor Merrill say, "Since we have Lord Jeffery here with us, there's no sense burning up the slide."

Morley looked up. There on the wall behind Professor Merrill's desk was the original portrait of Lord Jeffery. Morley squinted at the little gold plaque underneath the picture. The black letters said, "*Lord Jeffery Amherst,* John Singleton Copley, circa 1762."

Still in a daze, he recited the information on the plaque. He heard Professor Merrill say, "Good, good, that's three. Now for the significance."

Morley was paralyzed. He just sat staring at the picture. Twachtman was looking at his watch: "Only thirty seconds left, Mr. Morley. Do you have anything to say regarding the significance of the painting, or should we settle for a 59?"

Significance. Significance. What the hell was the significance of Lord Jeffery Amherst? The void in Morley's head was being filled by a sound. Professor Merrill was tapping his pencil on the desk. He could see Twachtman checking his watch, his grin growing. Tap, tap, tap. Morley looked back at Professor Merrill's pencil. Professor Merrill was trying to tell him something. Tap, tap, tap. Morley's foot started to twitch in rhythm. All of a sudden, he felt like singing. So he did.

"*Oh, Lord Jef-fer-y Am-herst was a sol-dier of the King, and he came from a-cross the sea. . . . *" Morley rose to his feet. Professor Merrill rose up with him. "*To the French-man and the In-di-ans, he did-n't do a thing In the wilds of this wild coun-try. . . .*

"*And for His Roy-al Ma-jes-ty, he fought with all his might For he was a sol-dier loy-al and true. . . . And he con-quered all the en-em-*

ies that came with-in his sight, And he looked a-round for more when he was through."

Twachtman stood up and walked out. He didn't even have the grace to shake Morley's hand.

"Oh—Am-herst! Brave Am-herst! 'Twas a name known to fame in days of yor-ore-ore. May it ev-er be glor-ious—Till the sun shall climb the heav'ns no more."

Professor Merrill offered Morley his hand. "Edward, you are now a gentleman, an athlete, and something of a scholar. Do well, and keep our phones humming."

"Yes, sir! And thank you. I owe you one for this."

"Nonsense," said the Professor, still clasping his medallion. "I'd say we're about even."

Morley couldn't wait to get back to Beta. He was going to ask Miss Malle to call and tell the brothers to put on a keg, but she was on the phone when he left. As he ran out, Morley stopped at the bust of Augustus P. Mead. He read the words one more time.

> I hope for such a study of Art at Amherst as may take the subject out of the realm of pedantry into the realm of actual life and keep it there as something that every educated man should follow with feeling, with emotion, and with love.

He walked up to the bust, grabbed Augustus P. Mead's bald brass bean with both hands, kissed it, and danced out the door into the Spring sunlight.

XII

The Amherst Common, like every other Common in New England, was encircled by a ring of *Ulmus Americanus.* For the last half-century, these majestic trees had given grace to both the people and the landscape. But in the late 50's and early 60's, the American Elm came under attack. The aggressor was a fungus from Holland. It had arrived, undetected, and attached itself to the elm's prime tenant, the bark beetle.

The bark beetle resided between the bark and the xylem, the wood of the elm. In this snug environment, the beetle laid its brood galleries. Eggs turned into grubs, which in turn evolved into more beetles, which in time emerged and moved on to their own elms.

When the Dutch fungus arrived, it immediately upset this long-standing relationship. While it didn't do any harm to the beetle, the fungus clogged the elm's plumbing by restricting the flow of water. Within as little as four weeks, the elm died, and the beetle, with no water, was forced to find a livelier tree, where once again, the fungus proved to be a deadly guest.

By May 30, 1966, just about every elm in New England was either dead or dying, and New Englanders were beginning to realize that without their elms, quaint New England didn't seem so quaint. The white clapboards, cobblestone walks, leaded windows, stone walls and granite steps that looked so great in the shade, withered like an aging beauty in the full sunlight.

It was a face New England had worn before. Henry Wadsworth Longfellow never thought of his village smithy standing under an elm tree. He had him shaded, quite properly, under a spreading *Castanea Americanus*. It was the American Chestnut, not the elm, that had cast the first shadow over New England's towns and commons, but during the early 1900's, it too had fallen victim to a blight. New Englanders reluctantly had uprooted their chestnuts and replaced them with elms, which now were giving ground to another tree, one that literally tasted like New England.

Memorial Day 1966 was indeed going to be memorable for the Town of Amherst. From that day forth, the Amherst Town Common would be ringed by a band of *Aceraceae Saccharum,* the sugar maple. If these new trees could resist the onslaught of pestilence and blight, their broad leaves and brilliant colors would adorn the Common for the next two hundred and fifty years.

All that morning, while Morley had been squirreled away in his room up in North studying for his comps, chain saws had been buzzing in front of Beta, stripping away limbs and trunks that had served the Town so well. As elm after elm thudded to the ground, so did the spirits of the volunteers who had assembled for this cleansing of the Common. By noon, the centerpiece of this once postcard-perfect town was desolate and forlorn as it hovered uninvitingly under a cloud of blue smoke. Depression was the main dish at a communal lunch. Then, during desert, just as Morley was walking into the Mead Art Building, the Town's spirit was rekindled when two trucks pulled up carrying fifty young, rock hard sugar maples, fresh from Vermont. There was a flurry of activity as the volunteers dropped their plates, picked up their shovels and set to work digging for the future. This was the scene that greeted Morley as he strode down the hill from Mead Art Building.

The tree planting on the Common was quickly overshadowed by the standing ovation Morley received from the big crowd on the porch of Beta. Miss Malle had called ahead with the good news, and the brothers had responded by charging a keg at Russell's. No one had thought he'd had a chance. How could he possibly pass his comps without any knowledge of the Fine Arts?

The Harts handed him his first beer. It tasted great, the second even better. Morley was as happy as he had ever been, and it showed. He even looked better. The swelling in his cheek was going down. The cut on his lower lip was almost healed. When he got his stitches out, he'd be back to normal.

His victory celebration was interrupted by the sound of sirens coming up Route 9. It was the Great Bike Race. What could be better. Between the Senior Chapel and his comps, he'd forgotten all about the Great Bike Race. This definitely would be his night to shine.

The Great Bike Race took place every Memorial Day. Pledges from the Psi U and Beta houses at Dartmouth would ride two bicycles all the way from the Hanover Inn to the Smith Quad, a distance of some 130 miles. The race took the better part of a day, so each house had a hospitality wagon that followed the racers. These wagons kept things well oiled by liberally dispensing libations to both the bikers and the brothers. Plus, enterprising publicans along the trail were continually offering the riders a free refueling. They knew that if they could get the riders to stop, their entourages would pull in behind them, and that crew could drop a C note in a matter of minutes. But having the Indians stop for a drink was a calculated risk. If they came in, chucked down a couple of rounds, paid the bill, and peddled away, it was pure profit. If they stayed, it was nothing but trouble.

In 1958, the Great Bike Race never reached the Smith Quad. Due to an unseasonably hot day, the hospitality wagons coming from Hanover were running on empty by the time they rolled into Greenfield. Normally, the riders wobbled right through Greenfield. The Smith Quad was only twelve miles down Route 5, and after a long day on the trail, the Indians were anxious to chase some beaver. But in 1958, the riders were so thirsty that they pulled into the Young Men's Polish Club of Greenfield.

Once inside, the Indians exhibited a dose of Dartmouth's legendary insensitivity by shooting off a quiver full of Polish jokes. These barbs did not tickle the regulars at the Y.M.P.C. Things began to unravel when a big Polish fist introduced itself to an

Indian nose. Although they were too drunk to realize it, the braves never stood a chance. After being pummeled by several humorless but humongous Polish farmers, the entire Dartmouth contingent was arrested. When the Sheriff, who happened to be President of the Young Men's Polish Club, discovered that the bruised and battered brothers wouldn't fit in the Greenfield jail, he locked them up in the old Louie & Abercrombie brewery. The only way that the Town of Greenfield could feed the Indians was to work out a deal with a new hamburger joint called McDonald's.

The judge, who was also Polish and proud of it, kept the Great Race locked in the basement of the brewery until a somewhat inflated restitution had been made to the Young Men's Polish Club. He demanded more wampum for fines, and, of course, many pelts were owed to McDonald's. The total bill was in excess of $5,000. It took The Big Chief from Dartmouth until Tuesday to spring his braves from the bowels of Louie & Abercrombie.

After what became known as the Greenfield Massacre, the Indians were not allowed to hold their post-race celebration in any of the local parks. That meant that the Dartmouth Psi U's and Betas had to impose on their brothers at Amherst. The annual party alternated between the Psi U and Beta houses; the price for this hospitality was fourteen kegs of beer, cash on the barrelhead. Mr. Russell loved it.

This year, the party was at Beta, which was just fine with Morley. He'd discovered that the squaws who followed the Great Bike Race were every bit as wild as the braves, especially when they drank too much of Mr. Russell's firewater, and despite the fact that Lord Jeffrey had wiped out the Indians by giving them blankets infested with smallpox, these young maidens seemed to have no qualms about nestling under an Amherst spread.

There was a big round of applause from the Common just as the riders came over the top of the hill. The last tree had been planted by the volunteers, and baptized by the Amherst Fire Department. The mayor was mounting a portable podium that had been placed on the Common directly in front of Beta. The tree planters were clustering around the podium. Off to the side, all 23 members of the Amherst Regional High School Marching Band and Ensemble stood ready to hit the first chord of *God Bless America.* Beyond them, Shortpecker and the boys from the V.F.W. were milling around, waiting to lead the traditional Memorial Day parade. At the far end of the Common, near Grace Episcopal Church, Elliot and his troops were preparing to protest the traditional Memorial Day Parade. Now, thanks to Commager's speech, the protestors outnumbered the marchers from the V.F.W.

At the first cord of *God Bless America,* all hell broke loose. Elliot and the protestors started marching towards the podium, chanting "One, Two, Three, Four, We don't Want your Fucking War." At the same time, the riders, seeing the large crowd in front of Beta, naturally assumed that the ceremony was for them. After all, to a pledge, what could be more important than the Great Bike Race.

Both riders jumped the curb and made a beeline for the Mayor. The hospitality wagons followed. The director of the Amherst Regional High School Marching Band and Ensemble, fearing for the safety of his tootlers, cut *God Bless America* at "Stand Beside Us" and led his 23 charges in a lively two step out of the way. They ended up marching directly into the path of Elliot's protestors, who by now had moved in front of Shortpecker and the boys from the V.F.W..

When the Mayor started waving his hands at the hospitality wagons, he unintentionally designated himself as the finale for the Great Bike Race. Both riders zipped by, tagging his outstretched arms. The hospitality wagons rolled to a stop in front of the podium. A phalanx of cars and motorcycles that had been accompanying the Great Race poured onto the Common behind them. Racers, volunteers, protestors, the boys from the V.F.W., and the 23 members of the Amherst Regional High School Marching Band and Ensemble became entangled in one big clump. The mayor was jumping up and down in a blue rage.

The two riders got off their bikes and tried to embrace the Mayor. The Indians were all hooting and hollering, obviously delighted that their brothers from Amherst had arranged such

151

a grand welcome. They were far too drunk to realize that they had crashed the tree ceremony and that the townspeople were hopping mad. It wasn't until the cops and some irate volunteers started pushing them off the Common that the Dartmouth crowd began to suspect that there might be some mistake.

The Betas couldn't believe what was happening. This was the best show they'd seen since Professor Roller hit town. The Mayor was screaming, "Remove this rabble from the Common! Remove this rabble from the Common!" Soon everybody was pushing and shoving everybody else. The cops began throwing anyone who was young, sweaty, and dirty off the Common. That was a mistake, since many of the Town's volunteers were young, sweaty and dirty from having just planted fifty trees.

Then the scene turned ugly. In an effort to clear the Common, a hospitality wagon recklessly backed into a new tree. There was a sickening rip as the bark peeled away from the trunk. When the tree snapped, so did the volunteers. They reacted like someone had intentionally run over one of their babies. They pulled the drunken driver from the wagon and started beating him. The cops took out their night sticks and started whacking anyone who wasn't wearing a uniform.

After a couple of whacks, the Common was quickly cleared. The Dartmouth crowd sought sanctuary on the Beta porch from which they began taunting the cops. Town cops usually stayed off College property, but they were so pissed at the Dartmouth guys, Morley figured that there might be another Greenfield Massacre. Fortunately, at that very moment, Mr. Russell's truck pulled into the Beta driveway and began unloading fourteen kegs of Schlitz. The clank of the first keg was enough for the Indians. It sent them stampeding to the Beta Bar.

With the Indians out of the way, the Mayor finally was able to restore order and start the Memorial Day parade. The Amherst Regional High School Marching Band and Ensemble began tootling, the boys from the V.F.W. began marching, the protestors began chanting, and a handful of spectators began waving little American flags as they headed off through town.

Morley decided to stay on the porch until his own keg kicked. He didn't give a damn about the Great Bike Race, Shortpecker's parade, or Elliot's protest. He'd passed his comps. He was going to sit on the Beta porch by himself, sip a few brews, watch the late afternoon sun set upon the new trees, and think about getting laid. As he looked out over the Common, he suddenly realized how much he missed the elms. Even dead, they had more class than these dinky little maples. It would be twenty years before these trees were worth a bucket of sap.

As Morley was refilling his cup, two big bastards wearing Beta T-shirts came up the driveway. They appeared to be talking to each other, but when they got closer, Morley realized that all they were saying was "quack, quack." He assumed that they were pledges from Dartmouth acting out some kind of initiation bit. They walked up onto the porch, stopped, and surveyed the Common. Morley offered them a beer. With fourteen more kegs downstairs, he could afford to be generous. They took the beers, said "quack, quack," and waddled off.

Morley watched the two Dartmouth guys quack their way up to an empty cop car. Its driver must have gone off with the parade. The bigger of the two delivered a forearm shiver to the mirror on the driver's side. There was a tinkle as the mirror shattered onto the sidewalk. The other duck casually kicked in the left headlight. This was real trouble. The one rule Shortpecker preached to all the Betas was never to mess with the Town cops. They didn't give a shit what you did on campus, but they'd kick your ass if you made trouble for the Town. Morley reloaded his beer and retreated to the Beta Bar.

Morley claimed his usual seat at the end of the bar. The more the brothers congratulated him, the more he drank. He had done it all. Now he could just sit back and get gloriously drunk. He was pleased to see that so many fine young squaws had followed the Indians. By six o'clock, he was convinced that every one of them was eager to climb under his blanket.

"Facilis Descensus Averno." Normally, Morley would just move along the bar asking each honey if she wanted to "rack it." Eventually, somebody always said yes. Unescorted women didn't descend into the Beta bar unless they were seriously thinking about getting laid, so picking off some honey was no big deal, provided you weren't too shitfaced.

Unfortunately, Morley was too shitfaced. Instead of discreetly asking some honey if she wanted to rack it, he was weaving around the bar, bellowing about how he wanted to get laid. He was so bad that even some Dartmouth guys were getting upset. When they complained, the brothers told them to stuff it. They made it clear that Morley could be as obnoxious as he wanted. He had passed his comps and was going to graduate. If the Dartmouth guys didn't like it, they could take a hike.

The Dartmouth guys took great umbrage at being told that they could take a hike. After all, they'd bought the beer. It began to look like the Great Bike Race was going to end in a fight, but nobody was too surprised. The Great Bike Race ended up in a fight every year.

Knowing that Morley would probably touch it off and seeing that he was in no condition to defend himself, Harts decided that it was time to pack Morley away for the night. He knew just how to do it. He took Morley aside and told him that Margie was waiting for him up at his room in North. That was all Morley needed to hear. He grabbed a couple of beers and staggered out.

It took him nearly twenty minutes to negotiate what was normally a five minute walk. By the time he reached his room, he'd forgotten all about Margie. He'd forgotten about everything. He carefully placed a beer on his dresser, accidentally knocked it over, and promptly passed out on his bed. The pictures from Janson's *History of Art* stared down at their conquering hero. Even though the bells in Johnson Chapel had yet to ring seven, his day was over, and somehow, he'd won.

But his day wasn't over, and he hadn't won.

"Heeeeey Ed." The bells had just chimed 1:30 A.M. when a familiar cry rose up from beneath his window. It was Rube.

That was not good. Every time Morley and Rube got together, it meant trouble. They just couldn't stay out of it. It had started the first weekend their freshman year. Morley was walking with his date over to the football game. This girl had been a camp counselor with him during the summer. She was going to be a freshman at Skidmore and was impressed that Morley was going to Amherst. By the end of the summer, Morley had gotten all the way to third base with this honey, and when she agreed to come to Amherst for the weekend, he'd rented a motel room with the expectation that he was about to hit his first home run.

Part of the seduction was to wow her with the view from the top of Memorial Hill. They were standing there, billing and cooing, when Rube drove up in a big new Dodge. Freshman weren't supposed to drive on campus, and nobody was supposed to drive on the top of Memorial Hill. Rube stopped and asked Morley if he wanted a ride. A sensuous looking blond was sitting on his lap. From the looks of her, Rube had hit a lot of home runs.

"Sure, why not," Morley had said, hoping to further impress his date. They had no sooner snuggled in the back seat when Rube pointed the Dodge down Memorial Hill. The blond started screaming, Morley's date started screaming, even Morley started screaming. It looked like they were on top of a roller-coaster. Nobody in their right mind would drive a car down Memorial Hill.

Rube just laughed. He was having a great time until he tried to put on the brakes. The grass was wet and the car started to skid. If it turned sideways, it probably would flip. There was nothing Rube could do but straighten her out and let her rip. And rip she did. Morley was amazed at how much speed they were carrying when they reached the bottom of the hill.

Unbeknownst to Rube, there was a drainage ditch at the base of Memorial Hill. When the Dodge hit the ditch, it became airborne. It sailed about thirty feet before it landed and plowed through a soccer net. Morley and his date banged their heads on the roof, and crumpled to the floor. Rube never stopped. He hit the gas and kept the Dodge rolling until it was safely hidden behind the gym. There he got out and took stock of the damage. Except for some grass stuck to the bumpers and the soccer net on top, the car was fine.

Even though it was her father's car, Rube's date wasn't the least bit upset. She slapped a make on Rube that gave even Morley a hardon. It was the only hardon he'd get that weekend. His date was so shaken up that she demanded to be put on the next bus back to Saratoga Springs. That was the last Morley ever saw of his first chance to get laid, but he didn't care. He thought that Rube was the funniest guy he had ever met, and over the next four years, Rube continued to steer him downhill.

Rube wasn't a Beta, but whenever he got shitfaced, he'd come looking for Morley. Tonight, Rube was shitfaced. When there was no response to his cry, he decided to check Morley's room. He knew he was up there. He'd already been to Beta and Harts had told him that Morley had left hours ago. Rube found Morley sprawled out on his bed, the spilled beer on the floor. He knew that was not a good sign. Morley never wasted a beer.

He kicked the bed. Morley didn't move so he began to shake him. "Come on, you bastard. Get your ass up, you passed your comps. It's time to have some fun."

Morley opened one eye and tried to say something, but "whizza, whizza" was all that came out. Rube was getting impatient. "Hey, look, I'm telling you. Get up!" he shouted.

"Whizza, whizza."

He shook Morley again. It was no use, Morley's eye shut, he was losing him. Rube had never seen Morley this drunk. "Look you bastard, get up! I've got a bike outside."

Morley opened both eyes. Rube had been able to unscramble a circuit. "Whizza kind of bike."

"Ken Bacon's new ten-speed, you jerk. Now come on." That did it. Morley sat up. Rube knew he had him. Ken Bacon's bike was one of these brand-new models with a big sprocket and ten separate gears. Bacon had gotten it after Professor Roller had ratfucked his old bike. As far as anyone knew, it was the only ten-speed in the entire Four College area, and Bacon wasn't about to let anybody steal it. He always locked it up with a big chain and carried the front wheel off with him.

"You really got Bacon's bike?" Morley mumbled.

"Yeah, what do you think, I'm lying? Of course I've got it."

"Howzya get it?"

"I was walking along and it said 'Come steal me.' That's howzya get it."

"Bullshit."

"Listen, I'm tellin ya, I got it. They're having an all night meeting at the library. Something about McNamara. The bike was sitting out front, so I took it. Now come on, let's go. Beta's still on tap."

"Who's gonna drive?"

"What? Are you shittin me? You're so drunk you can't even stand up. I'm driving."

Morley fell back on the bed and shut his eyes. Rube was exasperated. Why did he have to put up with this shit? "You asshole."

Morley didn't move. He had gone back to sleep. "Okay, okay, you can drive, but only to Beta."

Morley opened his eyes. He couldn't help smiling. Rube laughed. "You bastard, let's go."

Morley got up. He was wearing a T-shirt and levis. He bumbled around looking for his shoes. When he opened the closet, he fell in. Rube had to pull him out. "You want to drive. Shit, you can't even walk." Rube dug through the closet and produced a pair of flip flops. "Here, put these on. Let's go. Beta's gonna kick before we get there."

They banged their way down the three flight of stairs. Morley might as well have been barefoot, but he was too drunk to know it. Rube was sure that he was going to fall and kill himself. He was weaving from side to side and his feet kept slipping out of the thongs. He kept looking at Rube and saying, "I can't believe ya got Bacon's bike."

Sure enough, when they got outside, there it was: Ken Bacon's ten-speed. Morley tried to pull himself onto the seat but he fell off. The seat wasn't like an American bike's, or even a Raleigh's. It was one of those long, thin racing jobs that let your balls hang over the side. The seat was set high, so getting on was almost like mounting a unicycle.

After Morley and the bike had fallen over a couple of times, Rube said. "C'mon Morley, let me drive. You're going to rip your stitches if you don't stop fooling around."

"No way." Morley said. He gave the bike a push, hopped on the seat, and was off.

Rube wasn't about to be left behind. "You son of a bitch," he said, jumping onto the crossbar. The bike wobbled, but righted itself as they began to pick up speed. Down they went, past the library, onto Route 9 and into the Beta driveway.

"Watch it!" Rube yelled, as they sideswiped a parked car and careened into an empty beer keg. When they passed the door to the Beta bar, he tried to jump off, but Morley kept going, turned out the driveway, and peddled back onto Route 9.

"What the hell are you doing?" Rube shouted, but he knew he was too late. There was no stopping now.

There is a good reason why Amherst is known as the College on the Hill. Starting at Johnson Chapel, every way is down. The longest descent is on the Route 9 side of campus. After passing Beta, the road drops off and runs straight downhill for about a mile. Morley was going to run Bacon's bike down that mile.

At 2 A.M. on Tuesday morning, the campus was deserted, but if anyone had been around, they would have heard Rube screaming at Morley. He was scared shitless, and with good reason. They were zipping down the road doing about 40 mph, and a pair of headlights were coming up the other way.

"Holy shit, there's a car. Stop this damn thing!"

"I can't. The brakes are broken, see?" Morley spun the pedals backward as if to prove his point.

"You asshole! The brakes are on the handlebars!" Rube was ripshit. There was no way to reason with Morley, but he had to keep trying. The car was coming closer. "A car! Morley, there's a car coming up the hill!"

"Yeah, we're heading right for it."

"You asshole! Let's NOT head right for it!"

"We have to. It's the only thing marking the road."

Morley was right. Now that they were past the College, the

road was totally dark. The wind, or maybe fear, was making Rube's eyes water. Morley could feel the tears blowing into his face. Rube was sure that it was all over. He, Morley, and Ken Bacon's bike were about to become a permanent ornament on the hood of that car. "Pull over you asshole! You're going to hit that fucker head on!"

Morley was too drunk to be scared, and he liked it that Rube was going crazy. "Maybe it's two motorcycles." he shouted. "We'll go between them."

"You shithead! I've had it with you!"

At the last moment, Morley veered off and they whooshed past the car. The driver slammed on his brakes. He'd never seen them coming. With no light and no moon, he must have thought he'd passed a ghost.

They started to slow down as the road flattened out. There was a big draining ditch at the bottom of the hill, and Morley was peddling right for it. "Don't do it, Morley." Rube said. "If you ratfuck Bacon's bike, you won't graduate."

Morley kept peddling. "Shit Morley, I'm telling you, don't do it." Morley didn't stop.

Rube began to threaten him. "Listen, asshole. You do this and you're all through. The Dean will have your ass. You'll never graduate. Your father will never see you get your diploma."

Morley stopped just short of the ditch. "Okay, but you have to push the bike back up the hill."

Rube got off. He was pissed, but relieved. His ass was killing him from sitting on the crossbar, but at least he was alive, and with any luck Beta would still be on tap.

As they headed down the steps to the Beta Bar, Rube heard voices and knew that they were in luck. The King of Smut gave them a warm greeting.

"Yeah, Morley, Rube, how ya doin'." The King's salutation was followed by a couple of "quack, quacks." Morley could vaguely remember hearing that sound before, and he knew it meant trouble. But he couldn't remember why. Then he saw the two guys from Dartmouth. They looked drunker and meaner than ever. Their clothes were dirty, and when one of them hand-ed Morley a beer, he noticed that the cup was sticky. The guy had glue or something all over his hands. Morley just hoped that it wasn't spermatozoa.

Morley reclaimed his seat at the end of the bar and looked around. It was a good bar group. The Harts, the King of Smut, Monk, Behole, Fleas, Dal Neth Ritchie Grauer, Bunnsie, Lenny the Lob, Ruxin, and, of course, the two guys from Dartmouth.

After a few beers, Rube said, "Hey, Lob. How about getting the cannon out and taking a few shots at the Chi Phi's?" The House had one of those little cannons that are used to start sail-boat races. It shot a ten-gauge blanks and made quite a noise, especially when discharged indoors. Lenny the Lob was the offi-cial cannoneer. When Lenny got real drunk, he liked loading the cannon with golf balls and shooting them at Chi Phi.

"Sorry, Rube," said Ruxin. "The Common is swarming with cops. We don't need any more trouble tonight."

"Yeah, Rube," the Lob said. "Good idea, but Ruxin's right. Too many cops. Maybe later." It wasn't like to Lob to pass up an invitation to shoot off the cannon, especially after fourteen kegs of beer.

"That's okay." said Rube. "Hey, Morley, grab a couple of beers and come on outside. I want to show you something." Morley was surprised. Rube usually didn't take being rejected this well.

"We'll fix those bastards," he said as they wobbled across the lawn to Chi Phi.

They stopped at the big beech tree right next to Chi Phi. When they got to the tree, Morley said, "Hey Rube, what's going on?"

Rube's eyes were glassy. This new round of beers was taking hold. "Come on, let's climb this tree," he said.

"What, are you shittin me? Let's go back and get another beer."

"Come on. I've got an idea."

Climbing the tree was no fun. It was sappy, dirty, and Rube refused to leave their beers at the bottom, which meant that they had to climb with only one hand. They managed to get about twenty feet up, putting them at eye level with the top floor of Chi Phi. They could look right into the bedrooms, but there was nothing to see since all the Chi Phis had gone to bed.

Then without any warning Rube started yelling, "Hey, Beta eats shit! Beta Sucks!" Morley joined in. "Yeah, Beta eats it! You assholes! Fuck Beta!"

After a few minutes, lights started to come on at Chi Phi, and a now familiar "quack, quack" could be heard coming across the lawn from Beta.

Morley and Rube kept yelling and with the lights on, it looked like the insults were coming from the Chi Phis. It never occurred to anyone to ask why the Chi Phis would be yelling insults at Beta at 3:30 in the morning. The quack quacking moved right under the tree. Morley and Rube looked down at the two guys from Dartmouth. Each of them had a baseball bat. Rube smiled at Morley and yelled down through the branches, "Hey you assholes, Beta eats it raw!"

There was a crash of glass. Some Chi Phis leaned out the window just in time to see the two quackers from Dartmouth knocking out the latticed windows around their porch. Rube stopped yelling when he heard the sound of shattering glass mixing with the quack quacking.

Shit, these two Dartmouth guys were nuts. They were doing some serious damage. When a squad car pulled up in front of Chi Phi, the quackers dropped their baseball bats and took off behind the Alumni Hall. All of the Chi Phis were awake and screaming at the cops to stop the guys from Dartmouth. Rube looked at Morley and said, "Let's get out of here."

As they scrambled down the tree, there was a tremendous BOOM from Beta. A golf ball bounced off the side of Chi Phi. Morley and Rube dropped out of the tree and landed right next to a cop. He gave them a strange look and said, "Put your hands up, you're under arrest."

Rube was quick on the defense. "Hey, we didn't do anything, we were just sitting in the tree."

The Chi Phis were still screaming at the cops to go after the guys from Dartmouth. Now the cop was really confused. He told Morley and Rube not to move and started after the quack, quacks which were coming from behind the Alumni Hall. As soon as the cops were out of sight, Rube grabbed Morley ran back towards Beta. BOOM! Another golf ball sailed over their heads.

When Morley and Rube got inside, they fell down on the couch in the front hall and tried to catch their breath. Beta was completely dark, but with each new BOOM, the house lit up as if it had been hit by lightning.

"Oh, Paulie, where are you?" It was Lenny the Lob calling from the darkness.

Ruxin yelled back from upstairs, "Come on, Lenny, there's cops all over the place. Stuff the cannon."

Lenny came creeping around the corner of the living room, followed by six brothers. Ruxin stuck his head over the top of the stairs. He was pissed. "Lenny. Knock it off. The House is already fucked."

BOOM. The entire house lit up. "Oh, Paulie! Where ARE you?"

"Screw you, Lob." Ruxin ran into Room 4 and bolted the door. "Quick, to the porch," said the King of Smut.

The brothers raced up the stairs. Rube went with them, but Morley had had it. He started to fall asleep on the couch. Rube came running back down the stairs. "Shit, there are cops everywhere. Whatever you do, don't go outside! Do you hear me?"

"Yeah, sure," Morley said. He was too tired to move. He fell asleep as soon as Rube left him, but was jerked awake by another BOOM. He could hear Lenny and the other brothers shouting things like "Take that, copper," and "This one's for the Gipper." They were having a great time.

Morley desperately needed to crash. He was exhausted. "The hell with this," he said to no one. "These guys are asking for trouble. I'm going to North." He pulled himself up and staggered out the front door.

No sooner had he stepped off the Beta lawn when he felt a sharp pain in his stomach. He keeled over. The next thing he knew, some big bastard was hanging all over him. A nightstick was pressed against the side of his face. Handcuffs bit into his wrists. A voice said, "We got you now, you stupid bastard. You college kids ain't gettin away with this shit."

Morley's mind was muddled. Where was he? What the hell was happening? When he lifted his head, he was blinded by flashlights. A voice said, "This has to be the guy, he's covered with sap. Take him down to the station."

The last thing Morley remembered was the sound of a cell door slamming shut. Clank. He was screwed.

XIII

Morley awoke to a steady stream of shrieks. His mouth was dry, his stomach ached, his head hurt. He wanted a shower, but he had no idea where he was. Given the hardness of the bed, he knew he wasn't at the Majestic Motel. He opened his eyes. Things looked a little blurry, but gradually he focused on a row of bars. What had he done to get himself thrown in jail? He started to remember bits and pieces of the previous day; passing his comps, drinking on the porch, two guys from Dartmouth going "quack, quack," Ken Bacon's bicycle, sitting in the tree with Rube, Lenny the Lob and the cannon. So what was wrong with that? He hadn't broken anything.

He tried to sit up, but couldn't. The pain in his head forced him back down. From the prone position, he studied the length of his body. All he was wearing was a pair of Levi's and a T shirt. He had no socks, shoes, or belt. He remembered the cops taking his belt, probably so he wouldn't hang himself. Hell, judging from the bars, he might have already hung himself.

Morley strained his blood shot eyes to read a clock that hung on the wall above a mirror. The mirror was probably one of those one-way jobs you saw in the movies. Watching the second hand made his stomach queazy. It was 7:13. That meant there were only 26 hours and 47 minutes until graduation. He had to do something. But he couldn't think. The shrieking from the next cell kept driving into his head like a nail.

Morley tried to stand up. It was no use. He was going to be sick. "I hope for such a study of art at Amherst as may take the subject out of the realm of pedantry into the realm of actual life and

165

keep it there as something that every educated man should follow with feeling, with emotion, with love." He'd passed his comps. Why the hell hadn't he just stayed in bed? Damn that Rube.

His whole body was shaking. He slid off the bunk and crawled to the commode. He wrapped his arms around its sides and lifted his head over the bowl. It was made of stainless steel, obviously for easy cleaning, but it hadn't been cleaned. There were pieces of soggy paper and pubic hairs stuck to the rim. Seeing them pushed his stomach over the edge.

He started to drool profusely, a sure sign that he was about to throw up. The shrieking was still coming from the next cell, but it no longer bothered him. Now, it seemed appropriate. This was the feeling of death. He was one of Signorelli's damned being cast into hell. He just wished it would come quickly. Only it never did.

Then it happened. His insides came spilling out.

"Again and Again and Again
Laah–la la–la la la la la la."

Morley let go of the bowl and rolled over onto the floor. He was too exhausted to move, but he felt better. From his spot on the floor, he could see himself in the mirror. He looked BAD. Puke was still dripping from his nose and mouth. He needed a shave. Once again, he tried to think, but once again, the shrieks distracted him. "Hey, asshole, shut up," were Morley's first words of the day. And they worked. The shrieking stopped.

"Hey Morley, that you?"

Morley recognized the voice, but he couldn't match it with a face. He rolled onto one knee, grabbed the bars, pulled himself up, and looked into the next cell. If he hadn't hurt so bad, he would have laughed. Ed Henry was sitting on the floor, wearing a big shiteating grin. He had a blanket wrapped around himself. If only he could see how ridiculous he looked, but that was impossible. Ed Henry had been totally blind from birth.

Morley had gotten to know Henry sophomore year. Starting as sophomores, kids on scholarship, like Morley, were expected to help pay for their education by converting part of their scholarship into a loan. The loan was to be repaid by working at one of the College's rinky dink jobs: busing at the dining hall, being a lab assistant, refereeing intramural sports, giving tours for the admissions office. Fortunately, Dean Wilson had found a special job for Morley.

Dean of Admissions Eugene S. (Bill) Wilson '29 chose students in a unique way. He looked at them not only as individuals, but as ingredients in a postpubescent stew. Like a master chef, he'd mix them together, let them simmer for four years, and hope that each new batch of Amherst men would be more interesting than the last. The spices in the Dean's recipe were his "experiments," kids who, on paper, never should have gotten into Amherst. Year after year, the Dean was able to go to public high schools, his favorite gardens, and top off his basket with an interesting assortment. Much to the faculty's amazement, these were often the students that gave each class its unique flavor.

Morley was an experiment, as was Henry; but, starting their second semester sophomore year, they were still pretty tasteless. Henry was messing up socially, Morley academically. Dean Wilson decided to stir the pot. He'd mix them together and see what happened. Morley's job was to be Henry's primary reader. At first Morley was hesitant. Everyone knew that Henry was a nut; that he'd gone off the deep end when his girlfriend dumped him.

For most of his freshman year, Henry seemed to be doing okay. He was happy, surprisingly well adjusted, and an above-average student. He'd even joined a fraternity, Phi Gam. Phi Gam had looked like a perfect place for Henry. It was full of all the campus goody-goodies. The head of the Student Council, the President of the Glee Club, and the editor of *The Amherst Student* were all Phi Gams. Everyone felt that Henry would fit right in at Phi Gam. They had an old fire engine that they drove around at the football games. Henry would have a great time riding it. He could ring the bell.

The night Henry received his Phi Gam pledge pin, he gave it to his girlfriend. She was some ugly honey from Mount Holyoke that Henry had met at the first freshman mixer. He was the only one blind enough to talk with her. Soon, they were an item. Morley later learned that Henry had never gotten anything before, so a little kiss face was enough to send him into orbit. When he gave her his pledge pin, she gave him a hand job. That's when he knew he was in love.

Most houses welcomed their pledges with a couple of kegs and a few tunes from the juke box. The Phi Gams' initiation was the "Fiji Island Party," their biggest event of the year. They decorated the house with palm trees, hired a black band from Springfield, dressed them up in Hawaiian shirts and had them play drums that sounded like tin cans. All the brothers and their dates had to wear bathing suits, even though it was March.

The key to the Fiji Island Party was the Fiji Island Punch. It would take the hair off a full-grown monkey. The supposedly goody-goodies at Phi Gam were, in reality, a bunch of devious bastards. Once the crowd got greased up on Fiji Island Punch, the Fiji Island band would break into the limbo. When the honeys tried to dance under the stick, the Phi Gams would get down on their knees and pretend to urge them on. What they were really doing was peeking at their snatches, and hoping to coax a tit or two out of their suits. The Phi Gams got a collective hard-on just thinking about the Fiji Island Party.

The Fiji Island Party was Henry's first taste of fraternity life. What he tasted most was the Fiji Island Punch. He was wolfing it down like water. Henry would have been a sloppy drunk even if he could see, but as a blind drunk, he was awful. He knocked over palm trees, broke lights, bumped into walls, and generally made a nuisance of himself. After a few shots of Fiji Island Punch, the Phi Gams were no longer their goody-goody selves. They stole Henry's cane and used it as the limbo stick. They just laughed when some fat girl slipped and squished Henry's cane into a right angle. Drunk and with his cane bent, Henry started walking around in circles. All the phony Phi Gams thought that was hilarious. Henry's initiation ended when he fell into a Fiji Island palm tree and passed out.

The Fiji Island Punch was so potent that even Henry's girl-friend started to look good, at least to the Phi Gams. That was too bad for Henry, because during a heart-to-heart pledge talk with his big brother, he had confided that she had given him a hand-job. Henry figured fraternity guys were supposed to get a lot of ass, and he wanted his big brother to know that he wasn't going to let the house down.

Henry's big brother was impressed, as well he should have been. This jerk was the countertenor for the Glee Club and had the worst case of acne Morley had ever seen. One look at him and anyone knew that he couldn't buy a piece of ass. But, of course, Henry had never had one look at him. Henry was convinced that all Phi Gams were super studs and that his big broth-er was just a high-pitched John Wayne.

Henry's big brother reasoned that if Henry could get a hand-job from this honey, so could he. Surely being an acned asshole wasn't any worse than being blind. Now, with his pledge son passed out, he was ready to make his move. He asked Henry's honey whether she would like another glass of Fiji Island Punch. It was the first time since coming to Mount Holyoke that any male besides Henry had acknowledged her. Ten minutes later, she was giving Henry's big brother a handjob. Twenty minutes later, he was drilling her. An hour later, they were pinned. The next day, Henry tried to commit suicide. Nobody saw him again until the following semester.

But when he came back, Henry just wasn't himself. He de-pledged Phi Gam. He cut classes, flunked tests, and didn't seem to care about anything. Mostly he just sat alone in his room. His grades for the fall semester were almost as bad as Morley's. It' was then that Dean Wilson got the idea of making Morley Hen-ry's primary reader. Any reading would be a step up for Morley, and maybe, just maybe, he could get Henry out of the dumps.

The Dean's plan worked to a T. Morley's grades began to nudge higher, while Henry's spirits soared. He liked having Morley as his reader. It gave him a different perspective. The fact that Luther wrote his proclamation after being constipated for days didn't impress Morley at all ("You always think better on the can"), nor did the concept of the Oedipus complex, ("That's the first snatch you see. Except in your case, of course. Too bad you missed it.")

A big breakthrough came when Henry asked Morley about the eternal triangle. Much to Henry's surprise, Morley used him as an example. "Take that dog you used to date and that asshole she dates now."

A glimmer of light came into Henry's dead eyes. He had never realized that the love of his life was a dog or that his former big brother was an asshole. Everybody had been too polite to tell him that he had fallen in love with a dog, and, of course, none of the Phi Gams considered themselves assholes. All this time Henry had been thinking that he was the asshole, that John Wayne had stolen his Marilyn Monroe, and that everyone was laughing at him. Now, with one sentence, Morley had turned things around.

Morley could see that Henry hadn't known any of this stuff. "Look, Henry, you're a pretty good-looking guy. You go to the first freshman mixer. Everybody's nervous, but since you can't see anything, you're really out of it. Naturally, you head for the safest place in the room, the corner. And where do you think the biggest dog in the room is going to hang out? Naturally, in the same safe corner.

"This honey looks like someone beat on her with an ugly stick. Everybody in the place knows it but you. She's nice to you because you're the only guy that'll talk to her. You ask her out. She accepts. You take her to plays, movies, lectures, even a few parties. You get a little ass, you think you're in love.

"Then along comes this guy with zits." Henry had never known that his big brother had zits. "He knows that this honey is good for a handjob because you've told him." Henry had spilled the whole story to Morley in one of their sessions. "Very dumb on your part. Never tell anybody what you're getting, because if you do, they'll want a piece."

"Anyway, the guy with the zits figures that since you've gotten shitfaced and are making a fool of yourself, he'll give it a shot. The Fiji Punch has done its job. They go into a dark room where she can't see his zits and he can't see how ugly she is and before you know it, slam, bam thank you ma'am." Morley could see Henry wince, but he was beginning to get the picture.

"My prediction is that your old honey will bolt the first time that some guy with no zits says hello to her. Likewise, your big brother will drop her as soon as he can find something better. But believe me, those two might have gone as high as they're gonna go. I mean, they are some kind of ugly."

"You, on the other hand, have plenty of running room. Go out and meet some honeys. There are dozens of girls who would like to date you hiding in the corners of Smith and Holyoke."

Before the end of sophomore year, Morley had convinced Henry to join another fraternity, Alpha Theta Xi. The Alpha Theta Xi's weren't big men on campus, but they were good guys who liked Henry. He fit right in and soon was his old self. Morley didn't read for Henry after sophomore year, but they'd stayed friends. On big weekends, Morley would tell Henry to tap his way up to Beta so Morley could give him a beer and a candid appraisal of his date. Henry's dates were always real dogs, but Morley always found something nice to say about them. He'd tell him that they had "great pins," "big tits," or a "super ass." Then he would ask Henry if he was getting anything. The inevitable shiteater that covered his face was a sure giveaway, but Henry never told. He had learned his lesson.

So now, what was Henry doing in jail? Morley hoped that he hadn't been caught boffing some unattractive, but under-aged, honey.

"Henry. What are you doing here?"

"The cops picked me up on the Common for protesting the war."

"Protesting the war! What have you got to protest? Nobody's going to draft you."

"No, but they're going to draft you, and a lot of other guys that have no business going over there."

"Geeez, Henry, you're starting to sound like Elliot. Why didn't they nab him?"

"I was drunk, he wasn't."

"They threw you in jail just for being drunk?"

"Well, it was a little more than that. Thanks to the booze, my protest got a little out of hand."

"Man, you are the worst drunk. What did you do?"

Henry got up off the floor and sat on his bunk. He looked very pleased with himself, like he enjoyed being in jail.

"The Alpha Theta Xis were having their 'Senior Sayonara.' That's when the underclassmen give the seniors their going away gifts. It's always a good show, but this year they were serving Kamikazes. I really got hammered." Morley shook his head. A Kamikaze was a collection of booze that supposedly launched a suicidal sneak attack on your brain. Just the thought of one made Morley feel sick again.

"My gift was a BB gun," Henry said. "It was inscribed 'To Deadeye Ed, the quickest draw in Alpha Theta Xi.' My pledge son printed it on the stock, in Braille, of course. Nice touch, huh?"

"Yeah, good bit," said Morley. The "Deadeye" part was obvious, but the reference to "quickdraw" was a bit more subtle. It highlighted Henry's hair trigger.

After coming out of his slump, Henry had gone on a roll. He became a man with a mission, and that was to clean out all of the corners of Smith and Mt. Holyoke. The brothers at Alpha Theta Xi often told Morley that Henry was pumping a fortune into the condom machine. His sexual prowess was becoming an Alpha Theta Xi legend.

Then Henry almost blew it. He asked the condom salesman if he could stock a brand of prophylactics known as "Delay." These safes had a special lubricant supposed to prevent premature ejaculation. When the Alpha Theta Xis discovered that Henry had trouble holding his wad, they started calling him "Quickdraw." Henry wasn't at all bothered by this recognition. He told everyone that a hair trigger was no problem if your gun was a repeater.

"Anyway, I'd been picketing the Memorial Day Parade all afternoon," Henry said, continuing his story, "so when I left the party, I figured, what the hell. If the Town wanted a war, I'd give them a war. I sat down on the Common and started firing away with my new BB gun. Then the cops showed up."

Morley had missed it, because he'd been passed out up in his room at North, but he later learned that Henry's arrest had caused quite a scene. At about 12:30, the police had received a report that there was some guy on the Common shooting a gun. Nobody had said that it was a blind kid with a BB gun. For all the police knew, it could have been another Charles Whitman, the psycho that had just gunned down twenty-three people from the Tower at the University of Texas. Elliot and his crowd already had the cops on edge. If these anti-war protestors were crazy enough to picket the Memorial Day Parade, who knew what they might do, especially now that Commager had told them they were right?

The cops called the Sheriff. The Sheriff decided that he wasn't going to take any chances. He didn't want any blood on his hands. He sealed off the road around the Common, ordered his men to put on flak jackets, armed them with riot guns, and set up some huge spotlights that illuminated Henry's every move. Meanwhile, Henry was just sitting there, plunking away, oblivious to the commotion that was going on around him.

The sound of the Sheriff's bullhorn caught Henry by complete surprise. At first he thought it was Elliot making another speech. The theme was about the same: "Stop shooting! Throw down your gun! I repeat. Stop shooting, and throw down your gun!"

The bullhorn was hurting Henry's ears. He realized that he was going to be sick, but what he didn't realize was that when he got up, there was a row of riot guns cocked and pointed right at him. If "Deadeye" could have seen the fingers that were nervously massaging those triggers, he would have been crapping his drawers as well as chucking his cookies.

The Sheriff had positioned himself behind one of the new trees. When he realized that Henry was blowing lunch, he decided to make his move, only he was too late. Elliot, seeing the glow that was coming from the Common, had immediately recessed his all-night meeting, and headed straight for the lights. He had circumvented the police barricade and run right to Henry. When it came to protesting, nobody was going to upstage Elliot.

Elliot wasn't the only one drawn to the bright lights. At 12:30, what was left of the Great Bike Race spilled out of Beta. The braves and their squaws, who were suppose to be back at Smith by 1:00, gathered around the Common. They were all as shitfaced as Henry and eager to dump much abuse on the Sheriff and the cops. This, in addition to Elliot's protests and Henry's ravings, led to another pushing and shoving match between the Indians and the cops. The Sheriff had had it. When he realized that Henry was not another Charles Whitman, but just some blind kid with a BB gun, he should have let him go and called it an evening. Instead, he whisked Henry off to jail. No wise ass college kid, blind or not, was going to make him look like a fool. He even ordered a strip search of Henry. All it produced was his wallet, a dollar and thirty-two cents, and five "Delays." When the Sheriff asked Henry what the hell he was doing with five "Delays," Henry told him that he would have had six but "with a hair trigger, he liked to leave his gun resting on an empty chamber." All of the cops except for the Sheriff thought Henry was a pisser.

"Why were you wailing just now?" Morley asked.

Henry started to rock back and forth, a sure sign he was getting excited. "Morley, I am going to drive that fat ass Sheriff crazy."

As if on cue, in came the Sheriff. "O.K., you guys, get cleaned up. We're going to court."

Henry started to wail. The Sheriff grimaced. "Hey you, shut up. You'll have plenty to cry about when the judge gets through with you." Then he looked at Morley. "And as for you, you may not want to tell me your name, but you'll sure as hell tell it to the judge."

As he slammed the door, Morley looked up at the clock. It read 7:32. Morley saw a ray of hope. If the Sheriff didn't know who he was, there might be a way out of this mess. They couldn't book him if they didn't know his name. As it stood now, some guy named John Doe was in a heap of trouble. He just had to make sure that John Doe never got connected with Edward D. Morley, and there was only one way to do that. He had to escape.

He looked around the cell. The only things in it were a blanket and a pair of cheap flip flops. How was he going to make his getaway in flip flops? He wished he had his Rydells. Morley remembered an article in *Sports Illustrated* about Terry Baker, the great quarterback from Oregon who had won the Heisman Trophy. Terry loved his Rydells so much that he had taken the cleats off and wore them around like sneakers. If Morley had been as smart as Terry Baker, he'd be preparing to make his break in a pair of sawed-off Rydells and not some cheap flip flops.

The door to the cell block opened. An old guy wearing a V.F.W. jacket came in with two trays. It was time for breakfast. The thought of escaping had revived Morley. He could use a little breakfast. Juice, eggs and bacon with an English muffin was just what he needed. He pulled his tray through a slot in the bars. The tray was covered by a checkered napkin, exactly like the ones in the Westerns. Morley pulled off the napkin. He couldn't believe it. There sat a bowl of Quaker Puffed Wheat, or Quaker Puffed Rice. Whatever it was, the kernels were floating on some milk that looked like water. Henry started to howl. Jail was the pits.

The Sheriff returned promptly at 8:30. He was going to take them to the District Court in Northampton, where everyone from Amherst went to court. The Sheriff unlocked their cells. "Okay, boys, let's go."

Henry began to wail as soon as the Sheriff came in, but Morley told him to save his lungs, that he would tell him when to turn it on. Morley had decided that Henry's wailing was just the diversion he needed for his escape. Henry tapped his way through the station, but Morley took his arm as they walked outside. The Sheriff was right behind them. The sun hurt Morley's eyes. It was going to be another beautiful day. It occurred to Morley that his parents were just leaving home. What would they do if they got to Amherst and found him in jail? He had to escape, right now.

The Sheriff bent over to unlock his car. As he fiddled with the door, Morley squeezed Henry's arm. Henry started to howl.

There were lots of people on the street at 8:35 in the morning, and they all stopped to see what was happening. The Sheriff quickly unlocked the back door and tried to push Henry into the back seat. Henry wouldn't go. He wedged himself between the frame and howled even louder. A crowd began to gather. The Sheriff was pushing and cursing and yelling into the station for some help. Once again, Henry was making him look like a fool.

This was the break Morley had been looking for. He pushed his way through the crowd and began to run. If he could get around the corner, he'd be on his way. Twenty yards, ten yards, five yards. He could hear the Sheriff yelling, "Stop that guy. Somebody grab him." But nobody had to. As Morley planted his foot to make the turn, the flip flop gave way. It flipped and he flopped. His big toe buckled under his foot. He could feel the concrete ripping the nail out of his toe. His hands reached out to break his fall. He remembered rolling over the curb into the gutter. There was a loud whack as the side of his head slapped against the pavement. He must have passed out for a moment.

When he opened his eyes, a pair of thick glasses with black frames were staring at him. It was Elliot. He had Morley's head cradled against his ample tummy. "Oh, shit!" was all Morley said.

"It's all right." Elliot reassured him. "These pigs can't touch you."

"Get away from him," the Sheriff ordered.

"Why?" Elliot said.

"'Cause I say so," the Sheriff said. He had drawn his gun and had it pointed at them. It was a pearl-handled revolver.

Morley was scared. This crazy bastard actually might blow their heads off. He looked mad enough to do it. Elliot appeared very calm. His hands were steady. Reluctantly, he moved Morley's head from his lap. Morley tried to get up. His left foot was covered with blood, his toe throbbing. His eyes fastened on the hole at the end of the pearl-handled revolver. One spit from it and he'd be gone before he ever got to Vietnam.

Henry, much to the crowd's delight, was making his own getaway. If the fat-ass Sheriff was off chasing Morley, he was going to hit the road. The crowd, made up partly of protestors who had run over from the Common, was shouting its encouragement as Henry tapped his way back to campus. Morley watched in disbelief. Henry might be nuts, but he had more balls than the whole Glee Club put together.

There was no way that Henry was going to escape. The Sheriff was screaming bloody murder. Blue uniforms poured from the police station. The cops quickly chased Henry down, and amid taunts and jeers from the crowd and a harangue from Elliot, threw him into the back of the Sheriff's car. Once he saw that Henry was safe, the Sheriff put his gun away and slapped a pair of handcuffs on Morley. Morley offered no resistance. He just wanted to get into the car before somebody shouted his name.

When he had Morley inside the car, the Sheriff put another pair of cuffs on Henry, and then with a third pair, clamped Henry and Morley together. Then he slammed the back door, squeezed in behind the wheel, and pointed his cruiser towards Northampton.

Now Morley was really depressed. His toe hurt, the cuffs were killing him, and worst of all, he had blown his chance to escape. John Doe was about to become Edward D. Morley, who was about to get kicked out of Amherst one day before he was scheduled to graduate, still with no idea what he had done.

Henry wasn't the least bit upset. He was having a grand time. Being locked in the car with the Sheriff meant he could give him more shit. "Hey Mr. Sheriff, how's it feel to arrest a blind boy for shooting a BB gun?"

The back of the Sheriff's neck was crimson. He was driving very fast.

"Cop catches blind boy, hey, big stuff!"

Henry started to rock back and forth. He was getting excited. Morley was being pulled around by the cuffs. "Hey, take it easy," he said to Henry. "We're in enough trouble." But it was no use. Henry was all stoked up.

"Hey, Sheriff. You're good at catching blind boys. You ever catch any ass?"

The veins in the Sheriff's neck looked like they were about to pop. He was so mad, he could hardly keep the car on the road. Morley was glad when they reached the courthouse. The seven miles had seemed like seven hundred. He thought for sure the Sheriff would pull over and beat the hell out of Henry. He certainly would've had just cause.

XIV

After a three-day weekend, Tuesday morning at Northampton District Court looked like a recruiting station for Alcoholics Anonymous. Drunks were everywhere, smelling of urine and puke. Their clothes were disheveled and dirty. These were guys who had reached the bottom of the bottle.

Most of them kept nodding off. When someone came by, they would look up with bloodshot eyes, pleading for a cigarette, or, better yet, a drink. They made quite an impression on Morley, especially now that he was one of them.

They made absolutely no impression on Henry, who, of course, couldn't see them. "Hey Morley, this place smells like crap," he said as they found a spot on the defendant's bench.

"You ought to see it," Morley said. "It looks like crap."

Henry put on his big stupid grin. He couldn't have been happier. Morley felt sorry for the poor bastard. How could he possibly understand life if he couldn't see it? But then, maybe Henry didn't have it so bad. He was the only person in the whole building who was smiling.

Morley forgot about Henry and started to think about himself. How was he going to get out of this mess? The Sheriff still didn't know who he was. He had planned to sign in as John Doe, but Henry had screwed up both their signatures. Henry told the Sheriff that he couldn't write with the cuffs on, that he needed unrestricted movement because he was blind. Morley knew this was bullshit. Henry could sign his name in a straitjacket, but when the Sheriff refused to remove the cuffs, Henry scribbled all over the page. As a result, everyone's signature became illegible, which was fine with Morley.

The big Regulator clock on the wall had clicked to 9:05. The Clerk stood up. "Hear ye, hear ye, the District Court of Northampton, County of Hampshire, the Commonwealth of Massachusetts, is now in session, the Honorable Francis X. Mahoney presiding. All rise." Morley grabbed Henry and pulled him to his feet.

The Honorable Francis X. Mahoney entered with something less than a flourish. Morley could see why. Who would want to walk into a room filled with thirty-two stinking drunks? It would be better to be a garbage collector than the Judge for the District Court of Northampton. Garbage couldn't smell any worse, and at least you wouldn't have to listen to it. How could the Judge do this every day?

The answer was easy. Francis X. Mahoney drank as much as anyone else in the courtroom. He was just careful to do it at the right places, namely, the Democratic Club of Western Massachusetts. It was his association with the Democratic Club and one big break that had placed Francis X. Mahoney on the bench.

If you were a member of the Democratic Party and a judge in Massachusetts, it could mean only one thing: you knew the Kennedys. Francis X. Mahoney not only knew the Kennedys, he worked for them. Nobody ever accused Francis X. Mahoney of being too bright, but he was lucky enough to get onto the Kennedy bandwagon early and smart enough to push it as hard as he could. Joe Kennedy liked that kind of loyalty.

It was Old Joe himself who told Francis X. Mahoney to go to law school. During the days, Francis worked for the Kennedys. At night he went to Suffolk Law. It took him eleven years to graduate, which was a school record. It then took him eighteen tries to pass the Massachusetts Bar. That too was a record, one that had never been broken.

Francis X. Mahoney was 43 years old by the time the Commonwealth pronounced him fit to practice law. But Francis X. Mahoney never practiced law. Instead, he worked to make John Fitzgerald Kennedy the 38th President of the United States, and his little brother, Edward Moore Kennedy, the Junior Senator from Massachusetts. In return, Joe Kennedy made Francis X. Mahoney the Assistant District Attorney for Hampshire County and the President of the Democratic Club of Western Mass. This was what Francis X. Mahoney was doing in 1964 when Ted Kennedy's small plane crashed on a campaign run to Northampton.

Francis X. Mahoney became Joe Kennedy's man on the spot. He handled the situation perfectly. He made all the right calls, he got all the right doctors, and, most importantly, he got all the right press. By the time Edward Moore Kennedy limped out of Cooley Dickinson Hospital, Francis X. Mahoney was the Honorable Francis X. Mahoney, Judge for the Northampton District Court.

Joe Kennedy couldn't have picked a better man. Presiding over the Northampton District Court wasn't all that different from presiding over a meeting of the Democratic Club of Western Mass. Judge Mahoney's primary job was to take good care of good Democrats so that they would continue to vote for the Kennedys. Except for the power, the prestige, and the license plate that said "JUDGE," it was a lousy job. Three-day weekends made it even worse. It was the three-day weekends that pushed marginal drunks over the edge.

The Judge knew that he had a full docket, so he got right to work. "The Town of Hadley versus Tony Skibilski. Mr. Skibilski, it is alleged that on the night of May 29, you left the Polish American Club of Hadley and proceeded to drive your pickup truck into the water fountain on the Hadley Town Common. How do you plead?"

Morley had noticed that the fountain was knocked over as the Sheriff zoomed through Hadley on the way to court. The Betas liked this fountain. It had been constructed by the Women's Temperance Union and was located right in front of the Presbyterian Church. On their way home from Smith on Saturday nights, the brothers used to stop and fill the pipe in the fountain with beer. The hope was that some elderly matron on her way to church Sunday morning would stop to get a drink and discover

181

that the Temperance Union Fountain was pumping beer. Now Tony Skibilski had totaled the fountain.

Tony stepped forward with his head down. He held his cap with both hands. His stubby little frame looked like it threw potatoes and onions into a truck all day and drank most of the night.

Morley doubted if Tony spoke much English. Dick and Stanley had taken him drinking at the Hadley Polish-American Club a couple of times, and Morley hadn't understood a word. Not that it mattered. The beer was cheap.

The Judge asked Tony how he pleaded. After a considerable pause, Tony mumbled something in Polish. It made absolutely no sense to Morley, but Tony's plea didn't seem to faze the Judge. All the members of the Hadley Polish-American Club were good Democrats and supported the Kennedys. "The Court accepts your plea of *nolo contendere* and fines you $25.00."

"Bang!" The Judge rapped his gavel. Tony had had his day in court.

And so it went. The Judge kept banging his way through a series of nonsensical *nolo contenderes*. Nobody was innocent, nobody was guilty. They were just dirty, smelly, hung over, and $25.00 poorer.

Morley wasn't sure what he'd plead. He would have to wait and hear the charge. If it was just drunk and disorderly conduct, he'd think up some quote from the late John F. Kennedy and throw out a *nolo contendere*. If it was something worse, he'd maintain that he was innocent. Provided, of course, that he didn't pass out before then. The pain in his toe was becoming unbearable. He tried to put it out of his mind by listening to the current case.

The Judge was working over a repeat offender. He'd committed this guy to sixty days in a state institution less than a week ago. The poor guy must have been a Republican. No Democrat ever got sixty days.

"Mr. Russell, what are you doing back in my courtroom? You are supposed to be in a state institution."

Mr. Russell hung his head in shame. He looked like a little boy who had been caught peeing his pants. He was wearing a dirty white button down dress shirt, a pair of baggy chinos, dark socks, and scuffed-up Weejuns. He could have had some money at one time. Morley wondered whether he was any relation to the Mr. Russell at Russell's Package Store. He'd have to ask Short-pecker.

Mr. Russell started to cry. It was very embarrassing. Henry leaned over to Morley and asked too loudly, "What's happening?"

"Mr. Russell's crying."

"You've got to be shitting me." Again, he said it too loudly.

"No, he's actually crying, now shut up."

Henry was undeterred. "I bet he's going to throw himself on the mercy of the court. I've got this guy figured out."

Henry might have been right. Mr. Russell was sitting on the floor with his head in his hands, sobbing uncontrollably. Judge Francis X. Mahoney was not buying his act. He'd seen it too many times before.

"Mr. Russell, get on your feet and answer the question. How did you get out of the institution to which you were committed by this Court?"

Mr. Russell stumbled to his feet. Tears had cut two paths through the dirt on his face. He looked pitiful. If Mr. Russell were being tried by a jury, he'd have been out of there in a minute.

"My wife came to visit me." Mr. Russell said between sobs.

"Yes, please go on."

"She took me for a ride."

"Unlikely, but continue."

"She had to visit a friend, so she left me in a tavern and forgot to pick me up."

The Judge looked disgusted. "Mr. Russell, do you mean to tell this Court that your wife took you for a ride, left you at a bar, and then just forgot about you?"

"Yes, Your Honor." Mr. Russell sat down on the floor and started to cry again. What a story! This guy would have made a great Beta.

The arresting officer was sworn in. He testified that Mr. Russell was apprehended wandering around Chicopee. His wife had in fact come to visit him, but did not take him for a ride. Instead, Mr. Russell had rifled her purse while she went to the ladies' room and escaped as soon as she'd left. He'd used the money to go on a two-day binge which had culminated with his arrest in Chicopee. At that time of his arrest, all he was wearing were his Weejuns.

That was enough for the Judge. He entered a *nolo contendere* on behalf of Mr. Russell. Bang! It was back to the institution. The bailiffs scooped Mr. Russell off of the floor and carried him away. Morley could see a fresh stain on the floor. Mr. Russell must have peed his pants.

As Mr. Russell was being carried out of the courtroom, a raucous crowd surged in. Morley turned and saw Elliot leading a band of protestors. They all were carrying signs saying FREE HENRY and STOP THE WAR. In addition to the usual contingent of long haired guys and scuzzy girls, there were a lot of people who actually looked respectable. Apparently Henry had become a new hero of the antiwar movement. "What's happening?" Henry said.

"Your supporters have arrived."

"Really. How many?"

"Enough to upset the Judge."

The Judge banged his gavel while the Clerk shouted, "Order in the court! We must have order in the court."

While Elliot and his group milled around looking for seats, the Sheriff leaned over, took off their cuffs, got up and waddled to the bench. "Henry, get set, I think we're next," Morley whispered to Henry.

Henry started to rock back and forth. Morley could tell he was excited. Now that he had some support, there was no telling what he might do. "Hey Henry, don't screw around," Morley said. "I don't want to be sharing a room with Mr. Russell."

The Clerk announced, "Would Edward Henry please approach the bench." Good. They'd called Henry first. The Sheriff and the

Judge must have decided that the easiest way to get rid of Elliot and his gang was to dispense with Henry. The Sheriff would have looked pretty stupid calling Morley, since he still didn't know his name.

As it was, he looked plenty stupid calling up Henry. The Judge did a double take when Henry tapped his way toward the bench. It must have been the first time he realized that Henry was blind. The Judge glanced over at the Sheriff as if to say, "What's this?" It was bad enough that Amherst was the only Republican town in his district; now this jerkoff Sheriff had brought a blind kid into his court.

"Town of Amherst versus Edward Henry," the clerk droned. He was interrupted by a chorus of "Free Henry, Stop The War. Free Henry, Stop the War." The Judge banged his gavel. Elliot and his gang became silent. The clerk continued.

"Mr. Henry, it is charged that on the morning of May 31st you sat on the Amherst Common and proceeded to illegally discharge a weapon, to wit, a BB gun; were drunk and disorderly; resisted arrest; and attempted to escape. How do you plead?"

The Judge was on the edge of his chair. So was the entire courtroom. No one could believe what they were hearing. Resisting arrest! Attempted escape! These were serious charges. This kid from Amherst College was having the book thrown at him. The Sheriff had the political savvy of a gerbil. Couldn't he see that the kid was blind!

The protestors were back on their feet chanting, "Free Henry! Free Henry! Stop the War!" What would happen if the Republicans got wind of this story? The Judge could hear it now. "And from Chicago, this is Paul Harvey's News and Comment.

"And one last item from Northampton, Massachusetts. Today, thanks to Judge Francis X. Mahoney, we all can sleep a little more soundly. You see, today the Judge threw the book at one of America's most hardened criminals. After a late-night shooting spree in the town of Amherst, this one-man crime wave had first resisted arrest, then attempted a daring daylight escape. Thank goodness Judge Francis X. Mahoney has locked him away.

185

Now, the rest of us won't have to worry about this totally blind, that's right, TOTALLY BLIND, Amherst College senior and his BB gun, who, he says, was JUST PROTESTING THE WAR. This is Paul Harvey reporting from Chicago. Gooooood DAY!"

That's all the Kennedys would have to hear. His Honor would be history.

The Judge let out an audible groan. He wanted this blind kid out of his court, and he wanted him out NOW. He kept banging his gavel until he'd hammered Elliot and his group back into their seats. When they'd settled down, the Judge turned to Henry.

"How do you plead, Mr. Henry?" Henry was rocking back and forth like a hobby horse. Morley knew he was up to something, but he didn't know what.

"I beg your pardon, Your Honor," Henry said very respectfully, "but I wonder if I might ask the Court to clarify a legal term."

The Sheriff had seen enough of Henry to know that he was up to no good. He started to object, but the Judge quickly overruled him. He'd had it with this idiot Sheriff. He wasn't about to let anybody accuse him of railroading a blind kid. Besides, this was the first time in his two years on the bench that anyone had ever bothered to ask for a legal definition. Just because he'd gone to Suffolk Law nights and had taken eighteen tries to pass the bar didn't mean he wasn't legally conversant. If a smart college kid wanted a clarification, he'd give him a clarification. After all, he was the Judge.

"By all means, Mr. Henry, feel free to ask the Court any question that you might have pertaining to the law. It is the intent of this Court to give you every opportunity to defend yourself."

The Sheriff cringed. These damn micks were so stupid. Some smart-ass college kid asks him a question, so he pulls out his degree from Suffolk Night School. Let the kid ask all the questions he wanted. The evidence against Henry was overwhelming. No matter how much he flattered the Judge, or how many Commies came into court, the Sheriff was going to drill Henry a new asshole.

"Thank you very much, Your Honor." Henry said, his head bobbing up and down like a barnyard chicken. "What I would like to know is the difference between 'unlawful' and 'illegal.'"

All eyes turned toward the Judge. It was a hell of a question. What *was* the difference between "unlawful" and "illegal"?

The Judge sat up in his seat, straightened his robe, rubbed his chin and pondered the question. At that moment, he could have been Chief Justice Earl Warren deciding *Brown versus Board of Education.* He looked good. But he didn't have an answer.

He repeated the question out loud. "Unlawful and illegal." His mind muddled through eleven years of Suffolk Night School. "Illegal and unlawful." Damn, these college kids were tough.

Then, as if by accident, two wires crossed. A spark appeared in the Judge's eye. He had the answer. But it wasn't an answer, it was a question, a trick that the Judge had learned from the Kennedys, who in turn had learned it from Socrates. Whenever some wise-ass stumped you, just fire his own question back at him. Nine times out of ten, he'll end up shooting himself in the foot. Besides, the Judge had to do something. Henry looked like he was on the verge of an epileptic fit.

"Mr. Henry, you have asked the court an excellent question." Henry could hardly contain himself. He started rocking even more. "But since you seem to be a young man of great insight," the Judge paused after this little play on words, "the Court would be interested in hearing your thoughts on the question before it delivers its own opinion."

The Judge nodded at the reporter from the *Hampshire Gazette,* who, fortunately, was a good Democrat. They both realized that Henry was a political disaster just waiting to happen.

"Well, Your Honor," Henry said, clutching his cane in both hands. "I believe that 'unlawful' refers to a transgression against the law, but 'illegal' is a sick bird."

A stunned silence hung over the court. Suddenly one of the drunks started to laugh. Then all of the drunks started to laugh. Then Elliot and his protestors started to laugh. Then, even the Clerk started to laugh.

Soon the Judge, the Sheriff, and Morley were the only people in the courtroom who were not laughing. Francis X. Mahoney turned beet red. The Sheriff shook his head as if to say, "I told you so." Morley slumped back in his chair. Henry was still rocking back and forth with his big shiteating grin. They were screwed. What the hell was Henry thinking about? Henry deserved to be committed. Let Mr. Russell read to him from now on.

The Judge leaned over the bench and yelled to the Sheriff. "You get that nut out of here or I'm going to cite you for contempt of court!"

The Sheriff almost started to object, but then thought better of it. He grabbed Henry and headed for the door. Elliot and his group were jumping up and down, waving their signs and chanting, "Free Henry, Stop the WAR. Free Henry, Stop the WAR." The drunks were hooting and hollering. A few had gotten up and were rocking back and forth like Henry. The bailiffs were trying to push them down. It was going to be a long day for Judge Mahoney. He kept pounding his gavel while the Clerk kept shouting "Order in the Court! Order in the Court!"

Morley saw his chance. He fell in line behind the Sheriff and Henry. Nobody tried to stop him. The bailiffs were too preoccupied with trying to restore some "order in the Court."

Once outside the courtroom, Morley ducked behind a door. The Sheriff had forgotten all about him. Henry had started to wail again. The Sheriff was dragging him down the front steps of the courthouse. Elliot and his group had surrounded them. One of the scuzzy girls tried to pull him away from the Sheriff. Another one joined her. Soon, they were all tugging and pulling at Henry, who must have been in ecstasy. He was definitely going to get laid tonight.

The Sheriff gave up. He released Henry, threw up his arms and retreated to the safety of his car. There was a big cheer from the protestors as his squad car squealed out of the parking lot. Henry was a free man. The protestors triumphantly hoisted him into the back of a pickup that was draped with a sheet that read, STOP THE WAR! Elliot had a bullhorn and was announcing that there would be a rally on the Amherst Common celebrating Henry's acquittal. Cars covered with more signs protesting the war fell into line behind the pickup. The caravan proceeded through Northampton, heading for Amherst. Henry was sitting on top of the cab waving to an unseen crowd. Elliot wedged himself into the bed of the truck and was barking out news of the rally through his bullhorn. Springing Henry was a big coup for Elliot and the anti-war movement.

Morley looked at his toe. It was still killing him. He could have used a shot of Mr. Brown's Novocaine. The clock on the courthouse said 10:47. His parents would be at Amherst in less than an hour. How was he going to get back? He hadn't shaved and was disgustingly dirty. He looked even worse than when he'd left the Majestic. Nobody would ever pick him up.

"Morley! Come on, let's go." It was Harts. He was sitting in a brand new red Corvette, a graduation present from his parents. Morley ran over and jumped in. Harts handed him a cold beer. "Here you go, my boy. A little hair of the dog that bit ya." Morley took a big swig.

"So Harts, what the hell's going on? Why was I in jail?"

"Not good, Morley." Harts said, slipping the Vette into gear. "Someone cut down nine of the new trees on the Common. The cops are bullshit. They know the trees were there when they arrested Henry. They figure it has to be someone from Beta. We were the only house on tap." The Vette roared past the Women's Temperance Fountain in Hadley. It was still lying on its side, compliments of Tony Skibilski.

"So? What's that got to do with me?"

"The Dean came by this morning. Ruxin, of course, blamed everything on some rowdies from Dartmouth, but no one's buying that crap. The police told the Dean that they'd caught the guy who did it coming out of Beta, but he wouldn't give them his name, and the Sheriff had taken him to court. That, of course, is you. We saw it all from the roof."

"Thanks for the help."

"Hey, I came and got you as soon as we heard you'd gone to

court. What else could I do? If we'd tried to get you out last night, they'd have arrested us, too. Shortpecker says he's never seen the Town so mad."

Harts down shifted and gunned the Vette up the hill entering Amherst. The flag on Johnson Chapel was waving against a clear blue sky. The Alumni Office couldn't have ordered better weather. If the Canadian high could last one more day, so could Morley. They zoomed through the light at the corner of the Common. Morley saw what was left of the trees. He could understand why the Town was pissed. Cutting down nine trees on the Common was some major-league ratfucking.

"Who do you think did it?" Harts said as he pulled the Vette into the Beta driveway.

Morley didn't have to think. He just looked at Harts and went "Quack quack."

XV

Morley was sitting on a chair in the shower. The Harts's beer hadn't helped. He was still hung over, very tired, and his toe was killing him. A raw open wound was all that was left of the nail. The only thing that felt good was the steaming water pounding on his back. Beta had those big showerheads, like the ones down at the gym.

Morley would've liked to sit there all day, but he had to get up to meet his parents. He wondered if his father would perceive that something was wrong. J.P. was like an animal when it came to his boys. He could always smell when one of them was in trouble. Morley's mother wouldn't suspect a thing. She'd just go crazy when she saw his stitches. He'd blame it all on the Old Blue, the teeth, the stitches, even the toe. Talking about the game would be his cover. It might throw J.P off the scent.

As the water splashed over his head, across his stitches, through his chipped teeth and onto his mangled toe, Morley thought about the talk he'd just had with Shortpecker. According to Short, the Town was really pissed. Every year come June, they'd had it with college kids, even under the best of conditions. Elliot and his gang hadn't helped the situation. They'd stepped over the line when they moved their protest to the Common. That was like the College giving the Town the bird. "If these crackpots wanted to make trouble," Shortpecker had said, "let 'em do it on their own campus." Having the new trees rat-fucked was the last straw. Now the Town wanted a scalp, preferably the one from the kid the cops had tossed in jail with Henry.

"But Short, I didn't do it." Morley had protested.

"Doesn't matter," Short had told him. "You were the guy that got thrown in jail. If the Sheriff fingers ya, you're gone. Hell, the Dean ain't gonna help ya. The Alumni Office already's buggin him 'cause you screwed up the singing. I'm tellin ya Morley, stay out of town and whatever ya do, don't let the sheriff see ya."

Morley was gradually starting to feel a little better. Maybe things would just blow over. Or, as Calvin Coolidge, Amherst's most famous alumnus, used to say: "If you see ten problems coming your way, just sit still. Chances are nine of them will get derailed before they ever reach you." Morley would have loved to just sit still, but a familiar voice got him moving. "Edward, you've wrecked your chair. I'm telling Mom."

It wasn't Calvin Coolidge. It was Willie, his little brother, and he was right; Morley had wrecked his chair. He wrecked one every year. It was a bad habit he'd picked up as a freshman. The first time he'd gotten plastered at Amherst, he'd felt so terrible that he couldn't stand up in the shower. He didn't want his new classmates to think he was some degenerate, so rather than lie on the floor like a drunk in the detox unit, he lugged his desk chair into the shower. It soon became his trademark. When Morley's chair was in the shower, Morley was hung over.

While this procedure helped Morley, it didn't do much for his chairs. They soon assumed a white bleached color like bones lying in the sun. This chair was no exception, and now Willie was going to tell his mother. That would get Donna all upset. Donna collected antiques and was constantly disgusted with the way the brothers abused the furniture. Thanks to some good Betas who had gone to Wooglin, the House had inherited a lot of fine furniture. Queen Anne chairs were parked in the corners, while Chippendale sofas lined the walls. But they were a sad lot. Arms were missing, legs broken, springs popped from their cushions. Beta's furniture was kind of like Shortpecker, disabled but functional.

"Hey, Swillie, how's it going."

"Edward, you've taken all the varnish off your chair. Mom's going to be really mad."

192

"Not if you don't tell her. And besides, it's not my chair. Somebody left it here." Morley knew that Willie wasn't buying this explanation, but who cared. "Where's Mom and Dad?"

"They're in your room. Dad said to hurry up. He doesn't want to be late for the President's Reception."

"Go tell them to relax. Cal promised not to start without me."

Morley got out of the shower and reached for his towel. Willie gasped. "Edward, what's wrong with your eye?"

Willie sounded just like his mother. "Nothing. Don't worry about it."

"I'm going to tell Mom right now."

He could hear Willie running down the stairs. He was yelling, "Mom, Edward cut his eye, he has stitches in his face."

Poor Willie. His parents were wrecking him. They'd probably had him too late in life. Eight years was a big gap between kids. Morley thought about it as he toweled off. He was twenty-one, that made Willie thirteen. Why the hell would any thirteen-year-old kid give a rat's ass about a chair? He should be thinking about things like tits and the size of his pecker. But then, J.P. was grooming Willie for Harvard, and Harvard liked goody goodies. Willie could room with Rocky, the flying squirrel. Rocky would never ratfuck his chair.

Morley finished drying off and started to shave. He really didn't want to go to the President's Reception. All of the Administration and faculty would be there. He was going to have to be on his toes, even if one was hurting. He couldn't let anybody figure out that he was the guy who'd been in jail with Henry.

If he hadn't spent the night in jail, he would have been in for a pretty good day. Professor Merrill had invited Morley and his parents back to his house for cocktails after the Reception. That would be a real treat for his parents. J.P. would like rubbing shoulders with the cream of academia, and Donna would go nuts when she saw the Professor's antiques. Unlike Beta's, the Professor's furniture was seldom used and never abused.

Morley's mother actually shrieked when she saw him. Willie had primed her for the worst and she was giving an all-star per-

193

formance. Morley hadn't seen her this upset since he'd bought a motorcycle. "Edward, what happened to your face? Don't tell me you fell off that motorcycle. Oh Jack, I told you this would happen."

Morley's father didn't say a word. He'd learned to ignore Donna when she flew into orbit. Morley didn't know how he did it. She would wring her hands and rant like a banshee until the spell finally passed or someone managed to change the subject. Morley decided to change the subject.

"No, Mom. I sold my motorcycle. I got this playing rugby." Morley turned to his father, "Hey Dad, did you hear we beat the Old Blue?" He was hoping J.P. would be impressed.

"No, I don't understand rugby." he said. "Let's get going. I don't want to be late for the President's Reception." J.P. was not impressed. Baseball was the only sport he recognized in the Spring. Morley could not use the rugby game to cover his scent, but that was all right. Having to deal with his mother and Willie was keeping his father distracted.

As they walked out of Beta, a crew from the Town was cleaning up the remains of the trees. Morley tried to pick up the pace. "Dad, you're right, we are running late. Let's get moving." Willie, typical of all goody-goodies, wanted to know about the trees. "Mom, why are they cutting down those trees? It looks like they were just planted." Willie would do well at Harvard.

Morley's mother started to wring her hands. Having all sons was not good for her. She should have had at least one daughter. "Edward, what happened to those trees?"

She said it in the same tone of voice she used when she complained about the furniture at Beta. It implied that Morley was somehow responsible. "I don't know, Mom, it looks like the Town has taken them down for some reason. Let's keep moving."

"No, Will's right. Those trees were just planted. I think they were vandalized."

J.P. got them back on track. "Forget the damn trees and let's get to the Reception." If he smelled anything, he chose to ignore it.

There was a line winding up to the front of the President's house. People were happy and smiling, like they were going to a victory celebration. Morley and his family got in line behind the Greenblatts. Greenie had been the Captain of football, was President of the Class, and a top student. Greenie's father was a psychiatrist and Director of Public Health for the Commonwealth of Massachusetts. Donna and J.P. used to sit with him during the football games, but as much as they liked Dr. Greenblatt, he had the unsettling habit of analyzing every play in terms of a potential head injury. After a good tackle, he would say things like, "that's a possible stress to the cranium," or "too much pressure on the sixth vertebra." His diagnoses got Donna so upset that J.P. couldn't enjoy the game. Starting junior year, they sat with Myron Maurer, Evan's father. Myron Maurer was a criminal lawyer in Newark, N.J. and was used to seeing people getting banged up. To Myron Maurer, injuries were all part of the game.

After a warm greeting, Greenie's parents immediately focused on Morley's cut. Dr. Greenblatt examined Mr. Brown's needlework and launched into a long dissertation about the dangers of contact sports. While the Doc peppered his parents with medical jargon, Morley moved ahead to talk with Greenie. "I hear you were in jail last night." Greenie said. "What happened?"

Here was trouble. Greenie wasn't even a Beta. If Greenie knew that Morley had been in jail, who else knew? "Keep it down, will you?" Morley said to Greenie. "My little brother hears everything." Fortunately Willie had left the line and was messing around with some other kids on the President's side lawn. "Who told you?"

"It's getting around. Bill Joy was up at North looking for you this morning."

Here was real trouble. Bill Joy was head of campus police. Bill was a great guy, another World War II veteran who did his best to keep the Betas out of trouble. Bill would never come after Morley on his own. If Bill was looking for him, the Dean must suspect something.

The line moved ahead. Morley tried to regain his composure as he shook hands with President Plimpton. "Why, hello, Edward. That's a nasty looking cut you've got there, but we finally beat the Old Blue."

"Yes sir, it was a great game." Cal was old school, like Professor Merrill. He understood that academics weren't everything.

Morley proceeded to introduce his parents, who had moved ahead of the Greenblatts. J.P. knew that Dr. Greenblatt would want to share his thoughts on contact sports with the President, and that would hold up the whole line. "President Plimpton, I believe you know my parents."

"Why of course, Mr. and Mrs. Morley. We've certainly enjoyed having Edward with us these last four years, and isn't it nice that we finally beat the Old Blue. That's a wonderful ending to Edward's college career." J.P. and Donna beamed.

"Thank you, President Plimpton, we are very pleased that Edward could attend Amherst, and we appreciate your keeping an eye on him for us," J.P. said.

J.P. still treated Morley like a bad little boy, and for good reason. J.P. had first met Cal at the end of Morley's freshman year. Before that meeting, the Administration had pretty well decided that Morley needed to grow up, that he should enlist in the Marines for a couple of years. That's where students went if the Administration decided they needed to grow up.

Morley and his father had met with Cal and the Dean in the President's big office. Cal opened the meeting by reading the list of academic and social problems that Morley was having. It was all very factual, with little, if anything, left open to interpretation. One particularly embarrassing item had Morley playing the bass drum at D.U. with his penis. That had to be the death blow. Morley was sure that he'd be on the next bus for Parris Island.

When Cal finished, everybody looked to J.P. for some explanation. J.P.'s now-famous response was, "He appears to be a typical Morley. Naughty and dumb." Cal loved it. Morley was given a second chance, and Cal always went out of his way to say hello to his father. Morley hadn't forgotten that lesson. It's tough for people to beat on you when they're laughing with you.

The Morleys shook hands with the Plimptons and moved out into the yard. They could hear Dr. Greenblatt suggesting to Cal that all rugby players should be required to wear helmets. Morley saw the Hartmans and guided his parents over to where they were standing. They knew the Hartmans well. The Morleys and the Hartmans had talked on the phone numerous times trying to figure out what their sons were up to. Today, they could all sit back and relax, or so they thought.

"Dr. and Mrs. Hartman, how are you. You know my parents, Jack and Donna Morley." Morley sounded so unctuous that he reminded himself of Eddie Haskell on "Leave It To Beaver."

"Uh huh," was all Dr. Hartman said as he extended his hand. Dr. Hartman was also a psychiatrist, but he was in private practice. Unlike Dr. Greenblatt, who got paid to talk, Dr. Hartman got paid to listen, and he rarely expressed an opinion on anything.

Seeing the Hartmans launched Donna into her diatribe about the furniture at Beta. Mrs. Hartman immediately concurred. She thought that Beta was a pigsty and wondered how her Paul could live in such a mess. The Harts just stood there and smiled.

Morley saw Bill Joy standing over by the bar. "Hey, why don't we get you some drinks," Morley said, and after taking everyone's order, he and Harts headed for the bar.

"Harts, you get the drinks and take 'em back to our parents while I go talk to Bill Joy. Greenie said Bill was up at North looking for me this morning."

"Don't admit anything," Harts warned him. "You've only got twenty hours until graduation."

Morley grabbed a beer and walked over to Bill Joy. Bill saw him coming. "Hey, Morley, get over here. You're in big trouble." Morley's knees went soft. "The Town is up in arms over the trees. The Dean figures it was you that cut them down."

"Bill, come on, I had nothing to do with those trees."

"The Dean doesn't care. He wants to see you in his office at 8 A.M. tomorrow. If he can pull a case together, he's gonna throw ya out."

"He can't do that, I didn't do anything."

"He can do anything he wants. He's gonna have the Sheriff come in. If the Sheriff identifies you as the guy who was in jail with Henry, you're out."

Now Morley was in a state of near shock. "Look, Bill, I'll give it to you straight." Morley never bullshitted Bill, and Bill knew it. "I was the guy in jail with Henry, but I didn't do anything. It was two guys from Dartmouth that ratfucked the trees, honest."

Bill was as firm as Morley had ever seen him. "Morley, what I'm telling you is that it doesn't make any difference who did it. If the Sheriff fingers you as the guy in jail with Henry, you're history."

Morley's mind was racing. Obviously the Sheriff was the key. "Bill, you have to work a deal with the Sheriff."

"Can't do it, Morley. He's pissed you tried to escape, and your buddy Henry made him look like a fool. All the cops down at the station already are giving him shit about 'unlawful and illegal.'"

Morley sighed. "Yeah, Henry did a job on him."

"Forget Henry. He's got his excuse. He's blind. You're the one they're after. You'd better come up with something between now and eight A.M. tomorrow."

"Thanks, Bill. Help me if you can."

Bill shook his head. "Buddy, you might be beyond help."

When Morley got back to his parents, the Hartmans were gone and Donna and J.P. were talking with Professor Merrill. Professor Merrill couldn't have been nicer. He noticed right away that Morley was favoring his left leg. "Edward, what happened to your foot? I didn't know you hurt that, too."

"I must've caught a cleat, Professor. It didn't start to bother me until after the game."

The mere mention of the game got the Professor excited. He started fingering his medallion. "Oh, what a game," he said to J.P. "I assume that Edward told you all about it."

Now J.P. was impressed. "No, Professor, Edward was too busy explaining his injuries to his mother. But he did mention that they won."

"Won! Why, they not only won, they beat the Old Blue! Amherst is national champion."

Morley could see that Professor Merrill was about to replay the entire game, so he said, "Why don't I get some refills while you run through the game, Professor. I played it once and believe me, that was enough."

Professor Merrill chuckled and handed Morley his glass. "Good idea, Edward. A gin and tonic for me, and what might we get for you, Mrs. Morley?"

Donna seemed very relaxed. Hanging around with the Professor was good for her. "Oh, something light, I'm not much of a drinker, Professor Merrill."

"Certainly. Make it three gin and tonics, Edward." He looked back at Morley's mother. "Please call me Charlie. Now where was I? Oh yes, the Old Blue . . . "

As Morley was getting the drinks, he felt a hand on his shoulder. It belonged to Al Most '29, the Alumni Secretary. Morley didn't envy Al, especially at this time of year. As the Alumni Secretary, Al had to be nice to everyone, which is why even undergraduates could call him Al. It didn't matter to Al whether or not you graduated. Amherst's biggest donor had never graduated.

"Hey Al, what's up?" Morley asked.

"Gee, Ed, where have you been? Didn't you get my note?"

"Note? What note?"

"Oh, never mind. Damn, I'll be glad when this graduation is over."

"Al, you okay? You look a little frazzled."

"Well, funny you should mention it. I didn't get much sleep. What the hell were you Betas doing last night?" Al lived in a house that was owned by the College. It was next to the Alumni Hall, right behind Beta and Chi Phi. "That party went pretty late. And just when I thought things had settled down, the Chi

Phi's started yelling, and someone started shooting off a cannon. The next thing I knew, the police were stalking through my yard. When I went out to see what was going on, I found two guys hiding in my bushes. When I asked them what they were doing, they started quacking at me, like ducks. Can you believe it?"

"Yeah, I heard things got pretty wild. Fortunately, I spent the night up at North."

"Damn, that's where I left the note. I'm surprised you didn't get it. Anyway, we've got a little problem. As you might have guessed, it has to do with your singing."

"What's the problem?" Morley said.

Al looked uneasy. It was an unnatural act for him to say something uncomplimentary to an alumnus, or even a potential alumnus. "Well, Ed, it's not quite up to par."

"Hey, Al, I might have missed a few notes, but so what?"

"Look Ed, normally we wouldn't care, but this McNamara thing, and now the trees, well, people are getting upset and we want things to go smoothly."

"Which means?"

Al swallowed. "We don't want you to lead the singing at the Alumni Sing. Crumpett says Harvey Hayden, that kid who leads the Glee Club, has agreed to do it, but we need your permission, since you're the elected Class Choregus."

Morley felt sorry for Al. If alumni giving took a nosedive, John J. McCloy '16 would not be pleased. He was too good a guy to have to put up with all of this crap, plus, Morley didn't give a rat's ass who did the singing. If Hayden wanted to stretch his cords, that was fine with Morley. "Well, you know Al, being elected Choregus means a lot to me, but if you think it will help calm things down, sure, let Hayden do the singing."

Al looked relieved. "Now Ed, don't get me wrong. We still want you at all the parties, and you're still the Choregus. A lot of the Alumni will want to have a drink with you. They like the fact that we won a national championship and that will help alumni giving."

"Speaking of giving, Al, what did you have to give Crumpett to get Hayden to sing?"

Al obviously was impressed that Morley understood the quid pro quos of fundraising. "Well, let's put it this way." Al said. "You're the last elected Choregus in the history of Amherst. From now on, it automatically goes to the President of the Glee Club."

By now, the lawn was covered with seniors and their parents. Willie and a bunch of other kids were running around the edge of the lawn. His shirttail had fallen out, his tie was askew, he was having a good time. Morley picked up the three gin-and-tonics, grabbed himself another beer, and started back to where he had left his parents and Professor Merrill.

"Hey Ed, come say hello to my parents." It was Rube. His big blue eyes were sparkling. It was hard to believe that he had been totally shitfaced just eight hours earlier. "Mom, Dad, you remember Ed."

"Yeah, we remember Ed," Rube's father said. He obviously was pissed. "Ed probably was having breakfast with his parents while you were still in bed."

"Come on, Dad, relax, will you? I told you, my alarm didn't go off."

"Actually, I slept in, too." Morley said, trying to help Rube. "We've been pretty busy finishing up our papers and exams."

"Those exams must have been rough." Rube's father said, pointing at Morley's stitches. He wasn't buying their act. Rube's mother was wearing the same nervous look that Donna usually had.

"Dad, Ed got banged up beating the Old Blue."

"Oh great, so now he can go through life looking like Frankenstein." Rube's father was a plumber from Albany and a tough little bastard. "I'll be glad when you guys grow up. Here," he barked, handing Rube a glass, "get your mother a drink."

Rube was only too happy to oblige. "Come on, Ed." he said, excusing Morley from his parents. "So how the fuck did you get out of jail?" Rube asked when they were safely away.

"It's a long story, but I'm still screwed. Those two idiots from Dartmouth must have cut down the trees on the Common and now the Sheriff is trying to pin it on me."

"That's not good. What are you going to do?"

"I'm supposed to meet with the Dean at eight tomorrow morning. He's gonna have the Sheriff there. If the Sheriff says that I'm the guy they had in jail last night, then I guess they'll throw me out."

"Hell, they can't do that. You didn't touch those trees, I know that."

"Great, why don't you come up and tell that to the Dean."

"Yeah, right, he might take my word for it. 'Oh Dean, be nice to Morley, he's a good boy.' You know if I went in there, he'd throw us both out. But let me know if I can help."

"Thanks, Rube, but you've helped enough."

"Hey, anything for a friend." Rube said, heading for the bar. "I'd better get some drinks before the old man gets any more pissed off."

The ice in the gin and tonics had almost melted by the time Morley made it back to his parents and Professor Merrill, but nobody seemed to mind. Everyone was relaxed and happy, and with good reason. After four years, a big investment was about to pay off. Even Morley's mother was enjoying herself. She didn't say a thing when Willie came up all sweaty and disheveled and asked if he could go to the movies with his new friends. That was just fine. So what if his shirttail was hanging out.

The cocktail party at Professor Merrill's was more of the same. All the big names from the College were there: John J. McCloy, Archibald MacLeish, and, of course, Henry Steele Commager. As J.P. noted, if Robert Frost had been alive, he would have been there too. Morley's mother was floating. It could have been due to the gin and tonics, but more likely, it was Professor Merrill's furniture. She had never seen so many fine antiques outside of a museum. And on the living room wall, overlooking it all, was *Wind From the Sea*.

Professor Merrill was the perfect host. He introduced Morley's parents as if they were the guests of honor. Morley tagged along as the Professor gave his mother a peripatetic tour of the house. He enjoyed seeing her so happy. She deserved it.

The Professor was quick to apologize for a hundred or so old books which were piled on the 18th-century Chippendale dining room table. He'd been to an estate sale that morning and had bought out someone's library. He explained to Morley's parents that he had just stacked the books on the table until he had a chance to go through them. Right now, Henry Steele Commager was circling the table like a shark sizing up its prey. According to the Professor, by the time the party was over, Henry Steele would have devoured the entire pile, and if you asked him a question about any one of those books, he'd probably know the answer. Morley's father loved it. Imagine going through a hundred books at a cocktail party. Morley just shook his head. He hadn't looked at a hundred books in his four years at Amherst.

As they were leaving, Professor Merrill took Morley aside. "Edward, I enjoyed spending this time with your parents. They're very proud of you. Let's not disappoint them, especially now that you're so close. Stay away from Beta tonight." He said it like he knew something.

"Yes sir, I'll stay up at North, but whatever you've heard, I want you to know I'm innocent."

The Professor winked. "Don't worry. I know that. We boys from the gym stick together."

XVI

The bells woke him at 7:45. He had fifteen minutes to make his meeting with the Dean. As Morley carefully lifted Margie's arm from his neck, he exposed her breast. Once again, he was reminded that she had the most beautiful bust he'd ever seen. Margie's boobs would stack up with any Playmate's. If *Playboy* ever featured "The Girls of Smith," Margie would have to be the centerfold.

He didn't want to wake her, not after what had happened last night. Morley had gone to dinner with his parents and Willie and, as he had promised Professor Merrill, he'd headed straight to his room in North after they'd dropped him off. He had been sitting on the day bed packing up books when he heard someone open his door. According to the bells, it was just after eleven. When he looked up, there was Margie. It was obvious that she had been drinking, but she didn't seem too sloshed. "Hey, what's up?" he'd asked her.

"Hopefully you," she'd replied. "It's time for your graduation present." With that, she turned off all but one light and put on Jackie Gleason's album, "Music for Lovers Only." Then she told Morley to sit back on the workbench while she stood in front of him and started to undress.

She took off her sweater first. The one light cast her in a seductive shadow. Morley could see that her breasts were cradled in a black lace bra. It was cut very low in the front, exposing the top of her nipples. Morley could feel himself getting hard. Margie had never acted like this before. Maybe she was sloshed.

Next she kicked off her shoes, slipped her thumbs into the waistband of her slacks, and with a roll of her hips, eased them to the floor. Now, all she had on were her bra and panties. The panties were made of black lace, just like the bra. They accented the creamy white of her long sculptured thighs. He wished that she would just stand there for a while.

Margie reached back and undid her bra. Two gorgeous mounds tumbled out. They became silhouetted in the light as she turned to toss the bra onto the chair. There was no question she could be a centerfold.

She eased her hands into the sides of her panties and slowly slid them down to the floor. With one hand she started rubbing her breasts while the other stroked her thighs. Then, like a centerfold leaving the page, she moved over to the workbench. Morley could feel the heat from her body. He was tempted to ask her about the guy from Yale, but knew that now was not the time.

She sat down beside him and gently pushed him onto his back. When he was down, she unbuckled his belt, undid his pants and unzipped his fly. Her hands felt soft and warm as she reached into his drawers and pulled out his unit. She rubbed it slowly up and down as he squirmed out of his pants.

He tried to pull Margie on top of him, but she resisted. "Slow down, Morley, I want to give you something special," she whispered, as she nibbled on an earlobe.

Morley did as he was told. Margie knelt above him and lightly kissed his lips. Then she started to massage his temples. He watched her breasts sway back and forth in front of his face. Hanging down like this, her nipples were big and brown, like the ones on top of baby bottles. Morley lifted his head to suck on them. He could feel the hardness of her nipples as he flicked them with his tongue.

Margie undid the buttons of his shirt and helped him out of it. Now they were both naked. She rubbed his arms and caressed his chest and stomach, pulling gently at his hair. Then she moved down and started to softly knead the muscles of his thighs.

When a hand brushed his unit, he hoped she would grab it and beat him off, but after a few easy strokes, she let it go and moved on to his calves and feet. After working each of his toes, she started to work her way back up his legs. Her breath was coming faster. His whole body was tingling.

Morley was both surprised and delighted when a moist warmth covered the head of his penis. This must be the something special. He moaned with anticipation as she slowly explored his organ with her tongue. Then she opened her mouth and took him in. Morley had never felt anything like this before. Margie began moving her head up and down, consuming more of him with each stroke. Her tongue was finding nerves that he never dreamed existed. He wanted this feeling to last forever, but he knew that he was about to come. He reached for Margie's head and tried to slow her down, but it was too late. He'd lost control and Margie knew it. He arched his back and pushed with all his might as Margie took him to the top. Once he was there, she wouldn't let him down. He just kept coming and coming as she continued to suck the life out of him. That was the difference between a blowjob and getting laid. With a blowjob, you had no control, and that's why Morley loved it.

Finally, he collapsed onto the workbench, like a wrestler who'd broken his bridge. He was so exhausted he could barely open his eyes. When he did, he saw that Margie was smiling at him. "Congratulations," she said, "you just graduated."

"Thanks," he said, pulling her down on top of him. "Give me a minute and maybe we can do a little post grad work."

The feel of Margie's body against him was all it took to restart his juices flowing. Now he wanted to get laid, but when he made his move, Margie resisted. All he could figure was that she must be having her period. "Look," he said, "I don't mind if you're having your period. I'll be gentle, it'll be good."

"I'm not having my period," she said, turning her head away. "It's something else."

"What else?"

"I just can't do it with you anymore."

"What do you mean you 'just can't do it with me anymore.' What the hell was that we just did?"

"That was different."

"Different! Margie, what are you talking about?"

Margie looked back at him. Tears were dripping from her cheeks. "I'm engaged."

"You're what!" Morley said, bolting upright.

"I got engaged." she said, between sobs. "At dinner." Sob. "Tonight." Sob. Now, she was sloshed.

"To whom?"

"Winslow Barrett." Sob. "He just graduated from Yale."

"Why?"

"Because he asked me."

"Because he asked you! There's a thousand guys who'd ask you if they ever got to know you."

"You know me, why don't you ask?"

"Come on Margie, give me a break. I don't even know if I'm going to graduate. The Dean's probably going to throw my ass out of here first thing tomorrow. You want to be engaged to some guy that's going to Vietnam?"

"Ask and find out."

"It sounds like Ol' Winslow beat me to it," Morley said, lamely dodging the bullet. "What's he going to be doing next year?"

Margie had regained her composure. "He's going to Stanford Law."

"When does he want to get married?"

"Next June, after I graduate."

That was time enough for Morley. If he were working in Boston for Ma Bell and Winslow was three thousand miles away in California, it wouldn't make any difference if Margie were engaged. He'd still have the inside track.

"Look, I've got to get some sleep," Morley said. "Let's discuss this in the morning, but I'll tell you one thing. You ain't marrying Winslow Barrett."

With that, he'd turned over and shut his eyes, but he couldn't get to sleep. He was still thinking of the BJ Margie had just given him. "Hey, Margie," he'd said, even though he knew that he shouldn't ask, "did Winslow Barrett get the same graduation present?"

"No, Morley, I'd never give a blowjob to someone who wanted to marry me. I save those for guys who let me type their fuckin papers. Goodnight." She turned over and went to sleep.

That was how the evening had ended. Morley had no intention of reopening their discussion of marriage. Right now, he had to focus all his energies on graduating. Still, as he looked over at Margie's breasts, he thought it wouldn't be too bad waking up every morning next to them, especially if he'd gotten a BJ the night before.

Once he had his diploma, things would look different, and he had time. Margie wasn't going anywhere, at least for another year. Besides, she'd been drunk. Maybe she wasn't really engaged. Maybe Winslow had just been looking for another hummer. For now, he was just hoping that Margie woke up before his mother arrived to reclaim her daybed. Morley was going to have enough trouble explaining all the pecker tracts on the red corduroy cover. Margie, lying there bare ass, would be beyond explanation.

Morley carefully slid out of the daybed, limped down the hall, showered, shaved, trotted back to his room, got dressed, straightened his tie, put on his "A" blazer, blew Margie a kiss, and walked out into another glorious Spring morning. Hundreds of people were milling around in front of Johnson Chapel. Many were carrying signs that read, MCNAMARA GO HOME; HOW DO YOU SPELL DEATH? M-C-N-A-M-A-R-A; and, of course, PEACE and PEACE NOW. Nobody seemed too happy, but then, who could be happy at eight in the morning?

Bill Joy was guarding the door to the Chapel. Elliot Ginsberg was standing next to him. Both of them looked nervous, like a couple of kids who had just lit the fuse to a firecracker and were waiting for it to go off. Morley had to push his way up the steps. When he got to the top, he said, "Hey Bill, who are all of these people?"

"McNamara is supposed to speak at 8:30." Bill said.

"He must have a big set of balls," Morley said. "This crowd looks like a lynch mob."

"He might as well get used to it, "Bill said. "Commager, and Elliot here, have really stirred things up."

"Well, that's McNamara's problem. I've got enough troubles of my own. Can you let me in?"

"Yeah, sure, the Dean's up there waiting for you. But the Sheriff ain't here yet. Best of luck."

"Thanks, Bill." Bill opened the door and waved Morley in. As he entered the Chapel, he could hear some of the protestors grumbling. They wanted to know why he was allowed in early. Morley felt like telling them, "Hey, you want to take my place? Be my guest."

There was an eerie quiet as the big Chapel door shut behind him. He turned and started to climb the stairs to the Dean's office. The leather soles of his Weejuns scraping against the granite steps marked his ascent. He paused when he got to the top, slicked back his hair, knocked once on the Dean's door, and walked in. This was it. If he could get through this meeting with the Dean he would graduate. If not, he was off to McNamara's war. "Good morning, Mrs. Martula." Morley said to a pleasant looking lady sitting behind the reception desk.

"Good morning, Edward," Mrs. Martula said. Mrs. Martula knew all the Betas. Her husband was a good friend of Shortpecker's. All the Betas called him The Mouse. Morley had been there when he had earned his nickname. It had been in the Spring of his sophomore year. The King of Smut had gotten hold of a porno flick called "Eek, A Mouse," and had invited Shortpecker to bring up some of the boys from V.F.W. for a "cultural exchange evening."

It should have been a fun evening, especially when the boys from the Club arrived with a keg, but unfortunately, the premiere of "Eek a Mouse" had suffered a premature climax. Mrs. Martula's husband had gotten up to get a beer just as the leading lady saw the mouse, screamed, and fainted seductively onto the bed. A well nippled breast and luxurious thigh had so distracted him that he tripped over the cord to the projector. Both Mrs. Martula's husband and the projector had crashed to the floor, thus ending the premiere of "Eek a Mouse." When the lights went on, The King had looked down at Mrs. Martula's husband, shook his head, and said, "Way to go, Mouse." That was it, he was labeled for life.

"That's some crowd out there," Morley said.

"It certainly is." Mrs. Martula agreed. "This McNamara thing is causing quite a stink. The Dean is meeting with President Plimpton right now. They hope that having the Secretary speak this morning will cool things off. You boys have worked so hard, and your families are all here. With such a lovely day, it would be a shame to have this riff-raff disrupt your graduation."

Morley seized the initiative; it was worth a shot. "Look, Mrs. Martula, if the Dean's too busy to see me now, I'll be happy to come back right after graduation."

"I wish that it were that simple, Edward." Mrs. Martula said. She knew Morley. Once he had his diploma, he'd be gone. "The Dean told me to tell you to wait in his office. I'm to get him just as soon as the Sheriff arrives. That won't be too long. I just called down to the station and they said he was on his way."

Morley walked into the Dean's office and sat down by the open window. He could hear a murmur coming from the crowd below. It was getting bigger all the time. Morley looked out the window and saw the fat little Sheriff getting out of his car. A big black limousine pulled up beside him. Morley had never seen such a fancy car. Secret Service men were running alongside it. They looked as nervous as Bill Joy and Elliot.

The crowd immediately directed its attention to the limousine. A guy with a walkie-talkie opened the back door. There was a pause and then, out stepped Robert Strange McNamara. The secret service quickly closed around him while the campus police tried to clear a path to the Chapel's door. People began yelling abuses at McNamara and waving their signs. Elliot had moved off the steps into the crowd and was pumping his PEACE sign for all he was worth. He must have been in seventh heaven. Of the three to four hundred people in front of the Chapel, few looked in favor of the war.

Mrs. Martula came in and joined Morley at the window. "What's all that commotion?" she said.

"McNamara's just arrived." Morley said.

"Oh, and there's the Sheriff. I'd better get the Dean." Mrs. Martula said, as she bustled out of the office.

The Sheriff managed to make it to the Chapel before McNamara. Morley looked down and saw that he had stopped to say something to Bill Joy. Morley was a dead duck. As soon as the Sheriff came up the stairs, he would finger Morley as the guy who was in jail with Henry and the Dean, right or wrong, would kick him out.

Morley turned to the door just as the Dean came into his office. He was about to say "Good Morning" when the chant of "One, Two, Three, Four, We don't Want your Fucking War. One, Two, Three, Four, We don't Want your Fucking War," began floating through the window.

"You'd think those people would show some respect for the Secretary of Defense," the Dean said, scowling. He walked over and slammed the window just as Mrs. Martula came running back in.

"Dean, the President wants you downstairs immediately. He's afraid there's going to be a riot."

The Dean hesitated and looked at Morley. "Where's the Sheriff?" Morley could hear the sound of leather soles scraping their way up the stairs. Before Mrs. Martula could answer, the cry of "One, Two, Three, Four, We don't Want your Fucking War" came from inside the Chapel. "My God!" the Dean said. "Those nuts must have busted in!" He looked at Morley. "I'll be right back." The Dean hustled out of the office with Mrs. Martula fast on his heels.

This was the break Morley had been praying for. Elliot and his buddies had opened a hole for him, and he didn't waste any time going through it. He sprinted out of the Dean's office, but stopped at the door. The Sheriff was at the top of the stairs catching his breath. There was no way that Morley could get out of the Dean's office without the Sheriff seeing him. Then the sound of leather on granite started coming up the stairwell. It was accompanied by the chant, "One, Two, Three, Four, We don't Want your Fucking War!" The Sheriff was swept aside as a phalanx of protestors rushed for seats in the balcony. Morley fell in with them, barged his way past the Sheriff, hustled down the corridor to the back stairwell, glided down two flights of stairs, and burst out the back door of the Chapel. There was nothing but open field ahead of him. He'd done it, he'd escaped.

He cut across the quad and headed down the hill to Beta. His parents were sitting on the porch waiting for him. He'd told them the night before that he'd meet them at Beta at 8:30 so they could pack up his stuff. He didn't want them anywhere near North and the Dean's office that morning.

He noticed that Willie was over on the Common watching a crew from the Town chip up the last remains of the trees. Typically, the Town's crew had managed to stretch this simple task into a two-day job. Morley heard a sudden grinding and flinched as he saw the chips from one of the saplings being spit into the back of the truck. If it hadn't been for Elliot, that's what he would have felt like coming out of the Dean's office.

"Hey Mom, Dad, how's it going."

As usual, Morley's mother was first to respond. "Edward, you boys have destroyed all of this lovely furniture. An old alumnus just came by and was disgusted. Those antiques should never have been put in a fraternity."

The last thing Morley cared about was the furniture. He just wanted to get packed and out of Beta. "Mom, don't worry about the furniture. It works fine and besides, I'm out of here." With that he turned to his Dad. "Dad, where's the car? Graduation isn't until ten, so you and Mom can walk downtown and have a cup of coffee while I pack."

"What about the daybed?" Donna said. "I think we should put that in first."

Of course she was right, but Morley had to give Margie time to get up, dressed, and gone. "It's up in North, Mom, and there's no place to park around there now. McNamara's making a speech at the Chapel. Besides, I can't get someone to help me carry it down until after graduation, unless you want to help me, Dad."

"No, no. It can wait. We'll go get a cup of coffee." J.P hated packing, plus he had no desire to carry the daybed down four flights of stairs. "The car's right out front. It's open. Will's supposed to be keeping an eye on it. Just lock it up when you're through. We'll see you after the ceremony."

"Great. Try to park right next to the side door of the gym. I've got a couple of things I'd like to throw in on the way out."

Commencement at Amherst was not held in the main quad, but at the smaller, more intimate quad formed by the gym. Morley's Dad hesitated. He didn't need directions; whenever he came to Amherst, he usually parked at the gym. But today was different. "Are you sure that the car will be all right down there?" he said, pointing to *The Amherst Student.* "According to this article, there are going to be a lot of nuts protesting McNamara's honorary degree."

Morley scanned the article in the *Student.* "First," it read, "a petition protesting the war will be circulated among the crowd during the graduation ceremony. Second, there will be a picket line in front of the gymnasium. Third, members of the senior class who are opposed to McNamara's receiving an honorary degree will wear white armbands."

The article went on to report that most students felt it would be in poor taste to disrupt graduation. A few, including Elliot, disagreed. Elliot thought that they "should raise as big a stink as possible over this thing. The system keeps right on going, and I want to make it clear that I am not part of this system. I have no desire to receive a diploma from any institution that would honor McNamara."

Morley wasn't too concerned about his father's car. Elliot's group might look a little strange and probably would make a lot of noise, but they weren't like the guys from Dartmouth.

They weren't going to do anything violent. "Dad, don't worry about your car." Morley said, throwing down the paper. "McNamara's meeting with the protestors right now. He'll calm them down. Just park by the side door of the gym. Everything's going to be fine."

His father looked skeptical. "Well, okay, we'll meet you right after the ceremony. Do you want Will to stay and help?"

Morley could have used some help carrying his stuff down to the car, but Willie was too much like his mother, and there was no telling what he might find in Morley's room. "No, Willie will just slow me down," Morley said. "Why don't you take him with you."

"Okay. We're off," said J.P.

Having taken care of his parents and Willie, Morley walked into Beta. Harts, Bunnsie, Evan Maurer, Monk, Smee and Beachball were huddled at the bottom of the stairs. Shortpecker was sitting in the middle of them. He was holding a check. They were all staring at it in amazement.

No one looked up when Morley came in. That was strange. Even though Morley hadn't said anything about his meeting with the Dean, everyone must have suspected that he was in trouble. "What the hell's going on?" Morley said. "Don't tell me somebody actually paid their dues."

Shortpecker handed Morley the check. It was drawn on the Chase Manhattan Bank of New York, against the account of John J.McCloy, '16, and made out to Beta Iota, Beta Theta Pi. It was for $5,000.00. Morley had never seen so many zeroes. He counted them, then read the notation, which said, "Fix up Furniture."

"You've got to be shittin me."

"No, it's true," Beachball said. "Short and I were just sitting here when McCloy came storming through. He walked upstairs, downstairs, told us he was a Beta, and said the House looked like a dump. We agreed. Then I told him that we had planned to have the furniture redone, but we didn't have any money because the Trustees kept raising the tuition. Mentioning the tuition must have hit a sensitive nerve. He asked how much it would cost to get everything fixed up. Short said '$2,500.' McCloy said, 'Not enough,' pulled out his checkbook, and wrote us this baby for five."

Morley could see that Smee had been doing some thinking. "Look, what's the use of putting all this money into fixing up the furniture? Professor Roller will just show up and we'll be right back where we started. I say that we use Brother McCloy's donation to reestablish our credit with Mr. Russell." As an underclassman, Smee was thinking of the future and having credit with Mr. Russell was a lot more important than having the furniture fixed.

Monk was quick to second Smee's suggestion. "Hey, seriously, Smee's got a good idea. I mean what the hell. We could clear our account with Mr. Russell, and there's nothing wrong with the furniture. Let's face it, Brother McCloy just caught us on an off day."

As usual, Monk's support put an immediate cloud over Smee's suggestion. "Monk, what, are you shitting us." Bunnsie said. "Just look at this place, it's a dump. Every chair needs fixing."

At this point, Shortpecker took back John J. McCloy '16's check from Morley. "You Betas, let me handle this. Take my word for it. You don't fuck with John J. McCloy."

Smee gave one of his knowing chuckles. "Yeah, right Short. We give you the check, we'll come back in September, and the V.F.W. will have all new furniture, and we'll have this same shit with some glue on it." Smee had a point. Shortpecker was sure to get some of this money to the Club. The trick was not to let him steal it all. "At the very least," Smee pleaded, "let's show Mr. Russell Brother McCloy's check and see if he'll let us charge a keg for graduation."

Nobody could argue with that reasoning. But Morley didn't care what they did with John J. McCloy '16's check. He was packing up, graduating, emptying out his locker, and heading home. He went upstairs while the rest of the group, check in hand, headed for Russell's.

Morley started emptying his drawers. Right away he was glad that he had sent Willie off with his parents. What was he going to do with his supply of safes? He couldn't think of any place at home where his mother wouldn't eventually find them. He'd leave them for the next generation of Betas. They'd be his legacy to the House. He checked the one rubber he always carried with him. It was silhouetted against the side of his wallet like a bad case of ringworm. One rubber was all he needed. He doubted that he was going to meet too many Beta Honeys working for the phone company.

He rolled his laundry bag down the stairs. It knocked a spindle loose when it hit the railing, reminding him of Hondo's now-famous victory over the Gator. He wondered what Hondo would do after graduation. Hondo was made to play ball. It was the one thing that he did better than anybody else at Amherst. How could all of that ability suddenly be diverted into the law, medicine or business? For Hondo to do anything but play ball would be a waste of time and talent.

The van from Russell's came whizzing by just as Morley was locking the door to his Dad's car. It pulled into the Beta driveway. Smee's plan must have worked. John J. McCloy '16's check must have reinstated Beta's credit with Mr. Russell.

Morley walked back upstairs, put on his cap and gown, and checked himself out in the mirror. He was again amazed at how a cap and gown could make even him look academic. He headed downstairs for the last time. He could hear Smee pouring a round of beers as he passed the door to the basement. "Facilis Descensus Averno." Morley's mouth began to water. He'd worked up a sweat packing the car. One last beer with the brothers would taste good. He almost turned down the stairs, but the bells from Johnson Chapel called him back. They rang out 9:30. He had to get to graduation. As a class officer, he was supposed to be near the head of the line, and the procession would start promptly at 10 A.M.

Morley picked up his pace as he went past the library. Thank goodness he'd never have to go back to that place. He stopped at the Senior Fence, a row of 4" x 6" wooden beams which had been set up ages ago by some long-forgotten class. By tradition, only seniors could sit on the Senior Fence. The 4 x 6's weren't very comfortable, but the Senior Fence had nothing to do with comfort. It had to do with privilege, and Morley had earned that privilege. Now he thought he'd savor it for a moment. He took a seat on the closest rail and looked over at the statue of Henry Ward Beecher, whose sister, Harriet Beecher Stow, had written *Uncle Tom's Cabin*. Some historians claimed that Harriet's book had started the Civil War. If she were at Amherst today, she undoubtedly would be marching shoulder to shoulder with Elliot. Morley wondered what type of a stink Elliot would make at the graduation. Telling the *Student* you were pissed off was one thing; actually doing something about it was a different story. Who'd want to create a scene in front of all their parents, friends, the faculty, the whole College? And for what? Just to make a point? What did McNamara care if some fat little kid from Amherst didn't like his war? He was the Secretary of Defense for the whole damn country.

Morley squinted into the sun and peered more closely at the stains on Henry Ward Beecher's head. He decided he'd better get moving before a pigeon came by and crapped on his cap.

XVII

Morley joined the crowd moving across the campus and down the steps of the War Memorial. He paused at the top of Memorial Hill. There still wasn't a cloud in the sky. Mount Nowatuck had never seemed closer; he felt he could reach out and touch the old chief's nose. He looked down at the quad in front of the Gym. It was swarming with people.

The line for the procession was just starting to form when Morley reached the bottom of the hill. He was going to have trouble finding his spot. There were too many people packed into the quad. If the College had known that McNamara's honorary degree was going to cause such a stink, they could have moved the graduation ceremony to the main campus. But it was too late now.

The lineup for graduation was basically the same as for Senior Chapel, except for the honorary doctorates and the fact that the Sheriff of Amherst always led the procession. The Sheriff was the official representative of the Commonwealth of Massachusetts under whose charter the College operated. President Plimpton and John J. McCloy '16, Chairman of the Board of Trustees, followed the Sheriff. Then came the commencement speaker. This year's blowhard was the Honorable Paul Howard Douglas, United States Senator from Illinois. Senator Douglas was a Bowdoin graduate who had taught Economics at Amherst from 1924 until 1927.

The seven men receiving honorary degrees, including McNamara, were next in line, followed by the Administration and faculty, the six class officers, and the rest of the graduating seniors. The focus of the procession was sure to be Robert Strange McNamara.

Morley waded into the maelstrom of parents, kids, students, protestors, and secret service men with their walkie-talkies. When he reached the head of the line, he froze. There was the Sheriff talking to the Dean.

The Sheriff was dressed in a top hat and tails and was carrying a ceremonial mace with purple and white ribbons dangling from the top. Even Morley had to admit that he looked good. The Dean took the Sheriff by the arm and started to lead him back to where the students were assembling. Morley started to freak. They must still be after him. Why else would the Sheriff and the Dean be moving to the back of the line? Morley wasn't about to let the Sheriff finger him now. He'd come too far. In less than an hour, he'd have his diploma. He quickly ducked down behind a bush and pulled his gown up around his head. If anybody asked what he was doing, he'd tell them he was taking a pee. With all of the tension that was building, it was as good as an excuse as any. Everybody in line, including the Secretary of Defense, probably felt like taking a pee.

The Dean and the Sheriff were less than ten yards away when their progress was stopped by the secret service. These guys weren't fooling around. They weren't letting anybody near the Secretary. They didn't know who might be coming to the graduation. A lot of kids already had lost their lives in the jungles of Vietnam and someplace in this crowd, there could be a parent or friend who felt they had a score to settle with the Secretary. This was especially true now that Henry Steele Commager had declared the war illegal and immoral. Before Commager's speech, their sons had died heroes. Now, thanks to McNamara's flawed policies, these same kids were being called criminals.

The bells from Johnson Chapel began to chime. President Plimpton pulled his gold watch out from under his robe, flicked it open, and pronounced, "It's ten o'clock. Sheriff, let's get moving."

The Sheriff resumed his position at the head of the procession, puffed himself up, banged the bottom of the mace three times on the pavement and started off in a slow, measured step. When the line started to move, Morley darted from behind his bush and jumped in next to Charlie Firestone. "Where have you been?" Charlie said. "The Dean's been looking for you."

"Fuck the Dean," Morley said. "In one hour, I'm outta here."

Since the Sheriff was at the head of the line, the protestors were directing most of their abuse at him. The poor Sheriff must have wondered why he ever had anything to do with the College. All he ever got from Amherst was a bunch of crap, even when he was just leading the procession.

A body of secret service men had moved between the Secretary and the crowd. They looked competent, but Morley could see that with so many people packed into the quad, it was not a good situation. The image of Jack Ruby jumping out and shooting Lee Harvey Oswald must have been on everyone's mind. Any nut with a gun could have easily blasted the Secretary as he walked by.

As class officers, Morley and Charlie Firestone were in the first row, right in front of the dais. The Rt. Rev. George Leslie Cadigan '33 rose to give the opening prayer. He thanked the Lord for the day, for the beauty of the College, for family and friends. He asked the Lord to give His guidance to all of those receiving degrees. He thanked Him for His many blessings and ended with a simple reminder, "Visit the sick, be kind to the poor, and help the needy." He made no reference to the war.

President Plimpton then welcomed the family and friends of Amherst to the College's 145th Commencement and introduced Senator Paul Douglas. Morley settled back as Senator Douglas, like all Commencement speakers, began his platitudes, admonitions, and challenges to the Class. He heard the chapel bells ring 10:30. He felt the sun warming his robe and cap. Black absorbs heat, white reflects it; his two years of Freshman Physics hadn't been a total failure. He looked around at his classmates, capped and gowned; they'd come a long way since Slosher had challenged Professor Kinsey. Morley still couldn't believe he was about to graduate.

A bead of sweat trickled from his forehead around his eye and into his stitches. He brushed the sweat from his cheek. He wondered who'd take the stitches out. He wouldn't have time to see Mr. Brown before he left. No matter, Ma Bell would know a good doctor.

As the Senator droned on, Morley studied the stack of diplomas on a table directly in front of him. Each sheepskin was bound by a piece of purple and white ribbon. One of those hides belonged to Morley. He started to count them just to make sure there were two hundred and eighty-one, only his eyes refused to stay open. The tension he had felt for the last four days began to dissipate. His head fell back. He was out.

An elbow to the ribs woke him up. It belonged to Charlie Firestone. "Hey, Morley, wake up. The Dean and the Sheriff are looking at you."

Morley sat up straight. He pulled his tassel over his face, but it was too late. The Sheriff had a fix on him and was nodding to the Dean as if to say, "No question about it. That's the guy."

Morley had relaxed too soon. By falling asleep, he had given the Sheriff a clear shot at his face. Thanks to the stitches, he was a marked man. Now the Dean had the identification he needed. Morley was the guy that had been in jail with Henry. Morley was the guy that had had sap all over him. Morley was the guy the Dean had promised the Town he would expel. How could this happen? How could they throw him out. He'd executed his plan, he'd passed his comps, he was innocent. But he knew none of that mattered. If the Dean said you were out, you were out.

Here he was just ten feet from his diploma, but he might as well have been in Vietnam. He looked over at Robert Strange McNamara. He was sitting back in his chair, secure in his crimson cape, surrounded by his secret service, smiling superciliously at the Class of '66. Now Morley was scared. This arrogant son of a bitch was going to send him halfway around the world to shoot people he didn't know for reasons he didn't understand.

Morley tried to think through his options. There were none. He heard the snap of a camera. He looked down at his feet and saw Willie. Willie had crawled up the aisle to take his picture. "Get the hell out of here," Morley whispered. Willie took another picture. He had his Mom's Brownie. "Turn around." he said, "Dad wants a shot of your face."

Morley turned around. There was his father with his eye to his 8 MM Kodak movie camera. J.P.'s home movies were the worst. He always shot too high, too low, too fast and too long. The zoom lens was his real nemesis. J.P.'s movies continually zoomed in and out, in and out. Watching them was like being trapped in a small boat during a heavy sea. Morley's maternal grandmother had actually gotten sick during one of J.P.'s home movies. She, and the rest of the family, would have gladly paid the Mouse to knock over J.P.'s projector.

Morley could tell that his father was zooming in and out right now. His mother was standing next to him. She looked uncharacteristically calm. There was no sign of her usual nervousness, that fear that someone was going to come up and tell her that one of her boys was in trouble. She actually seemed to be enjoying herself. Morley turned his attention back to the diplomas on the table. Think. There had to be a way, he just had to think.

Senator Douglas was winding up his address. He was saying something about how the Class of '66 had an obligation to go forth and to make its mark on the world. "You have had the privilege of an Amherst education, but with privilege, comes responsibility. Now as you leave this bucolic and safe harbor, you must come to the fore and shoulder the responsibilities that are the price of privilege. This is the charge I leave with you today. Thank you, and best of luck to the Class of 1966."

Unless he could come up with something in a hurry, the only responsibility Morley would be shouldering would be an M-16. The Dean and the Sheriff were about to strip him of his privileges. Think. He had to think.

Senator Douglas sat down. President Plimpton stepped to the podium. He thanked the Senator for his inspiring address and proceeded with the awarding of the honorary degrees.

"To Senator Paul Howard Douglas, son of Bowdoin College, former member of the Amherst faculty, current statesman in our United States Senate. During your three terms in the Senate you have established yourself as an independent thinker, committed to liberal domestic programs and a strong foreign policy. The Trustees of Amherst College applaud your public service and are proud to bestow upon you the degree of Doctor of Laws." There was polite applause.

"Harold R. Johnson '18." Harold R. Johnson '18 was the major benefactor of Hampshire College, some new, weirdo experimental college that a group of radical educators were planning to plop down between Mount Holyoke and Amherst. Old Harold tottered off with his doctorate. There was polite applause.

"Dr. Samuel P. Hayes '31." Dr. Hayes was a prominent black who was President of the Foreign Policy Association. He had been showered with honorary degrees during the civil rights era. His hood had almost as many colors as Henry Steele Commager's. Dr. Hayes actually looked bored as he accepted his Doctorate of Humane Letters. There was polite applause.

This was it. The moment Morley was waiting for, his last hope. "Robert Strange McNamara." A smattering of boos, whistles, and catcalls, was followed by a very proper ovation. Where was the big stink that Elliot had promised in the *Student?* Morley looked over to where Elliot was sitting. Elliot wasn't doing anything. He seemed perfectly content to politely sit on his ass and watch the Secretary receive his honorary degree along with everyone else.

So much for Amherst's great activist. Wearing a white arm band was one thing, getting up in front of your parents and the College and challenging the system was something else. Elliot talked a good game, but when it came right down to it, he wasn't going to stray too far from the privileged path, the one that led to a safe job, a nice car, and a box in the suburbs. Elliot claimed to be different, but he was still part of the system.

When the applause died down, President Plimpton continued. "Robert Strange McNamara, Phi Beta Kappa, Son of the

University of California and the Harvard Business School, you have had nearly complete success as a teacher, soldier, and businessman. Now, to a position of incredible responsibility, in a situation of unimaginable difficulty, and to an unrecognized war of inexplicable dimensions, you have brought a dedicated devotion which inspires admiration for your efforts and awe for your courage. You have displayed an integrity so unquestioned that while I would still prefer to go myself, I am willing to entrust my sons to your administration."

What a joke. The sons of Amherst weren't going to Vietnam, they were going to graduate school. Thanks to the Dean and the Sheriff, Morley'd probably be the only son of Amherst that Cal was going to entrust to McNamara. "By the authority invested in me by the Trustees of Amherst College I confer on you the degree of Doctor of Laws." There was the customary polite applause, accented by a few boos, one of which came from Elliot, but that was the sum total of his big stink. McNamara took his degree and strolled back to his seat.

"Robert Morris Morgenthau '41." Morley didn't know what Robert Morris Morgenthau '41 was being honored for, and he didn't care. He stayed focused on Robert Strange McNamara. The word Strange echoed through his mind. Seeing McNamara sitting there, surrounded by the secret service men, was very strange. Everything about this guy was strange. He even looked strange. His lean, pointy features, rimless glasses and straight slicked back hair with a high part favoring the left side, gave him the appearance of someone out of the 40's. He looked so out of place, it occurred to Morley that maybe this guy had no idea of what was really going on. Maybe he'd missed a whole generation. Maybe he was still back in an era when Americans liked their wars. Maybe he thought he was still fighting World War II. Maybe he was as screwed up as the guys at the gym.

Morley noticed that his classmates were starting to receive their diplomas. The Dean would select a diploma from the pile and hand it to President Plimpton. Cal would read the full name of the graduate in his beautifully rich patrician voice and pass the diploma on to John J. McCloy '16. The graduate, upon hearing his name, would walk up to the dais where John J. McCloy '16 would give him his diploma and shake his hand. Morley knew that he would never hear Cal read his name, that he would never walk to the dais, that he would never shake hands with John J. McCloy '16. When the Dean came to Morley's diploma, he would simply shove it back into the bottom of the pile. To get it, Morley would have to go see the Dean after the ceremony; the Sheriff would be there to identify him, and the Dean would throw him out. Somehow, Morley had to get to his diploma before the Dean did.

There were three Summas. Next came the twenty-eight Magnas, then the Cum Laude's. There were over a hundred of them. The names kept rolling from Cal's lips as future doctors, lawyers, and men of commerce, all looking very privileged, traipsed across the dais in front of Morley. Many of them wore white armbands. None of them would have to worry about Vietnam. They would be safe in graduate school, while Morley would be in Southeast Asia getting his ass shot off.

At last they started conferring the plain old Bachelor of Arts. Robert Thorne Abbott . . . more A's . . . Andrew Zoltan Benkovich . . . more B's . . . C's, D's, E's, F's, some G's . . . John Victor Giarratana, Jr. . . . Then it happened.

"Elliot Stephen Ginsberg."

Elliot trudged to the dais, walked up to John J. McCloy '16, crossed his arms, stuck his nose up like Chief Nowatuck's, and refused to accept his diploma. John J. McCloy '16 was dumbfounded. He didn't know what to do. He tried to shove the diploma under Elliot's folded arms, but Elliot would have none of it. John J. McCloy '16 was getting red in the face. He started shaking Elliot's diploma at him.

At first there was just a murmur from the audience. Then a woman shrieked, "My God, Maury, he's not going to take his diploma! Elliot! ELLIOT!! TAKE THE DIPLOMA! IT COST YOUR FATHER A FORTUNE! Maury, make him take the diploma! Oh my God, what's happening?!" Morley assumed that it was Elliot's mother who was screaming, but it could have been anybody who appreciated the value of an Amherst education.

Morley moved to the edge of his seat. He was beginning to see an opening. If Elliot refused to move, somebody would have to move him. If they tried to move him, there were plenty of people there who would rise to Elliot's defense. By refusing to budge, Elliot could very well touch off a riot. In the confusion, Morley might be able to run up, grab his diploma, and hit the road.

"Attaboy Elliot," Morley whispered under his breath. "Fuck McNamara and his war. Hold your ground. Show'em who's right. Make'em carry you out, and save my ass one more time."

But Elliot didn't hold his ground. Having made his point, he peacefully walked off the dias, stopped directly in front of Morley, and waited while eighteen other members of the Class of '66 got up to join him. These nineteen were going to walk out of their own graduation. This was their protest to Amherst's awarding Robert Strange McNamara, the principle architect of an illegal and immoral war, an honorary degree. These nineteen had come to the fore and were about to shoulder the responsibilities that Senator Douglas maintained are the price of privilege. That was great, but what Morley needed was a riot.

Morley slumped back into his chair. He looked at the table with his diploma. He looked at the Dean and at the Sheriff. He looked back at his father. Then he looked at McNamara. The son of a bitch was still sitting there flashing his stupid supercilious smile. He must have thought that Elliot was just another impolite little piss ant that he could squash at any time. Didn't he realize that Elliot had just refused his diploma? That because of him, Elliot wasn't going to graduate?

Morley's next move surprised even himself. He jumped to his feet, put one arm around Elliot, thrust the other into the air and said, "Let's get out of here."

Elliot looked at him in disbelief. "Morley, what are you doing?"

"I'm getting the hell out of here, that's what I'm doing. Let's go."

There was some polite applause, but most people were still trying to figure out what was happening. As they started to walk out, questions swarmed through Morley's mind. What was he doing? What would the Dean do? How could he throw out some-one who already had walked out? What would Ma Bell say when he showed up without his diploma? Would she hire someone who openly opposed the war? Then he remembered his father. That was the question that really bothered him. What was he going to say when his father asked him, "Ed, where's your diploma?" Morley felt his knees turn to jelly. He didn't dare let go of Elliot's corpulent body. If he did, he was sure he would fall on his ass.

Classmates began shaking his hand and shouting congratulations. It reminded Morley of leaving the field after a big game, only this was different. Who had he beaten? McNamara? The Dean? The system? Some strength started to come back into his legs, but not enough to let go of Elliot. They must have beaten somebody because, suddenly, he felt GOOD.

He looked up into the crowd and saw Mr. Dunster on his feet, applauding. Mrs. Dunster was trying to pull him down. A big contingent from the press was lined up at the edge of the quad waiting to interview Elliot. Unlike the Secretary, these guys knew that something had just happened. They knew that McNamara's unrecognized war had just been formally rejected by a kid at Amherst, and that nineteen others had joined him. That was the start, now how many would follow?

Elliot stopped just before they reached the reporters. He turned to Morley. "Why?" was all he said.

This time, Morley didn't have to think. This time, he had the answer. "Because," he said, "McNamara's an asshole."